THE INTEGRAL YOGA

The Integral Yoga

Sri Aurobindo's
Teaching and Method of Practice

Selected Letters of
SRI AUROBINDO
Compiled by
Sri Aurobindo Ashram
Archives and Research Library

LOTUS PRESS
Box 325, Twin Lakes, WI 53181
USA

Compiled from the letters on yoga of Sri Aurobindo by
Sri Aurobindo Ashram Archives and Research Library, Pondicherry, India.
This edition is published and distributed in the United States by Lotus Press
P.O. Box 325, Twin Lakes, WI 53181 by arrangement with
Sri Aurobindo Ashram Trust, Publication Department,
Pondicherry 605 002, India.

ISBN 0-941524-76-0
Library of Congress Catalog Card Number 93-78233

Printed at Sri Aurobindo Ashram Press
Pondicherry, India

Printed in India

Contents

Publisher's Note

This compilation consists of letters by Sri Aurobindo on various aspects of his spiritual teaching and method of yogic practice. Parts 1 to 4 deal mainly with the philosophical and psychological foundations of the teaching, Parts 5 to 11 with the method of practice, and Part 12 with elements of both.

Sri Aurobindo called his system the "Integral Yoga" because it proposed "a union [*yoga*] in all parts of our being with the Divine and a consequent transmutation of all their now jarring elements into the harmony of a higher divine consciousness and existence".

Sri Aurobindo wrote most of the letters during the 1930s to men and women living in his ashram in Pondicherry, India. At this time he was concentrated on his own spiritual practice and saw and spoke with practically no one; but he kept in touch with the seekers who had gathered around him by means of correspondence. The disciples sent him letters or diaries recounting events in their inward and outward lives. He replied, sometimes at length, sometimes simply by making marginal notations.

The letters included in this compilation have been selected from the more than two thousand pages of letters published in various volumes of the *Sri Aurobindo Birth Centenary Library*. References to these volumes are given at the end of the compilation. Generally the entire published letter has been reproduced. A few long letters dealing with two or more subjects have been split up and reproduced in different sections. Some material not thought relevant to the compilation has been cut out. Such omissions are indicated by ellipsis points (. . .).

Readers should keep in mind that each letter was written to a particular individual on a particular occasion. Sri Aurobindo once cautioned:

The tendency to take what I lay down for one and apply it without discrimination to another is responsible for much misunderstanding. A general statement, too, true in itself, cannot be applied to everyone alike or applied now and immediately without consideration of condition or circumstance or person or time.

In all his writings Sri Aurobindo used words from Sanskrit and other Indian languages. He also employed certain English words ("psychic", "vital") in his own way and coined a number of terms ("supermind", "environmental consciousness"). Readers not familiar with Sri Aurobindo's terminology are encouraged to consult the Glossary at the end of the volume.

This compilation was prepared by Peter Heehs and Bob Zwicker of the Sri Aurobindo Ashram Archives and Research Library.

Sri Aurobindo

Sri Aurobindo was born on 15 August 1872 in Calcutta. At the age of seven he was taken to England to be educated. After a brilliant career at St Paul's School, London, and King's College, Cambridge, he returned to India in 1893. For the next fourteen years he worked in the Princely State of Baroda, serving in various government departments, as a personal assistant to the Maharaja, and as a professor in Baroda College. During this period he mastered Sanskrit and Bengali and wrote much poetry and literary criticism. He also made secret preparations for an armed uprising against the British Raj.

After the Partition of Bengal in 1905, Sri Aurobindo quit his post in Baroda and went to Calcutta, where he became one of the leaders of the nationalist movement. As the editor of the newspaper *Bande Mataram* he boldly put forward the idea of complete independence for India. Arrested three times for sedition or treason, he was released each time for lack of evidence.

Sri Aurobindo began the practice of yoga in 1905. In 1910 he went to Pondicherry with the idea of devoting a year or two to meditation; but soon he realized that his spiritual work required his full attention and gradually cut off all connection with the revolutionary movement he had helped to initiate. During his forty years in Pondicherry, he worked out a new system of spiritual development, which he called the Integral Yoga. In 1926, with the help of his spiritual co-worker, the Mother, he founded an ashram where his motto, "All life is Yoga", could be put into practice. Among his many writings of the Pondicherry period the best known are *The Life Divine*, *The Synthesis of Yoga* and *Savitri*. Sri Aurobindo passed away on 5 December 1950.

It is the lesson of life that always in this world everything fails a man — only the Divine does not fail him, if he turns entirely to the Divine. It is not because there is something bad in you that blows fall on you, — blows fall on all human beings because they are full of desire for things that cannot last and they lose them or, even if they get, it brings disappointment and cannot satisfy them. To turn to the Divine is the only truth in life.

Sri Aurobindo

'21·4·33

Sri Aurobindo (1920 *c.*)

Sri Aurobindo (1950)

The changes we see in the world today are intellectual, moral, physical in their ideal and intention: the spiritual revolution waits for its hour and throws up meanwhile its waves here and there. Until it comes the sense of the others cannot be understood and till then all interpretations of present happenings and forecast of man's future are vain things. For its nature, power, event are that which will determine the next cycle of our humanity.

SRI AUROBINDO

Introduction

The teaching of Sri Aurobindo* starts from that of the ancient sages of India that behind the appearances of the universe there is the Reality of a Being and Consciousness, a Self of all things, one and eternal. All beings are united in that One Self and Spirit but divided by a certain separativity of consciousness, an ignorance of their true Self and Reality in the mind, life and body. It is possible by a certain psychological discipline to remove this veil of separative consciousness and become aware of the true Self, the Divinity within us and all.

Sri Aurobindo's teaching states that this One Being and Consciousness is involved here in Matter. Evolution is the method by which it liberates itself; consciousness appears in what seems to be inconscient, and once having appeared is self-impelled to grow higher and higher and at the same time to enlarge and develop towards a greater and greater perfection. Life is the first step of this release of consciousness; mind is the second; but the evolution does not finish with mind, it awaits a release into something greater, a consciousness which is spiritual and supramental. The next step of the evolution must be towards the development of Supermind and Spirit as the dominant power in the conscious being. For only then will the involved Divinity in things release itself entirely and it become possible for life to manifest perfection.

But while the former steps in evolution were taken by Nature without a conscious will in the plant and animal life, in man Nature becomes able to evolve by a conscious will in the instrument. It is not, however, by the mental will in man that this can be wholly done, for the mind goes only to a

---

* In this statement Sri Aurobindo speaks of himself in the third person.

certain point and after that can only move in a circle. A conversion has to be made, a turning of the consciousness by which mind has to change into the higher principle. This method is to be found through the ancient psychological discipline and practice of Yoga. In the past, it has been attempted by a drawing away from the world and a disappearance into the height of the Self or Spirit. Sri Aurobindo teaches that a descent of the higher principle is possible which will not merely release the spiritual Self out of the world, but release it in the world, replace the mind's ignorance or its very limited knowledge by a supramental Truth-Consciousness which will be a sufficient instrument of the inner Self and make it possible for the human being to find himself dynamically as well as inwardly and grow out of his still animal humanity into a diviner race. The psychological discipline of Yoga can be used to that end by opening all the parts of the being to a conversion or transformation through the descent and working of the higher still concealed supramental principle.

This, however, cannot be done at once or in a short time or by any rapid or miraculous transformation. Many steps have to be taken by the seeker before the supramental descent is possible. Man lives mostly in his surface mind, life and body, but there is an inner being within him with greater possibilities to which he has to awake — for it is only a very restricted influence from it that he receives now and that pushes him to a constant pursuit of a greater beauty, harmony, power and knowledge. The first process of Yoga is therefore to open the ranges of this inner being and to live from there outward, governing his outward life by an inner light and force. In doing so he discovers in himself his true soul which is not this outer mixture of mental, vital and physical elements but something of the Reality behind them, a spark from the one Divine Fire. He has to learn to live in his soul and purify and orientate by its drive towards the Truth the rest of the nature. There can follow afterwards an opening upward and descent of a higher principle of the

Being. But even then it is not at once the full supramental Light and Force. For there are several ranges of consciousness between the ordinary human mind and the supramental Truth-Consciousness. These intervening ranges have to be opened up and their power brought down into the mind, life and body. Only afterwards can the full power of the Truth-Consciousness work in the nature. The process of this self-discipline or Sadhana is therefore long and difficult, but even a little of it is so much gained because it makes the ultimate release and perfection more possible.

There are many things belonging to older systems that are necessary on the way — an opening of the mind to a greater wideness and to the sense of the Self and the Infinite, an emergence into what has been called the cosmic consciousness, mastery over the desires and passions; an outward asceticism is not essential, but the conquest of desire and attachment and a control over the body and its needs, greeds and instincts are indispensable. There is a combination of the principles of the old systems, the way of knowledge through the mind's discernment between Reality and the appearance, the heart's way of devotion, love and surrender and the way of works turning the will away from motives of self-interest to the Truth and the service of a greater Reality than the ego. For the whole being has to be trained so that it can respond and be transformed when it is possible for that greater Light and Force to work in the nature.

In this discipline, the inspiration of the Master, and in the difficult stages his control and his presence are indispensable — for it would be impossible otherwise to go through it without much stumbling and error which would prevent all chance of success. The Master is one who has risen to a higher consciousness and being and he is often regarded as its manifestation or representative. He not only helps by his teaching and still more by his influence and example but by a power to communicate his own experience to others.

This is Sri Aurobindo's teaching and method of practice. It is not his object to develop any one religion or to amalgamate the older religions or to found any new religion – for any of these things would lead away from his central purpose. The one aim of his Yoga is an inner self-development by which each one who follows it can in time discover the One Self in all and evolve a higher consciousness than the mental, a spiritual and supramental consciousness which will transform and divinise human nature.

1

The Integral Yoga and
the Ordinary Life

THE ONE THING NEEDFUL

It is the lesson of life that always in this world everything
fails a man — only the Divine does not fail him, if he turns
entirely to the Divine. It is not because there is something
bad in you that blows fall on you — blows fall on all human
beings because they are full of desire for things that cannot
last and they lose them or, even if they get, it brings disappointment and cannot satisfy them. To turn to the Divine is
the only truth in life.

*

To find the Divine is indeed the first reason for seeking the
spiritual Truth and the spiritual life; it is the one thing
indispensable and all the rest is nothing without it. The
Divine once found, to manifest Him, — that is, first of all to
transform one's own limited consciousness into the Divine
Consciousness, to live in the infinite Peace, Light, Love,
Strength, Bliss, to become that in one's essential nature and,
as a consequence, to be its vessel, channel, instrument in
one's active nature. To bring into activity the principle of
oneness on the material plane or to work for humanity is a
mental mistranslation of the Truth — these things cannot be
the first true object of spiritual seeking. We must find the
Self, the Divine, then only can we know what is the work the

Self or the Divine demands from us. Until then our life and action can only be a help or means towards finding the Divine and it ought not to have any other purpose. As we grow in the inner consciousness, or as the spiritual Truth of the Divine grows in us, our life and action must indeed more and more flow from that, be one with that. But to decide beforehand by our limited mental conceptions what they must be is to hamper the growth of the spiritual Truth within. As that grows we shall feel the Divine Light and Truth, the Divine Power and Force, the Divine Purity and Peace working within us, dealing with our actions as well as our consciousness, making use of them to reshape us into the Divine Image, removing the dross, substituting the pure gold of the Spirit. Only when the Divine Presence is there in us always and the consciousness transformed, can we have the right to say that we are ready to manifest the Divine on the material plane. To hold up a mental ideal or principle and impose that on the inner working brings the danger of limiting ourselves to a mental realisation or of impeding or even falsifying by a halfway formation the true growth into the full communion and union with the Divine and the free and intimate outflowing of His will in our life. This is a mistake of orientation to which the mind of today is especially prone. It is far better to approach the Divine for the Peace or Light or Bliss that the realisation of Him gives than to bring in these minor things which can divert us from the one thing needful. The divinisation of the material life also as well as the inner life is part of what we see as the Divine Plan, but it can only be fulfilled by an outflowing of the inner realisation, something that grows from within outwards, not by the working out of a mental principle.

*

The realisation of the Divine is the one thing needful and the rest is desirable only in so far as it helps or leads towards that or when it is realised, extends or manifests the realisation. Manifestation or organisation of the whole life for the

Divine work: first, the Sadhana personal and collective necessary for the realisation and a common life of the God-realised men, secondly, for help to the world to move towards that and to live in the Light, is the whole meaning and purpose of my Yoga. But the realisation is the first need and it is that round which all the rest moves, for apart from it all the rest would have no meaning.

*

Yoga is directed towards God, not towards man. If a divine supramental consciousness and power can be brought down and established in the material world, that obviously would mean an immense change for the earth including humanity and its life. But the effect on humanity would only be one result of the change; it cannot be the object of the sadhana. The object of the sadhana can only be to live in the divine consciousness and to manifest it in life.

*

Sadhana must be the main thing and sadhana means the purification of the nature, the consecration of the being, the opening of the psychic and the inner mind and vital, the contact and presence of the Divine, the realisation of the Divine in all things, surrender, devotion, the widening of the consciousness into the cosmic Consciousness, the Self one in all, the psychic and the spiritual transformation of the nature.

*

. . . the principle of this Yoga is not perfection of the human nature as it is but a psychic and spiritual transformation of all the parts of the being through the action of an inner consciousness and then of a higher consciousness which works on them, throws out their old movements or changes them into the image of its own and so transmutes lower into higher nature. It is not so much the perfection of the intellect as a transcendence of it, a transformation of the mind,

the substitution of a larger greater principle of knowledge —
and so with all the rest of the being.

This is a slow and difficult process; the road is long and it
is hard to establish even the necessary basis. The old existing
nature resists and obstructs and difficulties arise one after
another and repeatedly till they are overcome. It is therefore
necessary to be sure that this is the path to which one is
called before one finally decides to tread it.

THE OBJECT OF THE INTEGRAL YOGA

The object of the yoga is to enter into and be possessed by
the Divine Presence and Consciousness, to love the Divine
for the Divine's sake alone, to be tuned in our nature into
the nature of the Divine, and in our will and works and life
to be the instrument of the Divine. Its object is not to be a
great yogi or a Superman (although that may come) or to
grab at the Divine for the sake of the ego's power, pride or
pleasure. It is not for Moksha though liberation comes by it
and all else may come, but these must not be our objects.
The Divine alone is our object.

*

To come to this yoga merely with the idea of being a
superman would be an act of vital egoism which would
defeat its own object. Those who put this object in the front
of their preoccupations invariably come to grief, spiritually
and otherwise. The aim of this yoga is, first, to enter into the
divine consciousness by merging into it the separative ego
(incidentally, in doing so one finds one's true individual self
which is not the limited, vain and selfish human ego but a
portion of the Divine) and, secondly, to bring down the
supramental consciousness on earth to transform mind, life
and body. All else can be only a result of these two aims, not
the primary object of the yoga.

*

The only creation for which there is any place here is the supramental, the bringing of the divine Truth down on the earth, not only into the mind and vital but into the body and into Matter. Our object is not to remove all "limitations" on the expansion of the ego or to give a free field and make unlimited room for the fulfilment of the ideas of the human mind or the desires of the ego-centred life-force. None of us are here to "do as we like", or to create a world in which we shall at last be able to do as we like; we are here to do what the Divine wills and to create a world in which the Divine Will can manifest its truth no longer deformed by human ignorance or perverted and mistranslated by vital desire. The work which the sadhak of the supramental yoga has to do is not his own work for which he can lay down his own conditions, but the work of the Divine which he has to do according to the conditions laid down by the Divine. Our yoga is not for our own sake but for the sake of the Divine. It is not our own personal manifestation that we are to seek, the manifestation of the individual ego freed from all bounds and from all bonds, but the manifestation of the Divine. Of that manifestation our own spiritual liberation, perfection, fullness is to be a result and a part, but not in any egoistic sense or for any ego-centred or self-seeking purpose. This liberation, perfection, fullness too must not be pursued for our own sake, but for the sake of the Divine.

*

This yoga demands a total dedication of the life to the aspiration for the discovery and embodiment of the Divine Truth and to nothing else whatever. To divide your life between the Divine and some outward aim and activity that has nothing to do with the search for the Truth is inadmissible. The least thing of that kind would make success in the yoga impossible.

You must go inside yourself and enter into a complete dedication to the spiritual life. All clinging to mental preferences must fall away from you, all insistence on vital aims and interests and attachments must be put away, all egoistic clinging to family, friends, country must disappear if you want to succeed in yoga. Whatever has to come as outgoing energy or action, must proceed from the Truth once discovered and not from the lower mental or vital motives, from the Divine Will and not from personal choice or the preferences of the ego.

YOGA AND THE ORDINARY LIFE

In the yoga practised here the aim is to rise to a higher consciousness and to live out of the higher consciousness alone, not with the ordinary motives. This means a change of life as well as a change of consciousness. But all are not so circumstanced that they can cut loose from the ordinary life; they accept it therefore as a field of experience and self-training in the earlier stages of the sadhana. But they must take care to look at it as a field of experience only and to get free from the ordinary desires, attachments and ideas which usually go with it; otherwise, it becomes a drag and hindrance on their sadhana. When one is not compelled by circumstances there is no necessity to continue the ordinary life.

*

It is not helpful to abandon the ordinary life before the being is ready for the full spiritual life. To do so means to precipitate a struggle between the different elements and exasperate it to a point of intensity which the nature is not ready to bear. The vital elements in you have partly to be met by the discipline and experience of life, while keeping the spiritual aim in view and trying to govern life by it progressively in the spirit of Karmayoga.

*

The best way to prepare oneself for the spiritual life when one has to live in the ordinary occupations and surroundings is to cultivate an entire equality and detachment and the *samatā* of the Gita with the faith that the Divine is there and the Divine Will at work in all things even though at present under the conditions of a world of Ignorance. Beyond this are the Light and Ananda towards which life is working, but the best way for their advent and foundation in the individual being and nature is to grow in this spiritual equality. That would also solve your difficulty about things unpleasant and disagreeable. All unpleasantness should be faced with this spirit of *samatā*.

*

I may say briefly that there are two states of consciousness in either of which one can live. One is a higher consciousness which stands above the play of life and governs it; this is variously called the Self, the Spirit or the Divine. The other is the normal consciousness in which men live; it is something quite superficial, an instrument of the Spirit for the play of life. Those who live and act in the normal consciousness are governed entirely by the common movements of the mind and are naturally subject to grief and joy and anxiety and desire or to everything else that makes up the ordinary stuff of life. Mental quiet and happiness they can get, but it can never be permanent or secure. But the spiritual consciousness is all light, peace, power and bliss. If one can live entirely in it, there is no question; these things become naturally and securely his. But even if he can live partly in it or keep himself constantly open to it, he receives enough of this spiritual light and peace and strength and happiness to carry him securely through all the shocks of life. What one gains by opening to this spiritual consciousness, depends on what one seeks from it; if it is peace, one gets peace; if it is light or knowledge, one lives in a great light and receives a knowledge deeper and truer than any the normal mind of man can acquire; if it is strength or power, he gets a spiritual strength for the inner life or Yogic power to govern the outer work and action; if it is happiness, he enters into a beatitude far greater than any joy or happiness that the ordinary human life can give.

There are many ways of opening to this Divine Consciousness or entering into it. My way which I show to others is by a constant practice to go inward into oneself, to open by aspiration to the Divine and once one is conscious of it and its action, to give oneself to it entirely. This self-giving means not to ask for anything but the constant contact or union with the Divine Consciousness, to aspire for its peace, power, light and felicity, but to ask nothing else and in life and action to be its instrument only for whatever work it gives one to do in the world. If one can once open and feel the Divine Force, the Power of the Spirit working in the mind and heart and body, the rest is a matter of remaining faithful to it, calling for it always, allowing it to do its work when it comes and rejecting every other and inferior force that belongs to the lower consciousness and the lower nature.

*

Apart from external things there are two possible inner ideals which a man can follow. The first is the highest ideal of ordinary human life and the other the divine ideal of yoga. . . . The ideal of human life is to establish over the whole being the control of a clear, strong and rational mind and a right and rational will, to master the emotional, vital and physical being, create a harmony of the whole and develop the capacities whatever they are and fulfil them in life. . . . The object of the divine life, on the other hand, is to realise one's highest self or to realise God and to put the whole being into harmony with the truth of the highest self or the law of the divine nature, to find one's own divine capacities great or small and fulfil them in life as a sacrifice to the highest or as a true instrument of the divine Shakti.

*

The spiritual life (*adhyātma-jīvana*), the religious life (*dharma-jīvana*) and the ordinary human life of which morality is a part are three quite different things and one must know which one desires and not confuse the three together. The ordinary life is that of the average human consciousness separated from its own true self and from the Divine and led by the common habits of the mind, life and body which are the laws of the Ignorance. The religious life is a movement of the same ignorant human consciousness, turning or trying to turn away from the earth towards the Divine, but as yet without knowledge and led by the dogmatic tenets and rules of some sect or creed which claims to have found the way out of the bonds of the earth-consciousness into some beatific Beyond. The religious life may be the first approach to the spiritual, but very often it is only a turning about in a round of rites, ceremonies and practices or set ideas and forms without any issue. The spiritual life, on the contrary, proceeds directly by a change of consciousness, a change from the ordinary consciousness, ignorant and separated from its true self and from God, to a greater consciousness in which one finds one's true being and comes first into direct and living contact and then into union with the Divine. For the spiritual seeker this change of consciousness is the one thing he seeks and nothing else matters.

Morality is a part of the ordinary life; it is an attempt to govern the outward conduct by certain mental rules or to form the character by these rules in the image of a certain mental ideal. The spiritual life goes beyond the mind; it enters into the deeper consciousness of the Spirit and acts out of the truth of the Spirit.

*

The principle of life which I seek to establish is spiritual. Morality is a question of man's mind and vital, it belongs to a lower plane of consciousness. A spiritual life therefore cannot be founded on a moral basis, it must be founded on a spiritual basis. This does not mean that the spiritual man must be immoral – as if there were no other law of conduct than the moral. The law of action of the spiritual conscious-ness is higher, not lower than the moral – it is founded on union with the Divine and living in the Divine Conscious-ness and its action is founded on obedience to the Divine Will.

ASCETICISM AND THE INTEGRAL YOGA

You have apparently a call and may be fit for Yoga; but there are different paths and each has a different aim and end before it. It is common to all the paths to conquer the desires, to put aside the ordinary relations of life, and to try to pass from uncertainty to everlasting certitude. One may also try to conquer dream and sleep, thirst and hunger, etc. But it is no part of my Yoga to have nothing to do with the world or with life or to kill the senses or entirely inhibit their action. It is the object of my Yoga to transform life by bringing down into it the Light, Power and Bliss of the divine Truth and its dynamic certitudes. This Yoga is not a Yoga of world-shunning asceticism, but of divine life. Your object, on the other hand, can only be gained by entering into Samadhi and ceasing in it from all connection with world-existence.

*

There is, of course, also the ascetic idea which is necessary for many and has its place in the spiritual order. I would myself say that no man can be spiritually complete if he cannot live ascetically or follow a life as bare as the barest anchorite's. Obviously, greed for wealth and money-making has to be absent from his nature as much as greed for food or any other greed and all attachment to these things must be renounced from his consciousness. But I do not regard the ascetic way of living as indispensable to spiritual perfection or as identical with it. There is the way of spiritual self-mastery and the way of spiritual self-giving and surrender to the Divine, abandoning ego and desire even in the midst of action or of any kind of work or all kinds of work demanded from us by the Divine.

*

My own life and my yoga have always been, since my coming to India, both this-worldly and other-worldly without any exclusiveness on either side. All human interests are, I suppose, this-worldly and most of them have entered into my mental field and some, like politics, into my life, but at the same time, since I set foot on the Indian soil on the Apollo Bunder in Bombay, I began to have spiritual experiences, but these were not divorced from this world but had an inner and infinite bearing on it, such as a feeling of the Infinite pervading material space and the Immanent inhabiting material objects and bodies. At the same time I found myself entering supraphysical worlds and planes with influences and an effect from them upon the material plane, so I could make no sharp divorce or irreconcilable opposition between what I have called the two ends of existence and all that lies between them. For me all is Brahman and I find the Divine everywhere. Everyone has the right to throw away this-worldliness and choose other-worldliness only, and if he finds peace by that choice he is greatly blessed. I, personally, have not found it necessary to do this in order to have peace. In my yoga also I found myself moved to include both worlds in my purview – the spiritual and the material – and to try to establish the Divine Consciousness and the Divine Power in men's hearts and earthly life, not for a personal salvation only but for a life divine here. This seems to me as spiritual an aim as any and the fact of this life taking up earthly pursuits and earthly things into its scope cannot, I believe, tarnish its spirituality or alter its Indian character. This at least has always been my view and experience of the reality and nature of the world and things and the Divine: it seemed to me as nearly as possible the integral truth about them and I have therefore spoken of the pursuit of it as the integral yoga. Everyone is, of course, free to reject and disbelieve in this kind of integrality or to believe in the spiritual necessity of an entire other-worldliness altogether, but that would make the exercise of my yoga impossible. My yoga can include indeed a full experience of the other worlds, the plane of the Supreme Spirit and the other planes in between and their possible effects upon our life and the material world; but it will be quite possible to insist only on the realisation of the Supreme Being or Ishwara even in one aspect, Shiva, Krishna as Lord of the world and Master of ourselves and our works or else the Universal Sachchidananda, and attain to the essential results of this yoga and afterwards to proceed from them to the integral results if one accepted the ideal of the divine life and this material world conquered by the Spirit.

MOTIVES FOR SEEKING THE DIVINE

Obviously to seek the Divine *only* for what one can get out of Him is not the proper attitude; but if it were absolutely forbidden to seek Him for these things, most people in the world would not turn towards Him at all. I suppose therefore it is allowed so that they may make a beginning – if they have faith, they may get what they ask for and think it a good thing to go on and then one day they may suddenly stumble upon the idea that this is after all not quite the one thing to do and that there are better ways and a better spirit in which one can approach the Divine. If they do not get what they want and still come to the Divine and trust in Him, well, that shows they are getting ready. Let us look at it as a sort of infants' school for the unready. But of course that is not the spiritual life, it is only a sort of elementary religious approach. For the spiritual life to give and not to demand is the rule. The sadhak, however, can ask for the Divine Force to aid him in keeping his health or recovering it if he does that as part of his sadhana so that his body may be able and fit for the spiritual life and a capable instrument for the Divine Work.

*

Let us first put aside the quite foreign consideration of what we would do if the union with the Divine brought eternal joylessness, Nirananda or torture. Such a thing does not exist and to drag it in only clouds the issue. The Divine is Anandamaya and one can seek him for the Ananda he gives; but he has also in him many other things and one may seek him for any of them, for peace, for liberation, for knowledge, for power, for anything else of which one may feel the pull or the impulse. It is quite possible for someone to say: "Let me have Power from the Divine and do His work or His Will and I am satisfied, even if the use of Power entails suffering also." It is possible to shun bliss as a thing too tremendous or ecstatic and ask only or rather for peace, for liberation, for Nirvana. You speak of self-fulfilment, — one may regard the Supreme not as the Divine but as one's highest Self and seek fulfilment of one's being in that highest Self; but one need not envisage it as a self of bliss, ecstasy, Ananda — one may envisage it as a self of freedom, vastness, knowledge, tranquillity, strength, calm, perfection — perhaps too calm for a ripple of anything so disturbing as joy to enter. So even if it is for something to be gained that one approaches the Divine, it is not a fact that one can approach Him or seek union only for the sake of Ananda and nothing else.

That involves something which throws all your reasoning out of gear. For these are aspects of the Divine Nature, powers of it, states of his being, — but the Divine Himself is something absolute, someone self-existent, not limited by his aspects, — wonderful and ineffable, not existing by them, but they existing because of Him. It follows that if he attracts by his aspects, all the more he çan attract by his very absolute selfness which is sweeter, mightier, profounder than any aspect. His peace, rapture, light, freedom, beauty are marvellous and ineffable, because he is himself magically, mysteriously, transcendently marvellous and ineffable. He can then be sought after for his wonderful and ineffable self and not only for the sake of one aspect or another of his. The only thing needed for that is, first, to arrive at a point when the psychic being feels this pull of the Divine in himself and, secondly, to arrive at the point when the mind, vital and each thing else begins to feel too that that was what it was wanting and the surface hunt after Ananda or what else was only an excuse for drawing the nature towards that supreme magnet.

Your argument that because we know the union with the Divine will bring Ananda, therefore it must be for the Ananda that we seek the union, is not true and has no force. One who loves a queen may know that if she returns his love it will bring him power, position, riches and yet it need not be for the power, position, riches that he seeks her love. He may love her for herself and could love her equally if she were not a queen; he might have no hope of any return whatever and yet love her, adore her, live for her, die for her simply because she is she. That has happened and men have loved women without any hope of enjoyment or result, loved steadily, passionately after age has come and beauty has gone. Patriots do not love their country only when she is rich, powerful, great and has much to give them; love for country has been most ardent, passionate, absolute when the country was poor, degraded, miserable, having nothing to give but loss, wounds, torture, imprisonment, death as the wages of her service; yet even knowing that they would never see her free, men have lived, served and died for her — for her own sake, not for what she could give. Men have loved Truth for her own sake and for what they could seek or find of her, accepted poverty, persecution, death itself; they have been content even to seek for her always, not finding, and yet never given up the search. That means what? That man, country, Truth and other things besides can be loved for their own sake and not for anything else, not for any circumstance or attendant quality or resulting enjoyment, but for something absolute that is either in them or behind their appearance and circumstance. The Divine is more than a man or woman, a stretch of land or a creed, opinion, discovery or principle. He is the Person beyond all persons, the Home and Country of all souls, the Truth of which truths are only imperfect figures. And can He then not be loved and sought for his own sake, as and more than these have been by men even in their lesser selves and nature?

What your reasoning ignores is that which is absolute or tends towards the absolute in man and his seeking as well as in the Divine – something not to be explained by mental reasoning or vital motive. A motive, but a motive of the soul, not of vital desire; a reason not of the mind, but of the self and spirit. An asking too, but the asking that is the soul's inherent aspiration, not a vital longing. That is what comes up when there is the sheer self-giving, when "I seek you for this, I seek you for that" changes to a sheer "I seek you for you." It is that marvellous and ineffable absolute in the Divine that X means when he says, "Not knowledge nor this nor that, but Krishna." The pull of that is indeed a categorical imperative, the self in us drawn to the Divine because of the imperative call of the greater Self, the soul ineffably drawn towards the object of its adoration because it cannot be otherwise, because it is it and He is He. That is all about it.

I have written all that only to explain what we mean when we speak of seeking the Divine for himself and not for anything else – so far as it is explicable. Explicable or not, it is one of the most dominant facts of spiritual experience. The will to self-giving is only an expression of this fact. But this does not mean that I object to your asking for Ananda. Ask for that by all means, so long as to ask for it is a need of any part of your being — for these are the things that lead towards the Divine so long as the absolute inner call that is there all the time does not push itself to the surface. But it was really that that has drawn from the beginning and is there behind — it is the categorical spiritual imperative, the absolute need of the soul for the Divine.

I am not saying that there is to be no Ananda. The self-giving itself is a profound Ananda and what it brings, carries in its wake an inexpressible Ananda — and it is brought by this method sooner than by any other, so that one can say almost, "A self-less self-giving is the best policy." Only one does not do it out of policy. Ananda is the result, but it is done not for the result, but for the self-giving itself and for the Divine himself — a subtle distinction, it may seem to the mind, but very real.

2

The Integral Yoga and Other Systems of Yoga and Philosophy

METAPHYSICAL THOUGHT AND THE SUPREME TRUTH

European metaphysical thought – even in those thinkers who try to prove or explain the existence and nature of God or of the Absolute – does not in its method and result go beyond the intellect. But the intellect is incapable of knowing the supreme Truth; it can only range about seeking for Truth, and catching fragmentary representations of it, not the thing itself, and trying to piece them together. Mind cannot arrive at Truth; it can only make some constructed figure that tries to represent it or a combination of figures. At the end of European thought, therefore, there must always be Agnosticism, declared or implicit. Intellect, if it goes sincerely to its own end, has to return and give this report: "I cannot know; there is, or at least it seems to me that there may be or even must be Something beyond, some ultimate Reality, but about its truth I can only speculate; it is either unknowable or cannot be known by me." Or, if it has received some light on the way from what is beyond it, it can say too: "There is perhaps a consciousness beyond Mind, for I seem to catch glimpses of it and even to get intimations from it. If that is in touch with the Beyond or if it is itself the consciousness of the Beyond and you can find some way to reach it, then this Something can be known but not otherwise."

Any seeking of the supreme Truth through intellect alone must end either in Agnosticism of this kind or else in some intellectual system or mind-constructed formula. There have been hundreds of these systems and formulas and there can be hundreds more, but none can be definitive. Each may have its value for the mind, and different systems with their contrary conclusions can have an equal appeal to intelligences of equal power and competence. All this labour of speculation has its utility in training the human mind and helping to keep before it the idea of Something beyond and Ultimate towards which it must turn. But the intellectual Reason can only point vaguely or feel gropingly towards it or try to indicate partial and even conflicting aspects of its manifestation here; it cannot enter into and know it. As long as we remain in the domain of the intellect only, an impartial pondering over all that has been thought and sought after, a constant throwing up of ideas, of all the possible ideas, and the formation of this or that philosophical belief, opinion or conclusion is all that can be done. This kind of disinterested search after Truth would be the only possible attitude for any wide and plastic intelligence. But any conclusion so arrived at would be only speculative; it could have no spiritual value; it would not give the decisive experience or the spiritual certitude for which the soul is seeking. If the intellect is our highest possible instrument and there is no other means of arriving at supraphysical Truth, then a wise and large Agnosticism must be our ultimate attitude. Things in the manifestation may be known to some degree, but the Supreme and all that is beyond the Mind must remain forever unknowable.

It is only if there is a greater consciousness beyond Mind and that consciousness is accessible to us that we can know and enter into the ultimate Reality. Intellectual speculation, logical reasoning as to whether there is or is not such a greater consciousness cannot carry us very far. What we need is a way to get the experience of it, to reach it, enter into it, live in it. If we can get that, intellectual speculation and reasoning must fall necessarily into a very secondary place and even lose their reason for existence. Philosophy, intellectual expression of the Truth may remain, but mainly as a means of expressing this greater discovery and as much of its contents as can at all be expressed in mental terms to those who still live in the mental intelligence. . . .

In the East, especially in India, the metaphysical thinkers have tried, as in the West, to determine the nature of the highest Truth by the intellect. But, in the first place, they have not given mental thinking the supreme rank as an instrument in the discovery of Truth, but only a secondary status. The first rank has always been given to spiritual intuition and illumination and spiritual experience; an intellectual conclusion that contradicts this supreme authority is held invalid. Secondly, each philosophy has armed itself with a practical way of reaching to the supreme state of consciousness, so that even when one begins with Thought, the aim is to arrive at a consciousness beyond mental thinking. Each philosophical founder (as also those who continued his work or school) has been a metaphysical thinker doubled with a yogi. Those who were only philosophic intellectuals were respected for their learning but never took rank as truth-discoverers. And the philosophies that lacked a sufficiently powerful means of spiritual experience died out and became things of the past because they were not dynamic for spiritual discovery and realisation. . . .

It is not by "thinking out" the entire reality, but by a change of consciousness that one can pass from the ignorance to the Knowledge – the Knowledge by which we become what we know. To pass from the external to a direct and intimate inner consciousness; to widen consciousness out of the limits of the ego and the body; to heighten it by an inner will and aspiration and opening to the Light till it passes in its ascent beyond Mind; to bring down a descent of the supramental Divine through self-giving and surrender

with a consequent transformation of mind, life and body —
this is the *integral* way to the Truth.* It is this that we call the
Truth here and aim at in our yoga.

ILLUSIONIST ADWAITA (MAYAVADA)

I do not agree with the view that the world is an illusion,
mithyā. The Brahman is here as well as in the supracosmic
Absolute. The thing to be overcome is the Ignorance which
makes us blind and prevents us from realising Brahman in
the world as well as beyond it and the true nature of
existence.

*

If Shankara's conception of the undifferentiated pure Consciousness as the Brahman is your view of it, then it is not
the path of this yoga that you should choose; for here the
realisation of pure Consciousness and Being is only a first
step and not the goal. But an inner creative urge from within
can have no place in an undifferentiated Consciousness — all
action and creation must necessarily be foreign to it.

I do not base my yoga on the insufficient ground that the
Self (not soul) is eternally free. That affirmation leads to
nothing beyond itself, or, if used as a starting-point, it could
equally well lead to the conclusion that action and creation
have no significance or value. The question is not that but of
the meaning of creation, whether there is a Supreme who is
not merely a pure undifferentiated Consciousness and
Being, but the source and support also of the dynamic
energy of creation and whether the cosmic existence has for

* I have said that the idea of the supermind was already in existence from ancient times. There was in India and elsewhere the attempt to reach it by rising to
it; but what was missed was the way to make it integral for the life and to bring it
down for transformation of the whole nature, even of the physical nature. [Sri
Aurobindo's note]

It a significance and a value. That is a question which cannot be settled by metaphysical logic which deals in words and ideas, but by a spiritual experience which goes beyond Mind and enters into spiritual realities. Each mind is satisfied with its own reasoning, but for spiritual purposes that satisfaction has no validity, except as an indication of how far and on what line each one is prepared to go in the field of spiritual experience. If your reasoning leads you towards the Shankara idea of the Supreme, that might be an indication that the Vedanta Adwaita (Mayavada) is your way of advance.

This yoga accepts the value of cosmic existence and holds it to be a reality; its object is to enter into a higher Truth-Consciousness or Divine supramental Consciousness in which action and creation are the expression not of ignorance and imperfection, but of the Truth, the Light, the Divine Ananda. But for that, surrender of the mortal mind, life and body to that Higher Consciousness is indispensable, since it is too difficult for the mortal human being to pass by its own effort beyond mind to a supramental Consciousness in which the dynamism is no longer mental but of quite another power. Only those who can accept the call to such a change should enter into this yoga.

*

There is possible a realistic as well as an illusionist Adwaita. The philosophy of *The Life Divine** is such a realistic Adwaita. The world is a manifestation of the Real and therefore is itself real. The reality is the infinite and eternal Divine, infinite and eternal Being, Consciousness-Force and Bliss. This Divine by his power has created the world or rather manifested it in his own infinite Being. But here in the material world or at its basis he has hidden himself in what seem to be his opposites, Non-Being, Inconscience and Insentience. This is what we nowadays call the Inconscient which seems to have created the material universe by its inconscient Energy, but this is only an appearance, for we

_____
* Sri Aurobindo's principal work of spiritual philosophy.

find in the end that all the dispositions of the world can only have been arranged by the working of a supreme secret Intelligence. The Being which is hidden in what seems to be an inconscient void emerges in the world first in Matter, then in Life, then in Mind and finally as the Spirit. The apparently inconscient Energy which creates is in fact the Consciousness-Force of the Divine and its aspect of consciousness, secret in Matter, begins to emerge in Life, finds something more of itself in Mind and finds its true self in a spiritual consciousness and finally a supramental Consciousness through which we become aware of the Reality, enter into it and unite ourselves with it. This is what we call evolution which is an evolution of Consciousness and an evolution of the Spirit in things and only outwardly an evolution of species. Thus also, the delight of existence emerges from the original insentience, first in the contrary forms of pleasure and pain, and then has to find itself in the bliss of the Spirit or, as it is called in the Upanishads, the bliss of the Brahman. That is the central idea in the explanation of the universe put forward in *The Life Divine*.

THE YOGA OF THE GITA

I may say that the way of the Gita is itself a part of the yoga here and those who have followed it, to begin with or as a first stage, have a stronger basis than others for this yoga.

*

It is not a fact that the Gita gives the whole base of Sri Aurobindo's message; for the Gita seems to admit the cessation of birth in the world as the ultimate aim or at least the ultimate culmination of yoga; it does not bring forward the idea of spiritual evolution or the idea of the higher planes and the supramental Truth-Consciousness and the bringing down of that consciousness as the means of the complete transformation of earthly life.

The idea of the supermind, the Truth-Consciousness is there in the Rig Veda according to Sri Aurobindo's interpretation and in one or two passages of the Upanishads, but in the Upanishads it is there only in seed in the conception of the being of knowledge, *vijñānamaya purusa*, exceeding the mental, vital and physical being; in the Rig Veda the idea is there but in principle only, it is not developed and even the principle of it has disappeared from the Hindu tradition.

It is these things among others that constitute the novelty of Sri Aurobindo's message as compared with the Hindu tradition – the idea that the world is not either a creation of Maya or only a play, *līlā*, of the Divine, or a cycle of births in the ignorance from which we have to escape, but a field of manifestation in which there is a progressive evolution of the soul and the nature in Matter and from Matter through Life and Mind to what is beyond Mind till it reaches the complete revelation of Sachchidananda in life. It is this that is the basis of the yoga and gives a new sense to life.

*

Our yoga is not identical with the yoga of the Gita although it contains all that is essential in the Gita's yoga. In our yoga we begin with the idea, the will, the aspiration of the complete surrender; but at the same time we have to reject the lower nature, deliver our consciousness from it, deliver the self involved in the lower nature by the self rising to freedom in the higher nature. If we do not do this double movement, we are in danger of making a tamasic and therefore unreal surrender, making no effort, no tapas and therefore no progress; or else we may make a rajasic surrender not to the Divine but to some self-made false idea or image of the Divine which masks our rajasic ego or something still worse.

*

The Gita does not speak expressly of the Divine Mother; it speaks always of surrender to the Purushottama — it mentions her only as the Para Prakriti who becomes the Jiva, that is, who manifests the Divine in the multiplicity and through whom all these worlds are created by the Supreme and he himself descends as the Avatar. The Gita follows the Vedantic tradition which leans entirely on the Ishwara aspect of the Divine and speaks little of the Divine Mother because its object is to draw back from world-nature and arrive at the supreme realisation beyond it; the Tantric tradition leans on the Shakti or Ishwari aspect and makes all depend on the Divine Mother because its object is to possess and dominate the world-nature and arrive at the supreme realisation through it. This yoga insists on both the aspects; the surrender to the Divine Mother is essential, for without it there is no fulfilment of the object of the yoga.

THE TANTRIC TRADITION

Unless one realises the Supreme on the dynamic as well as the static side, one cannot experience the true origin of things and the equal reality of the active Brahman. The Shakti or Power of the Eternal becomes then a power of illusion only and the world becomes incomprehensible, a mystery of cosmic madness, an eternal delirium of the Eternal. Whatever verbal or ideative logic one may bring to support it, this way of seeing the universe explains nothing; it only erects a mental formula of the inexplicable. It is only if you approach the Supreme through his double aspect of Sat and Chit-Shakti, double but inseparable, that the total truth of things can become manifest to the inner experience. This other side was developed by the Shakta Tantriks. The two together, the Vedantic and the Tantric truth unified, can arrive at the integral knowledge.

*

Veda and Vedanta are one side of the One Truth; Tantra with its emphasis on Shakti is another; in this yoga all sides of the Truth are taken up, not in the systematic forms given them formerly but in their essence, and carried to the fullest and highest significance. But Vedanta deals more with the principles and essentials of the divine knowledge and therefore much of its spiritual knowledge and experience has been taken bodily into the *Arya.** Tantra deals more with forms and processes and organised powers – all these could not be taken as they were, for the integral yoga needs to develop its own forms and processes; but the ascent of the consciousness through the centres and other Tantric knowledge are there behind the process of transformation to which so much importance is given by me – also the truth that nothing can be done except through the force of the Mother.

The process of the Kundalini awakened rising through the centres as also the purification of the centres is a Tantric knowledge. In our yoga there is no willed process of the purification and opening of the centres, no raising up of the Kundalini by a set process either. Another method is used, but still there is the ascent of the consciousness from and through the different levels to join the higher consciousness above; there is the opening of the centres and of the planes (mental, vital, physical) which these centres command; there is also the descent which is the main key of the spiritual transformation. Therefore, there is, I have said, a Tantric knowledge behind the process of transformation in this yoga.

*

In the Tantra the centres are opened and Kundalini is awakened by a special process, its action of ascent is felt through the spine. Here it is a pressure of the Force from above that awakens it and opens the centres. There is an

---

* A philosophical journal (1914-21), in which most of Sri Aurobindo's major prose writings first appeared.

ascension of the consciousness going up till it joins the
higher consciousness above. This repeats itself (sometimes a
descent also is felt) until all the centres are open and the
consciousness rises above the body. At a later stage it
remains above and widens out into the cosmic consciousness
and the universal self. This is a usual course, but sometimes
the process is more rapid and there is a sudden and definite
opening above.

*

In our yoga there is no willed opening of the chakras, they
open of themselves by the descent of the Force. In the
Tantric discipline they open from down upwards, the Muladhar first; in our yoga, they open from up downward. But
the ascent of the force from the Muladhar does take place.

*

In the process of our yoga the centres have each a fixed
psychological use and general function which base all their
special powers and functionings. The *mūlādhāra* governs the
physical down to the subconscient; the abdominal centre —
svādhisthāna — governs the lower vital; the navel centre —
nābhipadma or *manipūra* — governs the larger vital; the
heart centre — *hrtpadma* or *anāhata* — governs the emotional
being; the throat centre — *visuddha* — governs the expressive
and externalising mind; the centre between the eye-brows —
ajñācakra — governs the dynamic mind, will, vision, mental
formation; the thousand-petalled lotus — *sahasradala* —
above commands the higher thinking mind, houses the still
higher illumined mind and at the highest opens to the intuition through which or else by an overflooding directness
the overmind can have with the rest communication or an
immediate contact.

*

The centres of consciousness, the chakras. It is by their opening that the yogic or inner consciousness develops — otherwise you are bound to the ordinary outer consciousness.

*

One can speak of the chakras only in reference to yoga. In ordinary people the chakras are not open, it is only when they do sadhana that the chakras open. For the chakras are the centres of the inner consciousness and belong originally to the subtle body. So much as is active in ordinary people is very little — for in them it is the outer consciousness that is active.

VAISHNAVA BHAKTI

The "human" vital consciousness has moved always between these two poles, the ordinary vital life which cannot satisfy and the recoil from it to the ascetic solution. India has gone fully through that seesaw, Europe is beginning once more after a full trial to feel the failure of the mere vital egoistic life. The traditional yogas — to which you appeal — are founded upon the movement between these two poles. On one side are Shankara and Buddha and most go, if not by the same road, yet in that direction; on the other are Vaishnava or Tantric lines which try to combine asceticism with some sublimation of the vital impulse. And where did these lines end? They fell back to the other pole, to a vital invasion, even corruption and a loss of their spirit. At the present day the general movement is towards an attempt at reconciliation, and you have alluded sometimes to some of the protagonists of this attempt and asked me my opinion about them, yours being unfavourable. But these men are not mere charlatans, and if there is anything wrong with them (on which I do not pronounce), it can only be because they are unable to resist the magnetic pull of this lower pole of the egoistic vital desire-nature. And if they are unable to resist, it is because they have not found the true force which will not only neutralise that pull and prevent deterioration and downward lapse, but transform and utilise and satisfy in their own deeper truth, instead of destroying or throwing away, the life-force and the embodiment in Matter; for, that can only be done by the supermind power and by no other. . . .

The tradition of later Vaishnava Bhakti is an attempt to sublimate the vital impulses through love by turning human love towards the Divine. It made a strong and intense effort and had many rich and beautiful experiences; but its weakness was just there, that it remained valid only as an inner experience turned towards the inner Divine, but it stopped at that point. Chaitanya's *prema* was nothing but a psychic divine love with a strong sublimated vital manifestation. But the moment Vaishnavism before or after him made an attempt at greater externalisation, we know what happened – a vitalistic deterioration, much corruption and decline.

*

It is a misunderstanding to suppose that I am against Bhakti or against emotional Bhakti – which comes to the same thing, since without emotion there can be no Bhakti. It is rather the fact that in my writings on yoga I have given Bhakti the highest place. All that I have said at any time which could account for this misunderstanding was against an *unpurified* emotionalism which, according to my experience, leads to want of balance, agitated and disharmonious expression or even contrary reactions and, at its extreme, nervous disorder. But the insistence on purification does not mean that I condemn true feeling and emotion any more than the insistence on a purified mind or will means that I condemn thought and will. On the contrary, the deeper the emotion, the more intense the Bhakti, the greater is the force for realisation and transformation. It is oftenest through intensity of emotion that the psychic being awakes and there is an opening of the inner doors to the Divine.

*

I have no objection at all to the worship of Krishna or the Vaishnava form of devotion, nor is there any incompatibility between Vaishnava Bhakti and my supramental yoga. There is in fact no special and exclusive form of supramental yoga: all ways can lead to the supermind, just as all ways can lead to the Divine.

*

It is not necessary to repeat past forms [of Bhakti Yoga] – to bring out the Bhakti of the psychic being and give it whatever forms come naturally in the development is the proper way for our sadhana.

*

The traditions of the past are very great in their own place, in the past, but I do not see why we should merely repeat them and not go farther. In the spiritual development of the consciousness upon earth the great past ought to be followed by a greater future.

THE INTEGRAL YOGA AND OTHER YOGAS

This yoga aims at the conscious union with the Divine in the supermind and the transformation of the nature. The ordinary yogas go straight from Mind into some featureless condition of the cosmic silence and through it try to disappear upward into the Highest. The object of this yoga is to transcend Mind and enter into the Divine Truth of Sachchidananda which is not only static but dynamic and raise the whole being into that truth.

*

Those who seek the Self by the old yogas separate themselves from mind, life and body and realise the self of it all as different from these things. It is perfectly easy to separate mind, vital and physical from each other without the aid of supermind. It is done by the ordinary yogas. The difference between this and the old yogas is not that they are incompetent and cannot do these things — they can do this perfectly well — but that they proceed from realisation of Self to Nirvana or some Heaven and abandon life, while this does not abandon life. The supramental is necessary for the transformation of terrestrial life and being, not for reaching the Self. One must realise Self first, only afterwards can one realise the supermind.

*

The realisation of Self and of the Cosmic being (without which the realisation of Self is incomplete) are essential steps in our Yoga; it is the end of other Yogas, but it is, as it were, the beginning of ours, that is to say, the point where its own characteristic realisation can commence.

*

The ordinary Yoga does not go beyond the spiritual mind — people feel at the top of the head the joining with the Brahman, but they are not aware of a consciousness above the head. In the same way in the ordinary Yoga one feels the ascent of the awakened lower consciousness (Kundalini) to the *brahmarandhra* where the Prakriti joins the Brahman-consciousness, but they do not feel the descent. Some may have had these things, but I don't know that they understood their nature, principle or place in a complete Sadhana. At least I never heard of these things from others before I found them out in my own experience. The reason is that the old Yogins when they went above the spiritual mind passed into Samadhi, which means that they made no attempt to be conscious in these higher planes — their aim being to pass away into the Superconscient and not to bring the Superconscient into the waking consciousness, which is that of my Yoga.

*

As for the depreciation of the old yogas as something quite easy, unimportant and worthless and the depreciation of Buddha, Yajnavalkya and other great spiritual figures of the past, is it not evidently absurd on the face of it?

*

Wonderful! The realisation of the Self which includes the liberation from ego, the consciousness of the One in all, the established and consummated transcendence out of the universal Ignorance, the fixity of the consciousness in the union with the Highest, the Infinite and Eternal is not anything worth doing or recommending to anybody – is "not a very difficult stage"!

Nothing new! Why should there be anything new? The object of spiritual seeking is to find out what is eternally true, not what is new in Time.

From where did you get this singular attitude towards the old yogas and yogis? Is the wisdom of the Vedanta and Tantra a small and trifling thing? Have then the sadhaks of the Ashram attained to self-realisation and are they liberated Jivanmúktas, free from ego and ignorance? If not, why then do you say, "it is not a very difficult stage", "their goal is not high", "is it such a long process?"

I have said that this yoga is "new" because it aims at the integrality of the Divine in this world and not only beyond it and at a supramental realisation. But how does that justify a superior contempt for the spiritual realisation which is as much the aim of this yoga as of any other?

*

I have never said that my yoga was something brand new in all its elements. I have called it the integral yoga and that means that it takes up the essence and many processes of the old yogas — its newness is in its aim, standpoint and the totality of its method. In the earlier stages which is all I deal with in books like the "Riddle" or the "Lights" or in the new book to be published* there is nothing in it that distinguishes it from the old yogas except the aim underlying its comprehensiveness, the spirit in its movements and the ultimate significance it keeps before it — also the scheme of its psychology and its workings: but as that was not and could not be developed systematically or schematically in these letters, it has not been grasped by those who are not already acquainted with it by mental familiarity or some amount of practice. The detail or method of the later stages of the yoga which go into little known or untrodden regions, I have not made public and I do not at present intend to do so.

I know very well also that there have been seemingly allied ideals and anticipations — the perfectibility of the race, certain Tantric sadhanas, the effort after a complete physical siddhi by certain schools of yoga, etc., etc. I have alluded to these things myself and have put forth the view that the spiritual past of the race has been a preparation of Nature not merely for attaining the Divine beyond the world, but also for this very step forward which the evolution of the earth-consciousness has still to make. I do not therefore care in the least — even though these ideals were, up to some extent parallel, yet not identical with mine — whether this yoga and its aim and method are accepted as new or not; that is in itself a trifling matter. That it should be recognised as true in itself by those who can accept or practise it and should make itself true by achievement is the one thing important; it does not matter if it is called new or a repetition or revival of the old which was forgotten. I laid emphasis on it as new in a letter to certain sadhaks so as to explain to them that a repetition of the aim and idea of the old yogas was not enough in my eyes, that I was putting for-

---

* *Bases of Yoga*. This and the other two books mentioned are short collections of letters by Sri Aurobindo on yoga.

ward a thing to be achieved that has not yet been achieved, not yet clearly visualised, even though it is the natural but still secret outcome of all the past spiritual endeavour.

It is new as compared with the old yogas:

1. Because it aims not at a departure out of world and life into Heaven or Nirvana, but at a change of life and existence, not as something subordinate or incidental, but as a distinct and central object. If there is a descent in other yogas, yet it is only an incident on the way or resulting from the ascent — the ascent is the real thing. Here the ascent is the first step, but it is a means for the descent. It is the descent of the new consciousness attained by the ascent that is the stamp and seal of the sadhana. Even the Tantra and Vaishnavism end in the release from life; here the object is the divine fulfilment of life.

2. Because the object sought after is not an individual achievement of divine realisation for the sake of the individual, but something to be gained for the earth-consciousness here, a cosmic, not solely a supra-cosmic achievement. The thing to be gained also is the bringing in of a Power of Consciousness (the supramental) not yet organised or active directly in earth-nature, even in the spiritual life, but yet to be organised and made directly active.

3. Because a method has been preconized for achieving this purpose which is as total and integral as the aim set before it, viz., the total and integral change of the consciousness and nature, taking up old methods but only as a part action and present aid to others that are distinctive. I have not found this method (as a whole) or anything like it professed or realised in the old yogas. If I had, I should not have wasted my time in hewing out a road and in thirty years of search and inner creation when I could have hastened home safely to my goal in an easy canter over paths already blazed out, laid down, perfectly mapped, macadamised, made secure and public. Our

yoga is not a retreading of old walks, but a spiritual adventure.

*

I meant by it the descent of the supramental consciousness upon earth; all truths below the supramental (even that of the highest spiritual on the mental plane, which is the highest that has yet manifested) are either partial or relative or otherwise deficient and unable to transform the earthly life; they can only at most modify and influence it. The supermind is the vast Truth-Consciousness of which the ancient seers spoke; there have been glimpses of it till now, sometimes an indirect influence or pressure, but it has not been brought down into the consciousness of the earth and fixed there. To so bring it down is the aim of our yoga.

But it is better not to enter into sterile intellectual discussions. The intellectual mind cannot even realise what the supermind is; what use, then, can there be in allowing it to discuss what it does not know? It is not by reasoning but by constant experience, growth of consciousness and widening into the Light that one can reach those higher levels of consciousness above the intellect from which one can begin to look up to the Divine Gnosis. Those levels are not yet the supermind, but they can receive something of its knowledge.

The Vedic Rishis never attained to the supermind for the earth or perhaps did not even make the attempt. They tried to rise individually to the supramental plane, but they did not bring it down and make it a permanent part of the earth-consciousness. Even there are verses of the Upanishad in which it is hinted that it is impossible to pass through the gates of the Sun (the symbol of the supermind) and yet retain an earthly body. It was because of this failure that the spiritual effort of India culminated in Mayavada. Our yoga is a double movement of ascent and descent; one rises to higher and higher levels of consciousness, but at the same time one brings down their power not only into mind and life, but in the end even into the body. And the highest of these levels, the one at which it aims is the supermind. Only when that can be brought down is a divine transformation possible in the earth-consciousness.

*

There are a thousand ways of approaching and realising the Divine and each way has its own experiences which have their own truth and stand really on a basis one in essence but complex in aspects, common to all but not expressed in the same way by all. There is not much use in discussing these variations; the important thing is to follow one's own way well and thoroughly. In this yoga, one can realise the psychic being as a portion of the Divine seated in the heart with the Divine supporting it there – this psychic being takes charge of the sadhana and turns the whole being to the Truth, the Divine, with results in the mind, the vital and the physical consciousness which I need not go into here – that is the first transformation. We realise next the one Self, Brahman, Divine, first *above* the body, life, mind and not only within the heart supporting them – above and free and unattached as the static Self in all and dynamic too as the active Divine Being and Power, Ishwara-Shakti, containing the world and pervading it as well as transcending it, manifesting all cosmic aspects. But what is most important for us is that it manifests as a transcending Light, Knowledge, Power, Purity, Peace, Ananda of which we become aware and which descends into the being and progressively replaces the ordinary consciousness itself by its own movements – that is the second transformation. We realise also the consciousness itself as moving upward, ascending through many planes, physical, vital, mental, overmental to the supramental and Ananda planes. This is nothing new; it is stated in the Taittiriya Upanishad that there are five Purushas, the physical, the vital, the mental, the Truth Purusha (supramental) and the Bliss Purusha; it says that one has to draw the physical self into the vital self, the vital into the mental, the mental into the Truth self, the Truth self into the Bliss self and so attain perfection. But in this yoga we become aware not only of this taking up but of a pouring down of the power of the higher Self, so that there comes in the possibility of a descent of the supramental Self and Nature to dominate and change our present nature and turn it from nature of Ignorance into nature of Truth-Knowledge (and through the supramental into nature of Ananda) — this is the third or supramental transformation. It does not always go in this order, for with many the spiritual descent begins first in an imperfect way before the psychic is in front and in charge, but the psychic development has to be attained before a perfect and unhampered spiritual descent can take place, and the last or supramental change is impossible so long as the two first have not become full and complete. That's the whole matter put as briefly as possible.

3

Planes of Consciousness and Parts of the Being

THE EVOLUTION OF CONSCIOUSNESS

In my explanation of the universe I have put forward this cardinal fact of a spiritual evolution as the meaning of our existence here. It is a series of ascents from the physical being and consciousness to the vital, the being dominated by the life-self, thence to the mental being realised in the fully developed man and thence into the perfect consciousness which is beyond the mental, into the supramental Consciousness and the supramental being, the Truth-Consciousness which is the integral consciousness of the spiritual being. Mind cannot be our last conscious expression because mind is fundamentally an ignorance seeking for knowledge; it is only the supramental Truth-Consciousness that can bring us the true and whole Self-Knowledge and world-Knowledge; it is through that only that we can get to our true being and the fulfilment of our spiritual evolution.

*

The Science of the West has discovered evolution as the secret of life and its process in this material world; but it has laid more stress on the growth of form and species than on the growth of consciousness: even, consciousness has been regarded as an incident and not the whole secret of the meaning of the evolution. An evolution has been admitted by certain minds in the East, certain philosophies and Scriptures, but there its sense has been the growth of the soul through developing or successive forms and many lives of the individual to its own highest reality. For if there is a conscious being in the form, that being can hardly be a temporary phenomenon of consciousness; it must be a soul fulfilling itself and this fulfilment can only take place if there is a return of the soul to earth in many successive lives, in many successive bodies.

The process of evolution has been the development from and in inconscient Matter of a subconscient and then a conscious Life, of conscious mind first in animal life and then fully in conscious and thinking man, the highest present achievement of evolutionary Nature. The achievement of mental being is at present her highest and tends to be regarded as her final work; but it is possible to conceive a still further step of the evolution: Nature may have in view beyond the imperfect mind of man a consciousness that passes out of the mind's ignorance and possesses truth as its inherent right and nature. There is a Truth-Consciousness as it is called in the Veda, a Supermind, as I have termed it, possessing Knowledge, not having to seek after it and constantly miss it. In one of the Upanishads a being of knowledge is stated to be the next step above the mental being; into that the soul has to rise and through it to attain the perfect bliss of spiritual existence. If that could be achieved as the next evolutionary step of Nature here, then she would be fulfilled and we could conceive of the perfection of life even here, its attainment of a full spiritual living even in this body or it may be in a perfected body. We could even speak of a divine life on earth; our human dream of perfectibility would be accomplished and at the same time the aspiration to a heaven on earth common to several religions and spiritual seers and thinkers.

The ascent of the human soul to the supreme Spirit is that soul's highest aim and necessity, for that is the supreme reality; but there can be too the descent of the Spirit and its powers into the world and that would justify the existence of the material world also, give a meaning, a divine purpose to the creation and solve its riddle. East and West could be reconciled in the pursuit of the highest and largest ideal, Spirit embrace Matter and Matter find its own true reality and the hidden Reality in all things in the Spirit.

*

The cycles of evolution tend always upward, but they are cycles and do not ascend in a straight line. The process therefore gives the impression of a series of ascents and descents, but what is essential in the gains of the evolution is kept or, even if eclipsed for a time, re-emerges in new forms suitable to the new ages. The creation has descended all the degrees of being from the Supermind to Matter and in each degree it has created a world, reign, plane or order proper to that degree. In the creating of the material world there was a plunge of this descending Consciousness into an apparent Inconscience and an emergence of it out of that Inconscience, degree by degree, until it recovers its highest spiritual and supramental summits and manifests their powers here in Matter. But even in the Inconscience there is a secret Consciousness which works, one may say, by an involved and hidden Intuition proper to itself.

*

Consciousness is a fundamental thing, the fundamental thing in existence — it is the energy, the motion, the movement of consciousness that creates the universe and all that is in it — not only the macrocosm but the microcosm is nothing but consciousness arranging itself. For instance, when consciousness in its movement or rather a certain stress of movement forgets itself in the action it becomes an apparently "unconscious" energy; when it forgets itself in the form it becomes the electron, the atom, the material object. In reality it is still consciousness that works in the energy and determines the form and the evolution of form.

When it wants to liberate itself, slowly, evolutionarily, out of Matter, but still in the form, it emerges as life, as animal, as man and it can go on evolving itself still farther out of its involution and become something more than mere man.

*

Consciousness is a reality inherent in existence. It is there even when it is not active on the surface, but silent and immobile; it is there even when it is invisible on the surface, not reacting on outward things or sensible to them, but withdrawn and either active or inactive within; it is there even when it seems to us to be quite absent and the being to our view unconscious and inanimate.

Consciousness is not only power of awareness of self and things, it is or has also a dynamic and creative energy. It can determine its own reactions or abstain from reactions; it can not only answer to forces, but create or put out from itself forces. Consciousness is Chit but also Chit Shakti.

Consciousness is usually identified with mind, but mental consciousness is only the human range which no more exhausts all the possible ranges of consciousness than human sight exhausts all the gradations of colour or human hearing all the gradations of sound — for there is much above or below that is to man invisible and inaudible. So there are ranges of consciousness above and below the human range, with which the normal human has no contact and they seem to it unconscious, — supramental or overmental and sub-mental ranges.

THE GRADATIONS OF CONSCIOUSNESS – THE GRADATION OF PLANES

The gradations of consciousness are universal states not dependent on the outlook of the subjective personality; rather the outlook of the subjective personality is determined by the grade of consciousness in which it is organised according to its typal nature or its evolutionary stage.

It will be evident that by consciousness is meant something which is essentially the same throughout but variable in status, condition and operation, in which in some grades or conditions the activities we call consciousness can exist either in a suppressed or an unorganised or a differently organised state; while in other states some other activities may manifest which in us are suppressed, unorganised or latent or else are less perfectly manifested, less intensive, extended and powerful than in those higher grades above our highest mental limit.

*

If we regard the gradation of worlds or planes as a whole, we see them as a great connected complex movement; the higher precipitate their influences on the lower, the lower react to the higher and develop or manifest in themselves within their own formula something that corresponds to the superior power and its action. The material world has evolved life in obedience to a pressure from the vital plane, mind in obedience to a pressure from the mental plane. It is now trying to evolve supermind in obedience to a pressure from the supramental plane. In more detail, particular forces, movements, powers, beings of a higher world can throw themselves on the lower to establish appropriate and corresponding forms which will connect them with the material domain and, as it were, reproduce or project their action here. And each thing created here has, supporting it, subtler envelopes or forms of itself which make it subsist and connect it with forces acting from above. Man, for instance, has, besides his gross physical body, subtler sheaths or bodies by which he lives behind the veil in direct connection with supraphysical planes of consciousness and can be influenced by their powers, movements and beings. What takes place in life has always behind it pre-existent movements and forms in the occult vital planes; what takes place in mind presupposes pre-existent movements and forms in the occult mental planes. That is an aspect of things which becomes more and more evident, insistent and important, the more we progress in a dynamic yoga.

But all this must not be taken in too rigid and mechanical a sense. It is an immense plastic movement full of the play of possibilities and must be seized by a flexible and subtle tact or sense in the seeing consciousness. It cannot be reduced to a too rigorous logical or mathematical formula.

*

The physical is not the only world; there are others that we become aware of through dream records, through the subtle senses, through influences and contacts, through imagination, intuition and vision. There are worlds of a larger subtler life than ours, vital worlds; worlds in which Mind builds its own forms and figures, mental worlds; psychic worlds which are the soul's home; others above with which we have little contact. In each of us there is a mental plane of consciousness, a psychic, a vital, a subtle physical as well as the gross physical and material plane. The same planes are repeated in the consciousness of general Nature. It is when we enter or contact these other planes that we come into connection with the worlds above the physical.

THE INNER BEING AND THE OUTER BEING

Men do not know themselves and have not learned to distinguish the different parts of their being; for these are usually lumped together by them as mind, because it is through a mentalised perception and understanding that they know or feel them; therefore they do not understand their own states and actions, or, if at all, then only on the surface. It is part of the foundation of yoga to become conscious of the great complexity of our nature, see the different forces that move it and get over it a control of directing knowledge. We are composed of many parts each of which contributes something to the total movement of our consciousness, our thought, will, sensation, feeling, action, but we do not see the origination or the course of these impulsions; we are aware only of their confused and pell-mell results on the surface upon which we can at best impose nothing better than a precarious shifting order.

*

There are, we might say, two beings in us, one on the surface, our ordinary exterior mind, life, body conscious-ness, another behind the veil, an inner mind, an inner life, an inner physical consciousness constituting another or inner self. This inner self once awake opens in its turn to our true real eternal self. It opens inwardly to the soul, called in the language of this yoga the psychic being which supports our successive births and at each birth assumes a new mind, life and body. It opens above to the Self or Spirit which is unborn and by conscious recovery of it we transcend the changing personality and achieve freedom and full mastery over our nature.

*

There are always two different consciousnesses in the hu-man being, one outward in which he ordinarily lives, the other inward and concealed of which he knows nothing. When one does sadhana, the inner consciousness begins to open and one is able to go inside and have all kinds of experiences there. As the sadhana progresses, one begins to live more and more in this inner being and the outer be-comes more and more superficial. At first the inner con-sciousness seems to be the dream and the outer the waking reality. Afterwards the inner consciousness becomes the reality and the outer is felt by many as a dream or delusion, or else as something superficial and external. The inner consciousness begins to be a place of deep peace, light, happiness, love, closeness to the Divine or the presence of

the Divine, the Mother. One is then aware of two consciousnesses, the inner one and the outer which has to be
changed into its counterpart and instrument – that also must
become full of peace, light, union with the Divine.

*

The outer being is a means of expression only, not one's self.
One must not identify with it, for what it expresses is a
personality formed by the old ignorant nature. If not identified one can change it so as to express the true inner
personality of the Light.

*

The individual is not limited to the physical body – it is only
the external consciousness which feels like that. As soon as
one gets over this feeling of limitation, one can feel first the
inner consciousness which is connected with the body, but
does not belong to it, afterwards the planes of consciousness
above the body, also a consciousness surrounding the body,
but part of oneself, part of the individual being, through
which one is in contact with the cosmic forces and with other
beings. The last is what I have called the environmental
consciousness.

*

By environmental consciousness I mean something that each
man carries around him, outside his body, even when he is
not aware of it, – by which he is in touch with others and
with the universal forces. It is through this that the thoughts,
feelings etc. of others pass to enter into one – it is through
this also that waves of the universal force – desire, sex, etc.
come in and take possession of the mind, vital or body.

*

They [the subconscient and the environmental conscious-
ness] are two quite different things. What is stored in the
subconscient – impressions, memories, rise up from there

into the conscious parts. In the environmental things are not stored up and fixed, although they move about there. It is full of mobility, a field of vibration or passage of forces.

THE MIND, THE VITAL AND THE PHYSICAL

There is a vital plane (self-existent) above the material universe which we see; there is a mental plane (self-existent) above the vital and material. These three together, — mental, vital, physical, — are called the triple universe of the lower hemisphere. They have been established in the earth-consciousness by evolution — but they exist in themselves before the evolution, above the earth-consciousness and the material plane to which the earth belongs.

*

On the surface, in the Ignorance, it is the mental, vital, physical Prakriti that acts and the Purusha is disfigured, as it were, in the action of the Prakriti. It is not our true mental being, our true vital being, our true physical being even that we are aware of; these remain behind, veiled and silent. It is the mental, vital, physical ego that we take for our being until we get knowledge.

*

Inertia, tamas, stupidity, narrowness and limitation, an inability to progress, doubt, dullness, dryness, a constant forgetfulness of the spiritual experiences received are the characteristics of the unregenerated physical nature, when that is not pushed by the vital and is not supported either by the higher mental will and intelligence.

*

What you describe is the material consciousness; it is mostly subconscient, but the part of it that is conscious is mechanical, inertly moved by habits or by the forces of the lower nature. Always repeating the same unintelligent and unenlightened movements, it is attached to the routine and established rule of what already exists, unwilling to change, unwilling to receive the Light or obey the higher Force. Or, if it is willing, then it is unable. Or, if it is able, then it turns the action given to it by the Light or the Force into a new mechanical routine and so takes out of it all soul and life. It is obscure, stupid, indolent, full of ignorance and inertia, darkness and slowness of *tamas*.

It is this material consciousness into which we are seeking to bring first the higher (divine or spiritual) Light and Power and Ananda, and then the supramental Truth which is the object of our yoga.

*

I put a value on the body first as an instrument, *dharma-sadhana*, or, more fully, as a centre of manifested personality in action, a basis of spiritual life and activity as of all life and activity upon the earth, but also because for me the body as well as the mind and life is a part of the Divine Whole, a form of the Spirit and therefore not to be disregarded or despised as something incurably gross and incapable of spiritual realisation or of spiritual use. Matter itself is secretly a form of the Spirit and has to reveal itself as that, can be made to wake to consciousness and evolve and realise the Spirit, the Divine within it. In my view the body as well as the mind and life has to be spiritualised or, one may say, divinised so as to be a fit instrument and receptacle for the realisation of the Divine. It has its part in the Divine Lila, even, according to the Vaishnava Sadhana, in the joy and beauty of Divine Love.

*

Vitality means life-force — wherever there is life, in plant or animal or man, there is life-force — without the vital there can be no life in matter and no living action. The vital is a necessary force and nothing can be done or created in the bodily existence, if the vital is not there as an instrument. Even sadhana needs the vital force.

But if the vital is unregenerated and enslaved to desire, passion and ego, then it is as harmful as it can otherwise be helpful. Even in ordinary life the vital has to be controlled by the mind and mental will, otherwise it brings disorder or disaster. When people speak of a vital man, they mean one under the domination of vital force not controlled by the mind or the spirit. The vital can be a good instrument, but it is a bad master.

The vital has not to be killed or destroyed, but purified and transformed by the psychic and spiritual control.

*

There are four parts of the vital being – first, the mental vital which gives a mental expression by thought, speech or otherwise to the emotions, desires, passions, sensations and other movements of the vital being; the emotional vital which is the seat of various feelings, such as love, joy, sorrow, hatred, and the rest; the central vital which is the seat of the stronger vital longings and reactions, e.g. ambition, pride, fear, love of fame, attractions and repulsions, desires and passions of various kinds and the field of many vital energies; last, the lower vital which is occupied with small desires and feelings, such as make the greater part of daily life, e.g. food desire, sexual desire, small likings, dislikings, vanity, quarrels, love of praise, anger at blame, little wishes of all kinds – and a numberless host of other things. Their respective seats are: (1) the region from the throat to the heart, (2) the heart (it is a double centre, belonging in front to the emotional and vital and behind to the psychic), (3) from the heart to the navel, (4) below the navel.

*

Higher vital usually refers to the vital mind and emotive being as opposed to the middle vital which has its seat in the navel and is dynamic, sensational and passionate and the lower which is made up of the smaller movements of human life-desire and life-reactions.

*

The nervous part of the being is a portion of the vital – it is the vital-physical, the life-force closely enmeshed in the reactions, desires, needs, sensations of the body. The vital proper is the life-force acting in its own nature, impulses, emotions, feelings, desires, ambitions, etc., having as their highest centre what we may call the outer heart of emotion, while there is an inner heart where are the higher or psychic feelings and sensibilities, the emotions or intuitive yearnings and impulses of the soul. The vital part of us is, of course, necessary to our completeness, but it is a true instrument only when its feelings and tendencies have been purified by the psychic touch and taken up and governed by the spiritual light and power.

*

The true vital consciousness is one in which the vital makes full surrender, converts itself into an instrument of the Divine, making no demand, insisting on no desire, answering to the Mother's force and to no other, calm, unegoistic, giving an absolute loyalty and obedience, with no personal vanity or ambition, only asking to be a pure and perfect instrument, desiring nothing for itself but that the Truth may prevail within itself and everywhere and the Divine Victory take place and the Divine Work be done.

*

The "Mind" in the ordinary use of the word covers indiscriminately the whole consciousness, for man is a mental being and mentalises everything; but in the language of this yoga the words "mind" and "mental" are used to connote specially the part of the nature which has to do with cognition and intelligence, with ideas, with mental or thought perceptions, the reactions of thought to things, with the truly mental movements and formations, mental vision and will, etc., that are part of his intelligence. The vital has to be carefully distinguished from mind, even though it has a mind element transfused into it; the vital is the Life-nature made up of desires, sensations, feelings, passions, energies of action, will of desire, reactions of the desire-soul in man and of all that play of possessive and other related instincts, anger, fear, greed, lust, etc., that belong to this field of the nature. Mind and vital are mixed up on the surface of the consciousness, but they are quite separate forces in themselves and as soon as one gets behind the ordinary surface consciousness one sees them as separate, discovers their distinction and can with the aid of this knowledge analyse their surface mixtures. It is quite possible and even usual during a time shorter or longer, sometimes very long, for the mind to accept the Divine or the yogic ideal while the vital is unconvinced and unsurrendered and goes obstinately on its way of desire, passion and attraction to the ordinary life. Their division or their conflict is the cause of most of the more acute difficulties of the sadhana.

*

The mind proper is divided into three parts – thinking Mind, dynamic Mind, externalising Mind – the former concerned with ideas and knowledge in their own right, the second with the putting out of mental forces for realisation of the idea, the third with the expression of them in life (not only by speech, but by any form it can give). The word "physical mind" is rather ambiguous, because it can mean this externalising Mind and the mental in the physical taken together.

Vital Mind proper is a sort of a mediator between vital emotion, desire, impulsion, etc. and the mental proper. It expresses the desires, feelings, emotions, passions, ambitions, possessive and active tendencies of the vital and throws them into mental forms (the pure imaginations or dreams of greatness, happiness, etc. in which men indulge are one peculiar form of the vital-mind activity). There is still a lower stage of the mental in the vital which merely expresses the vital stuff without subjecting it to any play of intelligence. It is through this mental vital that the vital passions, impulses, desires rise up and get into the Buddhi and either cloud or distort it.

As the vital Mind is limited by the vital view and feeling of things (while the dynamic Intelligence is not, for it acts by the idea and reason), so the mind in the physical or mental physical is limited by the physical view and experience of things, it mentalises the experiences brought by the contacts of outward life and things, and does not go beyond that (though it can do that much very cleverly), unlike the externalising mind which deals with them more from the reason and its higher intelligence. But in practice these two usually get mixed together. The mechanical mind is a much lower action of the mental physical which, left to itself, would only repeat customary ideas and record the natural reflexes of the physical consciousness to the contacts of outward life and things.

THE CENTRAL BEING –
THE JIVATMAN AND THE PSYCHIC BEING

The being of man is composed of these elements, the psychic behind supporting all, the inner mental, vital and physical, and the outer external nature of mind, life and body which is their instrument of expression. But above all is the central being (Jivatman) which uses them all for its manifestation, it is a portion of the divine Self and is hidden from the external man who replaces it by the mental and vital ego. It is only those who have begun to know themselves that become aware of their true central being; but it is there standing behind the action of mind, life and body and is most directly represented by the psychic which is itself a spark of the Divine. It is by the growth of the psychic element in one's nature that one begins to come into conscious touch with one's own central being. When that happens and the central being uses a conscious will to control and organise the movements of the nature it is then that one has a real, a spiritual self-mastery.

*

The phrase "central being" in our yoga is usually applied to the portion of the Divine in us which supports all the rest and survives through death and birth. This central being has two forms – above, it is Jivatman, our true being, of which we become aware when the higher self-knowledge comes, – below, it is the psychic being which stands behind mind, body and life. The Jivatman is above the manifestation in life and presides over it; the psychic being stands behind the manifestation in life and supports it.

*

The central being – the Jivatman which is not born nor evolves but presides over the individual birth and evolution – puts forward a representative of himself on each plane of the consciousness. On the mental plane it is the true mental being, *manomaya puruṣa*, on the vital plane the true vital being, *prāṇamaya puruṣa*, on the physical plane the true physical being, *annamaya puruṣa*. Each being, therefore is, so long as the Ignorance lasts, centred round his mental, vital or physical Purusha, according to the plane on which he predominantly lives, and that is to him his central being. But the true representative all the time is concealed behind the mind, vital and physical – it is the psychic, our inmost being.

When the inmost knowledge begins to come, we become aware of the psychic being within us and it comes forward and leads the sadhana. We become aware also of the Jivatman, the undivided Self or Spirit above the manifestation of which the psychic is the representative here.

*

The Jivatman, spark-soul and psychic being are three different forms of the same reality and they must not be mixed up together, as that confuses the clearness of the inner experience.

The Jivatman or spirit, as it is usually called in English, is self-existent above the manifested or instrumental being – it is superior to birth and death, always the same, the individual Self or Atman. It is the eternal true being of the individual.

The soul is a spark of the Divine which is not seated above the manifested being, but comes down into the manifestation to support its evolution in the material world. It is at first an undifferentiated power of the Divine Consciousness containing all possibilities which have not yet taken form, but to which it is the function of evolution to give form. This spark is there in all living beings from the lowest to the highest.

The psychic being is formed by the soul in its evolution. It supports the mind, vital, body, grows by their experiences, carries the nature from life to life. It is the psychic or *caitya purusa*. At first it is veiled by mind, vital and body, but as it grows, it becomes capable of coming forward and dominating the mind, life and body; in the ordinary man it depends on them for expression and is not able to take them up and freely use them. The life of the being is animal or human and not divine. When the psychic being can by sadhana become dominant and freely use its instruments, then the impulse towards the Divine becomes complete and the transformation of mind, vital and body, not merely their liberation, becomes possible.

The Self or Atman being free and superior to birth and death, the experience of the Jivatman and its unity with the supreme or universal Self brings the sense of liberation, it is this which is necessary for the supreme spiritual deliverance: but for the transformation of the life and nature the awakening of the psychic being and its rule over the nature are indispensable.

The psychic being realises its oneness with the true being, the Jivatman, but it does not change into it.

*

The Jiva is realised as the individual Self, Atman, the central being above the Nature, calm, untouched by the movements of Nature, but supporting their evolution though not involved in it. Through this realisation silence, freedom, wideness, mastery, purity, a sense of universality in the individual as one centre of this divine universality become the normal experience. The psychic is realised as the Purusha behind the heart. It is not universalised like the Jivatman, but is the individual soul supporting from its place behind the heart-centre the mental, vital, physical, psychic evolution of the being in Nature. Its realisation brings bhakti, self-giving, surrender, turning of all the movements Godward, discrimination and choice of all that belongs to the Divine Truth, Good, Beauty, rejection of all that is false, evil, ugly, discordant, union through love and sympathy with all existence, openness to the Truth of the Self and the Divine.

*

The psychic is not by definition,* that part which is in direct touch with the supramental plane, — although, once the

---

* Someone had asked what the psychic being was, whether it could be defined as that part of the being which is always in direct touch with the supramental. I replied that it could not be so defined. For the psychic being in animals or in most human beings is not in direct touch with the supramental — therefore it cannot be so described, *by definition*.

But once the connection between the supramental and the human consciousness is made, it is the psychic being that gives *the readiest response* — more ready than the mind, the vital or the physical. It may be added that it is also a purer response; the mind, vital and physical can allow other things to mix with their reception of the connection with the supramental is made, it gives to it the readiest response. The psychic part of us is something that comes direct from the Divine and is in touch with the Divine. In its origin it is the nucleus pregnant with divine possibilities that supports this lower triple manifestation of mind, life and body. There is this divine element in all living beings, but it stands hidden behind the ordinary consciousness, is not at first developed and, even when developed, is not always or often in the front; it expresses itself, so far as the imperfection of the instruments allows, by their means and under their limitations. It grows in the consciousness by Godward experience, gaining strength every time there is a higher movement in us, and, finally, by the accumulation of these deeper and higher movements, there is developed a psychic individuality, — that which we call usually the psychic being. It is always this psychic being that is the real, though often the secret cause of man's turning to the spiritual life and his greatest help in it. It is therefore that which we have to bring from behind to the front in the yoga.

The word 'soul', as also the word 'psychic', is used very vaguely and in many different senses in the English language. More often than not, in ordinary parlance, no clear distinction is made between mind and soul and often there is an even more serious confusion, for the vital being of desire — the false soul or desire-soul — is intended by the words 'soul' and 'psychic' and not the true soul, the psychic being. The psychic being is quite different from the mind or vital; it stands behind them where they meet in the heart. Its central place is there, but behind the heart rather than in the heart; for what men call usually the heart is the seat of emotion, and human emotions are mental-vital impulses, not ordinarily psychic in their nature. This mostly secret power behind, other than the mind and the life-force, is the true soul, the

---

supramental influence and spoil its truth. The psychic is pure in its response and allows no such mixture.

The supramental change can take place only if the psychic is awake and is made the chief support of the descending supramental power. [Sri Aurobindo's note]

psychic being in us. The power of the psychic, however, can act upon the mind and vital and body, purifying thought and perception and emotion (which then becomes psychic feeling) and sensation and action and everything else in us and preparing them to be divine movements.

*

Psychic is ordinarily used in the sense of anything relating to the inner movements of the consciousness or anything phenomenal in the psychology; in this case I have made a special use of it, relating it to the Greek word psyche meaning soul; but ordinarily people make no distinction between the soul and the mental-vital consciousness; for them it is all the same.

*

The contribution of the psychic being to the sadhana is: (1) love and bhakti, a love not vital, demanding and egoistic but unconditioned and without claims, self-existent; (2) the contact or the presence of the Mother within; (3) the unerring guidance from within; (4) a quieting and purification of the mind, vital and physical consciousness by their subjection to the psychic influence and guidance; (5) the opening up of all this lower consciousness to the higher spiritual consciousness above for its descent into a nature prepared to receive it with a complete receptivity and right attitude – for the psychic brings in everything, right thought, right perception, right feeling, right attitude.

*

Every soul is not evolved and active; nor is every soul turned directly to the Divine before practising yoga. For a long time it seeks the Divine through men and things much more than directly.

HIGHER MIND, ILLUMINED MIND, INTUITION, OVERMIND AND SUPERMIND

There are in fact two systems simultaneously active in the organisation of the being and its parts: one is concentric, a series of rings or sheaths with the psychic at the centre; another is vertical, an ascension and descent, like a flight of steps, a series of superimposed planes with the supermind-overmind as the crucial nodus of the transition beyond the human into the Divine. For this transition, if it is to be at the same time a transformation, there is only one way, one path. First, there must be a conversion inwards, a going within to find the inmost psychic being and bring it out to the front, disclosing at the same time the inner mind, inner vital, inner physical parts of the nature. Next, there must be an ascension, a series of conversions upwards and a turning down to convert the lower parts. When one has made the inward conversion, one psychicises the whole lower nature so as to make it ready for the divine change. Going upwards, one passes beyond the human mind and at each stage of the ascent, there is a conversion into a new consciousness and an infusion of this new consciousness into the whole of the nature. Thus rising beyond intellect through illuminated higher mind to the intuitive consciousness, we begin to look at everything not from the intellect range or through intel-lect as an instrument, but from a greater intuitive height and through an intuitivised will, feeling, emotion, sensation and physical contact. So, proceeding from Intuition to a greater overmind height, there is a new conversion and we look at and experience everything from the overmind consciousness and through a mind, heart, vital and body surcharged with the overmind thought, sight, will, feeling, sensation, play of force and contact. But the last conversion is the supra-mental, for once there – once the nature is supramentalised, we are beyond the Ignorance and conversion of consciousness is no longer needed, though a farther divine progression, even an infinite development is still possible.

*

The Self governs the diversity of its creation by its unity on all the planes from the Higher Mind upwards on which the realisation of the One is the natural basis of consciousness. But as one goes upward, the view changes, the power of consciousness changes, the Light becomes ever more intense and potent. Although the static realisation of Infinity and Eternity and the Timeless One remains the same, the vision of the workings of the One becomes ever wider and is attended with a greater instrumentality of Force and a more comprehensive grasp of what has to be known and done. All possible forms and constructions of things become more and more visible, put in their proper place, utilisable. Moreover, what is thought-knowledge in the Higher Mind becomes illumination in the Illumined Mind and direct intimate vision in the Intuition. But the Intuition sees in flashes and combines through a constant play of light – through revelations, inspirations, intuitions, swift discriminations. The overmind sees calmly, steadily, in great masses and large extensions of space and time and relation, globally; it creates and acts in the same way – it is the world of the great Gods, the divine Creators. Only, each creates in his own way; he sees all but sees all from his own viewpoint. There is not the absolute supramental harmony and certitude. These, inadequately expressed, are some of the differences. I speak, of course, of these planes in themselves – when acting in the human consciousness they are necessarily much diminished in their working by having to depend on the human instrumentation of mind, vital and physical. Only when these are quieted, they get a fuller force and reveal more their character.

*

The substance of knowledge is the same on all the overhead planes, but the higher mind gives only the substance and form of knowledge in thought and word — in the illumined mind there begins to be a peculiar light and energy and Ananda of knowledge which grows as one rises higher in the scale — or else as the knowledge comes from a higher and higher source. This light etc. are still rather diluted and diffused in the illumined mind; it becomes more and more intense, clearly defined and dynamic and effective on the higher planes so much so as to change always the character and power of the knowledge.

*

The Intuition is the first plane in which there is a real opening to the full possibility of realisation — it is through it that one goes farther — first to overmind and then to supermind.

*

It is hardly possible to say what the supermind is in the language of Mind, even spiritualised Mind, for it is a different consciousness altogether and acts in a different way. Whatever may be said of it is likely to be not understood or misunderstood. It is only by growing into it that we can know what it is and this also cannot be done until after a long process by which mind heightening and illuminating becomes pure Intuition (not the mixed thing that ordinarily goes by that name) and masses itself into overmind; after that overmind can be lifted into and suffused with supermind till it undergoes a transformation.

In the supermind all is self-known self-luminously, there are no divisions, oppositions or separated aspects as in Mind whose principle is division of Knowledge into parts and setting each part against another. Overmind approaches this at its top and is often mistaken for supermind, but it cannot reach it — except by uplifting and transformation.

*

By the supermind is meant the full Truth-Consciousness of the Divine Nature in which there can be no place for the principle of division and ignorance; it is always a full light and knowledge superior to all mental substance or mental movement. Between the supermind and the human mind are a number of ranges, planes or layers of consciousness – one can regard it in various ways – in which the element or substance of mind and consequently its movements also become more and more illumined and powerful and wide. The overmind is the highest of these ranges; it is full of lights and powers; but from the point of view of what is above it, it is the line of the soul's turning away from the complete and indivisible knowledge and its descent towards the Ignorance. For although it draws from the Truth, it is here that begins the separation of aspects of the Truth, the forces and their working out as if they were independent truths and this is a process that ends, as one descends to ordinary Mind, Life and Matter, in a complete division, fragmentation, separation from the indivisible Truth above. There is no longer the essential, total, perfectly harmonising and unifying knowledge, or rather knowledge for ever harmonious because for ever one, which is the character of supermind. In the supermind, mental divisions and oppositions cease, the problems created by our dividing and fragmenting mind disappear and Truth is seen as a luminous whole. In the overmind there is not yet the actual fall into Ignorance, but the first step is taken which will make the fall inevitable.

SUPERMIND AND SACHCHIDANANDA

Supermind is between the Sachchidananda and the lower creation. It alone contains the self-determining Truth of the Divine Consciousness and is necessary for a Truth-creation.

One can of course realise Sachchidananda in relation to the mind, life and body also – but then it is something stable, supporting by its presence the lower Prakriti, but not transforming it. The supermind alone can transform the lower nature.

*

It is the supramental Power that transforms mind, life and body – not the Sachchidananda consciousness which supports impartially everything. But it is by having experience of the Sachchidananda, pure existence-consciousness-bliss, that the ascent to the supramental and the descent of the supramental become (at a much later stage) possible. For first one must get free from the ordinary limitation by the mental, vital and physical formations, and the experience of the Sachchidananda peace, calm, purity and wideness gives this liberation.

The supermind has nothing to do with passing into a blank. It is the Mind overpassing its own limits and following a negative and quietistic way to do it that reaches the big blank. The Mind, being the Ignorance, has to annul itself in order to enter into the supreme Truth – or, at least, so it thinks. But the supermind being the Truth-Consciousness and the Divine Knowledge has no need to annul itself for the purpose.

*

1. I mean by the supracosmic Reality the supreme Sachchidananda who is above this and all manifestation, not bound by any, yet from whom all manifestation proceeds and all universe.

2. The supramental and the supracosmic are not the same. If it were so there could be no supramental world and no descent of the supramental principle into the material world – we would be brought back to the idea that the divine Truth and Reality can only exist beyond and the universe – any universe – can only be half-truth or an illusion of ignorance.

3. I mean by the supramental the Truth-Consciousness

whether above or in the universe by which the Divine knows not only his own essence and being but his manifestation also. Its fundamental character is knowledge by identity, by that the Self is known, the Divine Sachchidananda is known, but also the truth of manifestation is known, because this too is That – *sarvaṁ khalvidaṁ brahma, vāsudevaḥ sarvam,* etc. Mind is an instrument of the Ignorance trying to know – supermind is the Knower possessing knowledge, because one with it and the known, therefore seeing all things in the light of His own Truth, the light of their true self which is He. It is a dynamic and not only a static Power, not only a Knowledge, but a Will according to Knowledge – there is a supramental Power or Shakti which can manifest direct its world of Light and Truth in which all is luminously based on the harmony and unity of the One, not disturbed by a veil of Ignorance or any disguise. The supermind therefore does not transcend all possible manifestation, but it is above the triplicity of mind, life and Matter which is our present experience of this manifestation.

SUPERMIND AND THE EARTH

The interpenetration of the planes is indeed for me a capital and fundamental part of spiritual experience without which yoga as I practise it and its aim could not exist. For that aim is to manifest, reach or embody a higher consciousness upon earth and not to get away from earth into a higher world or some supreme Absolute. The old yogas (not quite all of them) tended the other way – but that was, I think, because they found the earth as it is a rather impossible place for any spiritual being and the resistance to change too obstinate to be borne; earth-nature looked to them in Vivekananda's simile like the dog's tail which, every time you straighten it, goes back to its original curl. But the fundamental proposition in this matter was proclaimed very definitely in the

Upanishads which went so far as to say that Earth is the foundation and all the worlds are on the earth and to imagine a clean-cut or irreconcilable difference between them is ignorance: here and not elsewhere, not by going to some other world, the divine realisation must come. This statement was used to justify a purely individual realisation, but it can equally be the basis of a wider endeavour.

*

The supramental is *not* grand, aloof, cold and austere; it is not something opposed to or inconsistent with a full vital and physical manifestation; on the contrary, it carries in it the only possibility of the full fullness of the vital force and the physical life on earth. It is because it is so, because it was so revealed to me and for no other reason that I have followed after it and persevered till I came into contact with it and was able to draw down some power of it and its influence. I am concerned with the earth, not with worlds beyond for their own sake; it is a terrestrial realisation that I seek and not a flight to distant summits. All other yogas regard this life as an illusion or a passing phase; the supramental yoga alone regards it as a thing created by the Divine for a progressive manifestation and takes the fulfilment of the life and the body for its object. The supramental is simply the Truth-Consciousness and what it brings in its descent is the full truth of life, the full truth of consciousness in Matter.

*

The earth is a material field of evolution. Mind and life, supermind, Sachchidananda are in principle involved there in the earth-consciousness; but only Matter is at first organized; then life descends from the life plane and gives shape and organization and activity to the life principle in Matter, creates the plant and animal; then mind descends from the mind plane, creating man. Now supermind is to descend so as to create a supramental race.

THE SUPRAMENTAL EVOLUTION

I have already spoken about the bad conditions of the world; the usual idea of the occultists about it is that the worse they are, the more is probable the coming of an intervention or a new revelation from above. The ordinary mind cannot know – it has either to believe or disbelieve or wait and see.

As to whether the Divine seriously means something to happen, I believe it is intended. I know with absolute certitude that the supramental is a truth and that its advent is in the very nature of things inevitable. The question is as to the when and the how. That also is decided and predestined from somewhere above; but it is here being fought out amid a rather grim clash of conflicting forces. For in the terrestrial world the predetermined result is hidden and what we see is a whirl of possibilities and forces attempting to achieve something with the destiny of it all concealed from human eyes. This is, however, certain that a number of souls have been sent to see that it shall be now. That is the situation. My faith and will are for the now. I am speaking of course on the level of the human intelligence – mystically-rationally, as one might put it. To say more would be going beyond that line. You don't want me to start prophesying, I suppose? As a rationalist, you can't.

*

If the supramental is decreed, nothing can prevent it; but all things are worked out here through a play of forces, and an unfavourable atmosphere or conditions can delay even when they cannot prevent. Even when a thing is destined, it does not present itself as a certitude in the consciousness here (overmind-mind-vital-physical) till the play of forces has been worked out up to a certain point at which the descent not only is, but appears as inevitable.

*

The descent of the supermind is a long process, or at least a process with a long preparation, and one can only say that the work is going on* sometimes with a strong pressure for completion, sometimes retarded by the things that rise from below and have to be dealt with before further progress can be made. The process is a spiritual evolutionary process, concentrated into a brief period; it could be done otherwise (by what men would regard as a miraculous intervention) only if the human mind were more flexible and less attached to its ignorance than it is. As we envisage it, it must manifest in a few first and then spread, but it is not likely to over-power the earth in a moment. It is not advisable to discuss too much what it will do and how it will do it, because these are things the supermind itself will fix, acting out of the Divine Truth in it, and the mind must not try to fix for it grooves in which it will run. Naturally, the release from subconscient ignorance and from disease, duration of life at will, and a change in the functionings of the body must be among the ultimate elements of a supramental change; but the details of these things must be left for the supramental Energy to work out according to the Truth of its own nature.

The descent of the supramental is an inevitable necessity in the logic of things and is therefore sure. It is because people do not understand what the supermind is or realise the significance of the emergence of consciousness in a world of inconscient Matter that they are unable to realise this inevitability. I suppose a matter-of-fact observer, if there had been one at the time of the unrelieved reign of inani-mate Matter in the earth's beginning, would have criticised any promise of the emergence of life in a world of dead earth and rock and mineral as an absurdity and a chimera; so too, afterwards he would have repeated this mistake and regard-ed the emergence of thought and reason in an animal world as an absurdity and a chimera. It is the same now with the

* Sri Aurobindo wrote this in December 1935.

appearance of supermind in the stumbling mentality of this world of human consciousness and its reasoning ignorance.

*

What the supramental will do the mind cannot foresee or lay down. The mind is ignorance seeking for the Truth, the supramental by its very definition is the Truth-Consciousness, Truth in possession of itself and fulfilling itself by its own power. In a supramental world imperfection and disharmony are bound to disappear. But what we propose just now is not to make the earth a supramental world but to bring down the supramental as a power and established consciousness in the midst of the rest — to let it work there and fulfil itself as Mind descended into Life and Matter and has worked as a Power there to fulfil itself in the midst of the rest. This will be enough to change the world and to change Nature by breaking down her present limits. But what, how, by what degrees it will do it, is a thing that ought not to be said now — when the Light is there, the Light will itself do its work — when the supramental Will stands on earth, that Will will decide. It will establish a perfection, a harmony, a Truth-creation — for the rest, well, it will be the rest — that is all.

*

The descent of the supramental means only that the Power will be there in the earth-consciousness as a living force just as the thinking mental and higher mental are already there. But an animal cannot take advantage of the presence of the thinking mental Power or an undeveloped man of the presence of the higher mental Power — so too anybody will not be able to take advantage of the presence of the supramental Power. I have also often enough said that it will be at first for the few, not for the whole earth, — only there will be a growing influence of it on the earth-life.

*

Your statement about the supramental evolution is correct except that it does not follow that humanity as a whole will become supramental. What is more likely to happen is that the supramental principle will be established in the evolution by the descent just as the mental principle was established by the appearance of thinking Mind and Man in earthly life. There will be a race of supramental beings on the earth just as now there is a race of mental beings. Man himself will find a greater possibility of rising to the planes intermediary between his mind and supermind and making their powers effective in his life, which will mean a great change in humanity on earth, but it is not likely that the mental stage will disappear from the ascending ladder and, if so, the continued existence of a mental race will be necessary so as to form a stage between the vital and the supramental in the evolutionary movement of the Spirit.

Such a descent of higher beings as you suggest may be envisaged as a part of the process of the change. But the main part of the change will be the appearance of the supramental being and the organisation of a supramental nature here, as a mental being has appeared and a mental nature organised itself during the last stage of the evolution. I prefer nowadays not to speak of the descent of the higher beings because my experience is that it leads to a vain and often egoistic romanticism which distracts the attention from the real work, that of the realisation of the Divine and the transformation of the nature.

*

As I have said, speculation on the results of the manifestation of a new supramental principle in the earth-consciousness organising itself there as mind, life and matter have already organised themselves — for that is what it comes to — is a little perilous and premature, because we must do it with the mind and the mind has not the capacity to forecast the action of what is above itself — just as a merely animal or vital perception of things could not have forecast what would be the workings of Mind and a mentalised race of beings here. The supermind is a different order of consciousness far removed from the mental – there are in fact several grades of higher consciousness between the human mind and the supramental. If the earth were not an evolutionary but a typal world, then indeed one could predict that the descent of a higher type of consciousness would swallow up or abolish the existing type. Ignorance would end and the creation in the ignorance disappear either by transmutation or by annihilation and replacement. The human mental kingdom would be transformed into the supramental; [the] vital and subhuman, if it existed in the typal world, would also be changed and become supramental. But, earth being an evolutionary world, the supramental descent is not likely to have such a devasting completeness. It would be only the establishment of a new principle of consciousness and a new order of conscious beings and this new principle would evolve its own forms and powers in the terrestrial order. Even the whole human kingdom need not and would not be transformed at once to the whole supramental extent. But at the same time the beginning of a supramental creation on earth is bound to have a powerful effect on the rest of terrestrial existence. Its first effect on mankind would be to open a way between the order of the Truth-light and the orders of the Ignorance here on earth itself, a sort of realised gradation by which it would be possible for mental man to evolve more easily and surely from the Ignorance towards the Light and, as he went, organise his existence according to these steps. For at present the grades of consciousness between mind and supermind act only as influences (the highest of them very indirect influences) on human mind and consciousness and cannot do more. This would change. An organised higher human consciousness could appear or several degrees of it, with the supermind-organised consciousness as the leader at the top influencing the others and drawing them towards itself. It is likely that as the supramental principle evolved itself the evolution would more and more take on another aspect – the Daivic nature would predominate, the Asuro-Rakshaso-Pishachic prakriti which now holds so large a place would more and more recede and lose its power. A principle of greater unity, harmony and light would emerge everywhere. It is not that the creation in the Ignorance would be altogether abolished, but it would begin to lose much of its elements of pain and falsehood and would be more a progression from lesser to higher Truth, from a lesser to a higher harmony, from a lesser to a higher Light, than the reign of chaos and struggle, of darkness and error that we now perceive. For according to all occult teaching the evolutionary creation could have been such but for the intervention of the Powers of Darkness – all traditions including that of the Veda and Upanishads point under different figures to the same thing. In the Upanishads it is the Daityas that smite with evil all that the gods create, in the Zoroastrian [teaching] it is Ahriman coming across the work of Ahura Mazda, the Chaldean tradition uses a different figure. But the significance is the same; it is the perception of something that has struck across the harmonious development of creation and brought in the principle of darkness and disorder. The occult tradition also foresees the elimination of this disturbing element by the descent of a divine Principle or Power on earth, but gives to it usually a sudden and dramatic form. I conceive that the supramental descent would effect the same event by a progressive elimination of the darkness and evolution of the Light, but with what rate of rapidity it would be rash to try to forecast or prefigure.

This is a very general statement, but perhaps it is a sufficient answer to your first question. I need only add that there is nothing to prevent the supramental creation, the creation in the higher Truth-Light from being evolutionary, a continuous efflorescence of the Divine Truth and Harmony in a manifold variety, not a final and decisive creation in a single fixed type. What would be decisive would be the crossing of the border between twilight and Light, the trans-

ference of the base of development from the consciousness
in the Ignorance to the Truth-consciousness. That would be,
on this level, final. The transition into a world of spirits
would only effectuate itself, first, if the whole earth-consciousness became thoroughly supramentalised, secondly, if
after that the turn were to a realisation here of the principle
of those worlds of Sachchidananda where determination
disappears in the interpenetration of All-in-All. But that
would be to look too far into the potentialities of the future.
In short, if the supramental principle came down it would
not be in order to reproduce Heaven here under celestial
conditions but to "create a new Heaven and a new earth" in
the earth-consciousness itself, completing and transmuting
but not abolishing the earth order.

It is evident that the creative process here could be greatly
modified and transmuted by the appearance of the supramental principle. What would be its exact forms is a more
difficult question, for the principle of a supramental creation
is obvious but the possibilities of its manifestation are many
and it is only the dynamic Truth itself that can choose and
determine.

4

The Divine, the Gods and
the Divine Force

THE DIVINE

The Divine is the Supreme Truth because it is the Supreme Being from whom all have come and in whom all are.

*

The Divine is that from which all comes, in which all lives, and to return to the truth of the Divine now clouded over by Ignorance is the soul's aim in life. In its supreme Truth, the Divine is absolute and infinite peace, consciousness, existence, power and Ananda.

*

The Divine has three aspects for us:

1. It is the Cosmic Self and Spirit that is in and behind all things and beings, from which and in which all is manifested in the universe — although it is now a manifestation in the Ignorance.

2. It is the Spirit and Master of our own being within us whom we have to serve and learn to express his will in all our movements so that we may grow out of the Ignorance into the Light.

3. The Divine is transcendent Being and Spirit, all bliss and light and divine knowledge and power, and towards that highest divine existence and its Light we have to rise and

bring down the reality of it more and more into our consciousness and life.

In the ordinary Nature we live in the Ignorance and do not know the Divine. The forces of the ordinary Nature are undivine forces because they weave a veil of ego and desire and unconsciousness which conceals the Divine from us. To get into the higher and deeper consciousness which knows and lives luminously in the Divine, we have to get rid of the forces of the lower nature and open to the action of the Divine Shakti which will transform our consciousness into that of the Divine Nature.

This is the conception of the Divine from which we have to start — the realisation of its truth can only come with the opening of the consciousness and its change.

*

The distinction between the Transcendental, the Cosmic, the Individual Divine is not my invention, nor is it native to India or to Asia — it is, on the contrary, a recognised European teaching current in the esoteric tradition of the Catholic Church where it is the authorised explanation of the Trinity, — Father, Son and Holy Ghost, — and it is very well-known to European mystic experience. In essence it exists in all spiritual disciplines that recognise the omnipresence of the Divine — in Indian Vedantic experience and in Mahomedan yoga (not only the Sufi, but other schools also) — the Mahomedans even speak of not two or three but many levels of the Divine until one reaches the Supreme. As for the idea in itself, surely there is a difference between the individual, the cosmos in space and time, and something that exceeds this cosmic formula or any cosmic formula. There is a cosmic consciousness experienced by many which is quite different in its scope and action from the individual consciousness, and if there is a consciousness beyond the cosmic, infinite and essentially eternal, not merely extended in Time, that also must be different from these two. And if the Divine is or manifests Himself in these three, is it not conceivable that in aspect, in His working, He may differentiate Himself so much that we are driven, if we are not to confound all truth of experience, if we are not to limit ourselves to a mere static experience of something indefinable, to speak of a triple aspect of the Divine?

In the practice of yoga there is a great dynamic difference in one's way of dealing with these three possible realisations. If I realise only the Divine as that, not my personal self, which yet moves secretly all my personal being and which I can bring forward out of the veil, or if I build up the image of that Godhead in my members, it is a realisation but a limited one. If it is the Cosmic Godhead that I realise, losing in it all personal self, that is a very wide realisation, but I become a mere channel of the universal Power and there is no personal or divinely individual consummation for me. If I shoot up to the transcendental realisation only, I lose both myself and the world in the transcendental Absolute. If, on the other hand, my aim is none of these things by itself, but to realise and also to manifest the Divine in the world, bringing down for the purpose a yet unmanifested Power, – such as the supermind, – a harmonisation of all three becomes imperative. I have to bring it down, and from where shall I bring it down – since it is not yet manifested in the cosmic formula – if not from the unmanifest Transcendence, which I must reach and realise? I have to bring it into the cosmic formula and, if so, I must realise the cosmic Divine and become conscious of the cosmic self and the cosmic forces. But I have to embody it here, – otherwise it is left as an influence only and not a thing fixed in the physical world, and it is through the Divine in the individual alone that this can be done.

These are elements in the dynamics of spiritual experience and I am obliged to admit them if a divine work has to be done.

*

The Divine we know is an Infinite Being in whose infinite manifestation these things [evil and suffering] have come — it is the Divine itself that is here, behind us, pervading the manifestation, supporting the world with its oneness; it is the Divine that is in us upholding itself the burden of the fall and its dark consequence. If above It stands for ever in its perfect Light, Bliss and Peace, It is also here; its Light, Bliss and Peace are secretly here supporting all; in ourselves there is a spirit, a central presence greater than the series of surface personalities which, like the supreme Divine itself, is not overborne by the fate they endure. If we find out this Divine within us, if we know ourselves as this spirit which is of one essence and being with the Divine, that is our gate of deliverance and in it we can remain ourselves even in the midst of this world's disharmonies, luminous, blissful and free. That much is the age-old testimony of spiritual experience.

*

It is in the inactive Brahman that one merges, if one seeks Laya or Moksha. One can dwell in the Personal Divine, but one does not merge in him. As for the Supreme Divine, he holds in himself the world-existence and it is in his consciousness that it moves, so by entering into the Supreme one rises above subjection to Nature, but one does not disappear from all consciousness of world-existence.

*

The Impersonal is Existence, Consciousness, Bliss, not a Person, but a state. The Person is the Existent, the Conscious, the Blissful; consciousness, existence, bliss taken as separate things are only states of his being. But in fact the two (personal being and eternal state) are inseparable and are one reality.

*

The personal realisation of the Divine may be sometimes with Form, sometimes without Form. Without Form, it is the Presence of the living Divine Person, felt in everything. With Form, it comes with the image of the One to whom worship is offered. The Divine can always manifest himself in a form to the bhakta or seeker. One sees him in the form in which one worships or seeks him or in a form suitable to the Divine Personality who is the object of the adoration. How it manifests depends on many things and it is too various to be reduced to a single rule.

*

When the Ananda comes into you, it is the Divine who comes into you, just as when the Peace flows into you, it is the Divine who is invading you, or when you are flooded with Light, it is the flood of the Divine himself that is around you. Of course, the Divine is something much more, many other things besides, and in them all a Presence, a Being, a Divine Person; for the Divine is Krishna, is Shiva, is the Supreme Mother. But through the Ananda you can perceive the Anandamaya Krishna, for the Ananda is the subtle body and being of Krishna; through the Peace you can perceive the Shantimaya Shiva; in the Light, in the delivering Knowledge, the Love, the fulfilling and uplifting Power you can meet the presence of the Divine Mother.

*

... I have started writing [about doubt], but I will begin not with doubt but with the demand for the Divine as a concrete certitude, quite as concrete as any physical phenomenon caught by the senses. Now, certainly, the Divine must be such a certitude not only as concrete but more concrete than anything sensed by ear or eye or touch in the world of Matter; but it is a certitude not of mental thought but of essential experience. When the Peace of God descends on you, when the Divine Presence is there within you, when the Ananda rushes on you like a sea, when you are driven like a leaf before the wind by the breath of the Divine Force, when Love flowers out from you on all creation, when Divine Knowledge floods you with a Light which illumines and transforms in a moment all that was before dark, sorrowful and obscure, when all that is becomes part of the One Reality, when the Reality is all around you, you feel at once by the spiritual contact, by the inner vision, by the illumined and seeing thought, by the vital sensation and even by the very physical sense, everywhere you see, hear, touch only the Divine. Then you can much less doubt it or deny it than you can deny or doubt daylight or air or the sun in heaven – for of these physical things you cannot be sure but they are what your senses represent them to be; but in the concrete experiences of the Divine, doubt is impossible.

*

The Divine gives itself to those who give themselves without reserve and in all their parts to the Divine. For them the calm, the light, the power, the bliss, the freedom, the wideness, the heights of knowledge, the seas of Ananda.

THE GODS

Of course, the gods exist – that is to say, there are Powers that stand above the world and transmit the divine workings. It is the physical mind which believes only what is physical that denies them. There are also beings of other worlds – gods and Asuras, etc.

*

There are gods everywhere on all the planes.

*

The dynamic aspect of the Divine is the Supreme Brahman, not the Gods. The Gods are Personalities and Powers of the dynamic Divine. You speak as if the evolution were the sole creation; the creation or manifestation is very vast and contains many planes and worlds that existed before the evolution, all different in character and with different kinds of beings. The fact of being prior to the evolution does not make them undifferentiated. The world of the Asuras is prior to the evolution, so are the worlds of the mental, vital or subtle physical Devas – but these beings are all different from each other. The great Gods belong to the overmind plane; in the supermind they are unified as aspects of the Divine, in the overmind they appear as separate personalities. Any godhead can descend by emanation to the physical plane and associate himself with the evolution of a human being with whose line of manifestation he is in affinity. But these are things which cannot be very easily understood by the mind, because the mind has too rigid an idea of personality – the difficulty only disappears when one enters into a more flexible consciousness above where one is nearer to the experience of One in all and All in one.

*

The Gods, as has already been said, are in origin and essence permanent Emanations of the Divine put forth from the Supreme by the Transcendent Mother, the Adya Shakti; in their cosmic action they are Powers and Personalities of the Divine each with his independent cosmic standing, function and work in the universe. They are not impersonal entities but cosmic Personalities, although they can and do ordinarily veil themselves behind the movement of impersonal forces. But while in the overmind and the triple world they appear as independent beings, they return in the supermind into the One and stand there united in a single harmonious action as multiple personalities of the One Person, the Divine Purushottama.

*

God is, but man's conceptions of God are reflections in his own mentality, sometimes of the Divine, sometimes of other Beings and Powers and they are what his mentality can make of the suggestions that come to him, generally very partial and imperfect so long as they are still mental, so long as he has not arrived at a higher and truer, a spiritual or mystic knowledge. The Gods already exist, they are not created by man, even though he does seem to conceive them in his own image; – fundamentally, he formulates as best he can what truth about them he receives from the cosmic Reality. An artist or a bhakta may have a vision of the Gods and it may get stabilised and generalised in the consciousness of the race and in that sense it may be true that man gives their forms to the Gods; but he does not invent these forms, he records what he sees; the forms that he gives are given to him.

*

As to the gods, man can build forms which they will accept but these forms too are inspired into man's mind from the planes to which the god belongs. All creation has the two sides, the formed and the formless, – the gods too are formless and yet have forms, but a godhead can take many forms, here Maheshwari, there Pallas Athene. Maheshwari herself has many forms in her lesser manifestation, Durga, Uma, Parvati, Chandi, etc. The gods are not limited to human forms – man also has not always seen them in human forms only.

*

Brahma, Vishnu, Shiva are only three Powers and Personalities of the One Cosmic Godhead.

*

Shiva is the Lord of Tapas. The power is the power of Tapas. Krishna as a godhead is the Lord of Ananda, Love and Bhakti; as an incarnation, he manifests the union of wisdom (Jnana) and works and leads the earth-evolution through this towards union with the Divine by Ananda, Love and Bhakti.

The Devi is the Divine Shakti – the Consciousness and Power of the Divine, the Mother and Energy of the worlds. All powers are hers. Sometimes Devi-power may mean the power of the universal World-Force; but this is only one side of the Shakti.

INVISIBLE FORCES AND THE DIVINE FORCE

Anyone with some intelligence and power of observation who lives more in an inward consciousness can see the play of invisible forces at every step which act on men and bring about events without their knowing about the instrumentation. The difference created by yoga or by an inner consciousness – for there are people like Socrates who develop or have some inner consciousness without yoga – is that one becomes conscious of these invisible forces and can also consciously profit by them or use and direct them. That is all.

*

If there are always forces around which are concerned to depress and discourage, there are always forces above and around us which we can draw upon, – draw into ourselves to restore, to fill up again with strength and faith and joy and the power that perseveres and conquers. It is really a habit that one has to get of opening to these helpful forces and either passively receiving them or actively drawing upon them – for one can do either. It is easier if you have the conception of them above and around you and the faith and the will to receive them – for that brings the experience and concrete sense of them and the capacity to receive at need or at will. It is a question of habituating your consciousness to get into touch and keep in touch with these helpful forces — and for that you must accustom yourself to reject the impressions forced on you by the others, depression, self-distrust, repining and all similar disturbances.

*

. . . it is part of the experience of those who have advanced far in Yoga that besides the ordinary forces and activities of the mind and life and body in Matter, there are other forces and powers that can act and do act from behind and from above; there is also a spiritual dynamic power which can be possessed by those who are advanced in the spiritual consciousness, though all do not care to possess or, possessing, to use it, and this power is greater than any other and more effective.

*

The invisible Force producing tangible results both inward and outward is the whole meaning of the Yogic consciousness. Your question about Yoga bringing merely a feeling of Power without any result was really very strange. Who would be satisfied with such a meaningless hallucination and call it Power? If we had not had thousands of experiences showing that the Power within could alter the mind, develop its powers, add new ones, bring in new ranges of knowledge, master the vital movements, change the character, influence men and things, control the conditions and functionings of the body, work as a concrete dynamic Force on other forces, modify events, etc., etc., we would not speak of it as we do. Moreover, it is not only in its results but in its movements that the Force is tangible and concrete. When I speak of feeling Force of Power, I do not mean simply having a vague sense of it, but feeling it concretely and consequently being able to direct it, manipulate it, watch its movement, be conscious of its mass and intensity and in the same way of that of other, perhaps opposing forces; all these things are possible and usual by the development of Yoga.

It is not, unless it is supramental Force, a Power that acts without conditions and limits. The conditions and limits under which Yoga or Sadhana has to be worked out are not arbitrary or capricious; they arise from the nature of things. These including the will, receptivity, assent, self-opening and surrender of the Sadhak have to be respected by the Yoga-force, unless it receives a sanction from the Supreme to override everything and get something done, but that sanction is sparingly given. It is only if the supramental Power came fully down, not merely sent its influences through the Overmind, that things could be very radically directed towards that object – for then the sanction would not be rare. For the Law of the Truth would be at work, not constantly balanced by the law of the Ignorance.

*

The Divine Force can act on any plane – it is not limited to the supramental Force. The supramental is only one aspect of the power of the Divine.

*

By Force I mean not mental or vital energy but the Divine Force from above - as peace comes from above and wideness also, so does this Force (Shakti). Nothing, not even thinking or meditating can be done without some action of Force. The Force I speak of is a Force for illumination, transformation, purification, all that has to be done in the yoga, for removal of hostile forces and the wrong movements – it is also of course for external work, whether great or small in appearance does not matter – if that is part of the Divine Will. I do not mean any personal force egoistic or rajasic.

THE DIVINE MOTHER

The Divine Mother is the Consciousness and Force of the Divine — which is the Mother of all things.

*

The Mother is the consciousness and force of the Divine — or, it may be said, she is the Divine in its consciousness-force. The Ishwara as Lord of the cosmos does come out of the Mother who takes her place beside him as the cosmic Shakti — the cosmic Ishwara is one aspect of the Divine.

*

The Supreme cannot create through the Transcendent because the Transcendent is the Supreme. It is through the Cosmic Shakti that the Divine creates.

*

It is a mistake to identify the Mother with the lower Prakriti and its mechanism of forces. Prakriti here is a mechanism only which has been put forth for the working of the evolutionary Ignorance. As the ignorant mental, vital or physical being is not itself the Divine, although it comes from the Divine — so the mechanism of Prakriti is not the Divine Mother. No doubt something of her is there in and behind this mechanism maintaining it for the evolutionary purpose; but what she is in herself is not a Shakti of Avidya, but the Divine Consciousness, Power, Light, Para Prakriti to whom we turn for release and the divine fulfilment.

*

It is possible to go towards the knowledge by beginning with the experience of dissolution in the One, but on condition that you do not stop there, taking it as the highest Truth, but proceed to realise the same One as the Supreme Mother, the Consciousness-Force of the Eternal. If, on the other hand, you approach through the Supreme Mother, she will give you the liberation in the silent One also as well as the realisation of the dynamic One, and from that it is easier to arrive at the Truth in which both are one and inseparable. At the same time, the gulf created by the mind between the Supreme and his manifestation is bridged, and there is no longer a fissure in the truth which makes all incomprehensible.

*

It is the Divine who is the Master – the Self is inactive, it is always a silent witness supporting all things – that is the static aspect. There is also the dynamic aspect through which the Divine works – behind that is the Mother. You must not lose sight of that, that it is through the Mother that all things are attained.

*

The Mother's consciousness is the divine Consciousness and the Light that comes from it is the light of the divine Truth, the Force that she brings down is the force of the divine Truth. One who receives and accepts and lives in the Mother's light, will begin to see the truth on all the planes, the mental, the vital, the physical. He will reject all that is undivine, – the undivine is the falsehood, the ignorance, the error of the dark forces; the undivine is all that is obscure and unwilling to accept the divine Truth and its light and force. The undivine, therefore, is all that is unwilling to accept the light and force of the Mother. That is why I am always telling you to keep yourself in contact with the Mother and with her Light and Force, because it is only so that you can come out of this confusion and obscurity and receive the Truth that comes from above.

*

Live always as if you were under the very eye of the Supreme and of the Divine Mother. Do nothing, try to think and feel nothing that would be unworthy of the Divine Presence.

*

Always behave as if the Mother was looking at you; because she is, indeed, always present.

THE MOTHER'S FORCE

When I speak of the Mother's force I do not speak of the force of Prakriti which carries in it things of the Ignorance but of the higher Force of the Divine that descends from above to transform the nature.

*

It [the Mother's Force] is the Divine Force which works to remove the ignorance and change the nature into the divine nature.

*

The Power above the head is of course the Mother's — it is the power of the Higher Consciousness which is preparing its way of descent. This Higher Consciousness carrying in it a sense of wide and boundless existence, light, power, peace, Ananda etc. is always there above the head and when something of the spiritual Force comes down to work upon the nature, it is from there that it comes. But nothing like the full descent of the peace, bliss etc. can come so long as the being is not ready.

*

What you feel streaming down must be the Mother's over-head Force. It flows usually from above the head and works at first in the mind-centres (head and neck) and afterwards goes down into the chest and heart and then through the movement of the whole body.

It is the effect of this working which you must be feeling in the head up to the shoulders. The Force that comes down from above is the one that works to transform the consciousness into that of a higher spiritual being. Before that the Mother's Force works in the psychic, mental, vital and the physical plane itself to support, purify and psychically change the consciousness.

*

The Mother's Force is not only above on the summit of the being. It is there with you and near you, ready to act whenever your nature will allow it. It is so with everybody here.

*

All has to be done by the working of the Mother's force aided by your aspiration, devotion and surrender.

THE DIVINE GRACE

For, as to this "Grace", we describe it in that way because we feel in the infinite Spirit or Self-existence a Presence or a Being, a Consciousness that determines, − that is what we speak of as the Divine, − not a separate person, but the one Being of whom our individual self is a portion or a vessel. But it is not necessary for everybody to regard it in that way. Supposing it is the impersonal Self of all only, yet the Upanishad says of this Self and its realisation: "This understanding is not to be gained by reasoning nor by tapasya nor by much learning, but whom this Self chooses, to him it reveals its own body". Well, that is the same thing as what we call the Divine Grace, − it is an action from above or from within independent of mental causes which decides its own movement. We can call it the Divine Grace; we can call it the Self within choosing its own hour and way to manifest to the mental instrument on the surface; we can call it the flowering of the inner being or inner nature into self-realisation and self-knowledge. As something in us approaches it or as it presents itself to us, so the mind sees it. But in reality it is the same thing and the same process of the being in Nature.

*

I should like to say something about the Divine Grace — for you seem to think it should be something like a Divine Reason acting upon lines not very different from those of human intelligence. But it is not that. Also it is not a universal Divine Compassion either, acting impartially on all who approach it and acceding to all prayers. It does not select the righteous and reject the sinner. The Divine Grace came to aid the persecutor (Saul of Tarsus), it came to St. Augustine the profligate, to Jagai and Madhai of infamous fame, to Bilwamangal and many others whose conversion might well scandalise the puritanism of the human moral intelligence; but it can come to the righteous also — curing them of their self-righteousness and leading to a purer consciousness beyond these things. It is a power that is superior to any rule, even to the Cosmic Law — for all spiritual seers have distinguished between the Law and Grace. Yet it is not indiscriminate — only it has a discrimination of its own which sees things and persons and the right times and seasons with another vision than that of the Mind or any other normal Power. A state of Grace is prepared in the individual often behind thick veils by means not calculable by the mind and when the state of Grace comes, then the Grace itself acts. There are these three powers: (1) The Cosmic Law, of Karma or what else; (2) the Divine Compassion acting on as many as it can reach through the nets of the Law and giving them their chance; (3) the Divine Grace which acts more incalculably but also more irresistibly than the others. The only question is whether there is something behind all the anomalies of life which can respond to the call and open itself with whatever difficulty till it is ready for the illumination of the Divine Grace – and that *something* must be not a mental and vital movement but an inner somewhat which can well be seen by the inner eye.

*

Without the Grace of the Divine nothing can be done, but for the full Grace to manifest the sadhak must make himself ready. If everything depends on the Divine intervention, then man is only a puppet and there is no use of sadhana, and there are no conditions, no law of things – therefore no universe, but only the Divine rolling things about at his pleasure. No doubt in the last resort all can be said to be the Divine cosmic working, but it is through persons, through forces that it works – under the conditions of Nature.

*

So many have done yoga relying on Tapasya or anything else, but not confident of any Divine Grace. It is not that, but the soul's demand for a higher Truth or a higher Life that is indispensable. Where that is, the Divine Grace whether believed in or not will intervene. If you believe, that hastens and facilitates things; if you cannot yet believe, still the soul's aspiration will justify itself, with whatever difficulty and struggle.

*

There is nothing unintelligible in what I say about strength and Grace. Strength has a value for spiritual realisation, but to say that it can be done by strength only and by no other means is a violent exaggeration. Grace is not an invention, it is a fact of spiritual experience. Many who would be considered as mere nothings by the wise and strong have attained by Grace; illiterate, without mental power or training, without "strength" of character or will, they have yet aspired and suddenly or rapidly grown into spiritual realisation, because they had faith or because they were sincere.

I do not see why these facts which are facts of spiritual history and of quite ordinary spiritual experience should be discussed and denied and argued as if they were mere matters of speculation.

Strength, if it is spiritual, is a power for spiritual realisation; a greater power is sincerity; the greatest power of all is Grace. I have said times without number that if a man is sincere, he will go through in spite of long delay and overwhelming difficulties. I have repeatedly spoken of the Divine Grace. I have referred any number of times to the line of the Gita:

"I will deliver thee from all sin and evil, do not grieve."

5

Bases of Yoga

THE CALL TO YOGA

The goal of yoga is always hard to reach, but this one is more difficult than any other, and it is only for those who have the call, the capacity, the willingness to face everything and every risk, even the risk of failure, and the will to progress towards an entire selflessness, desirelessness and surrender.

*

This yoga implies not only the realisation of God, but an entire consecration and change of the inner and outer life till it is fit to manifest a divine consciousness and become part of a divine work. This means an inner discipline far more exacting and difficult than mere ethical and physical austerities. One must not enter on this path, far vaster and more arduous than most ways of yoga, unless one is sure of the psychic call and of one's readiness to go through to the end.

*

By readiness, I did not mean capacity but willingness. If there is the will within to face all difficulties and go through, no matter how long it takes, then the path can be taken.

*

Nobody is fit for the sadhana — i.e. nobody can do it by his own sole capacity. It is a question of preparing oneself to bring in fully the Force not one's own that can do it with one's consent and aspiration.

*

When one enters into the true (yogic) consciousness then you see that everything can be done, even if at present only a slight beginning has been made; but a beginning is enough, since the Force, the Power are there. It is not really on the capacity of the outer nature that success depends, (for the outer nature all self-exceeding seems impossibly difficult,) but on the inner being and to the inner being all is possible. One has only to get into contact with the inner being and change the outer view and consciousness from the inner; that is the work of the sadhana and it is sure to come with sincerity, aspiration and patience.

*

For those who have within them a sincere call for the Divine, however the mind or vital may present difficulties or attacks come or the progress be slow and painful, — even if they fall back or fall away from the path for a time, the psychic always prevails in the end and the Divine Help proves effective. Trust in that and persevere — then the goal is sure.

THE INTEGRAL YOGA: NOT A SET METHOD

What is a perfect technique of yoga or rather of a world-changing or Nature-changing yoga? Not one that takes a man by a little bit of him somewhere, attaches a hook, and pulls him up by a pulley into Nirvana or Paradise. The technique of a world-changing yoga has to be as multiform, sinuous, patient, all-including as the world itself. If it does not deal with all the difficulties or possibilities and carefully deal with each necessary element, has it any chance of success? And can a perfect technique which everybody can understand do that? It is not like writing a small poem in a fixed metre with a limited number of modulations. If you take the poem simile, it is the Mahabharata of a Mahabharata that has to be done. And what, compared with the limited Greek perfection, is the technique of the Mahabharata?

*

The general principle of self-consecration and self-giving is the same for all in this yoga, but each has his own way of consecration and self-giving. The way that X takes is good for X, just as the way that you take is the right one for you, because it is in consonance with your nature. If there were not this plasticity and variety, if all had to be cut in the same pattern, yoga would be a rigid mental machinery, not a living power.

*

The way of yoga must be a living thing, not a mental principle or a set method to be stuck to against all necessary variations.

OPENING

The sadhana of this yoga does not proceed through any set mental teaching or prescribed forms of meditation, Mantras or others, but by aspiration, by a self-concentration inwards or upwards, by self-opening to an Influence, to the Divine Power above us and its workings, to the Divine Presence in the heart and by the rejection of all that is foreign to these things. It is only by faith, aspiration and surrender that this self-opening can come.

*

The object of the self-opening is to allow the force of the Divine to flow in bringing light, peace, Ananda, etc. and to do the work of transformation. When the being so receives the Divine Shakti and it works in him, produces its results (whether he is entirely conscious of the process or not,) then he is said to be open.

*

To be open is simply to be so turned to the Mother that her Force can work in you without anything refusing or obstructing her action. If the mind is shut up in its own ideas and refuses to allow her to bring in the Light and the Truth, if the vital clings to its desires and does not admit the true initiative and impulsions that the Mother's power brings, if the physical is shut up in its desires, habits and inertia and does not allow the Light and Force to enter in it and work, then one is not open. It is not possible to be entirely open all at once in all the movements, but there must be a central opening in each part and a dominant aspiration or will in each part (not in the mind alone) to admit only the Mother's "workings", the rest will then be progressively done.

*

In this yoga the whole principle is to open oneself to the Divine Influence. It is there above you and, if you can once become conscious of it, you have then to call it down into you. It descends into the mind and into the body as Peace, as a Light, as a Force that works, as the Presence of the Divine with or without form, as Ananda. Before one has this consciousness, one has to have faith and aspire for the opening. Aspiration, call, prayer are forms of one and the same thing and are all effective; you can take the form that comes to you or is easiest to you. The other way is concentration; you concentrate your consciousness in the heart (some do it in the head or above the head) and meditate on the Mother in the heart and call her in there. One can do either and both at different times — whatever comes naturally to you or you are moved to do at the moment. Especially in the beginning the one great necessity is to get the mind quiet, reject at the time of meditation all thoughts and movements that are foreign to the sadhana. In the quiet mind there will be a progressive preparation for the experience. But you must not become impatient, if all is not done at once; it takes time to bring entire quiet into the mind; you have to go on till the consciousness is ready.

*

In this yoga all depends on whether one can open to the Influence or not. If there is a sincerity in the aspiration and a patient will to arrive at the higher consciousness in spite of all obstacles, then the opening in one form or another is sure to come. But it may take a long or short time according to the prepared or unprepared condition of the mind, heart and body; so if one has not the necessary patience, the effort may be abandoned owing to the difficulty of the beginning. There is no method in this yoga except to concentrate, preferably in the heart, and call the presence and power of the Mother to take up the being and by the workings of her force transform the consciousness; one can concentrate also in the head or between the eyebrows, but for many this is a too difficult opening. When the mind falls quiet and the concentration becomes strong and the aspiration intense, then there is a beginning of experience. The more the faith, the more rapid the result is likely to be. For the rest one must not depend on one's own efforts only, but succeed in establishing a contact with the Divine and a receptivity to the Mother's Power and Presence.

*

There are two ways of doing Yoga, one by knowledge and one's own efforts, the other by reliance on the Mother. In the last way one has to offer one's mind and heart and all to the Mother for her Force to work on it, call her in all difficulties, have faith and bhakti. At first it takes time, often

a long time, for the consciousness to be prepared in this way
— and during that time many difficulties can come up, but if
one perseveres a time comes when all is ready, the Mother's
Force opens the consciousness fully to the Divine, then all
that must develop develops within, spiritual experience
comes and with it the knowledge and union with the Divine.

*

Keep yourself open to the Mother, remember her always
and let her Force work in you, rejecting all other influences
— that is the rule for yoga.

*

By remaining psychically open to the Mother, all that is
necessary for work or Sadhana develops progressively, that
is one of the chief secrets, the central secret of the Sadhana.

SURRENDER

There is not much spiritual meaning in keeping open to the
Mother if you withhold your surrender. Self-giving or surrender is demanded of those who practise this Yoga, because without such a progressive surrender of the being it is
quite impossible to get anywhere near the goal. To keep
open means to call in her Force to work in you, and if you do
not surrender to it, it amounts to not allowing the Force to
work in you at all or else only on condition that it will work
in the way you want and not in its own way which is the way
of the Divine Truth. A suggestion of this kind is usually
made by some adverse Power or by some egoistic element of
mind or vital which wants the Grace or the Force, but only
in order to use it for its own purpose, and is not willing to
live for the Divine Purpose, — it is willing to take from the
Divine all it can get, but not to give itself to the Divine. The
soul, the true being, on the contrary, turns towards the

Divine and is not only willing but eager and happy to surrender.

*

Surrender means to consecrate everything in oneself to the Divine, to offer all one is and has, not to insist on one's ideas, desires, habits, etc., but to allow the divine Truth to replace them by its knowledge, will and action everywhere.

*

Surrender is giving oneself to the Divine – to give everything one is or has to the Divine and regard nothing as one's own, to obey only the Divine will and no other, to live for the Divine and not for the ego.

*

It is the first principle of our sadhana that surrender is the means of fulfilment and so long as ego or vital demand and desire are cherished, complete surrender is impossible – the self-giving is incomplete. We have never concealed that. It may be difficult and it is; but it is the very principle of the sadhana. Because it is difficult it has to be done steadily and patiently till the work is complete.

You have to go on rejecting the vital mixture every time it rises. If you are steadfast in rejecting, it will lose more and more of its force and fade out.

*

If one wanted the Divine, the Divine himself would take up the purifying of the heart and develop the sadhana and give the necessary experiences; it can and does happen in that way if one has trust and confidence in the Divine and the will to surrender. For such a taking up involves one's putting oneself in the hands of the Divine rather than relying on one's own efforts alone and this implies one's putting one's trust and confidence in the Divine and a progressive self-giving. It is in fact the principle of sadhana that I myself followed and it is the central process of yoga as I envisage it. It is, I suppose, what Sri Ramakrishna meant by the method of the baby-cat in his image. But all cannot follow that at once; it takes time for them to arrive at it — it grows most when the mind and vital fall quiet.

What I mean by surrender is this inner surrender of the mind and vital. There is, of course, the outer surrender also: the giving up of all that is found to conflict with the spirit or need of the sadhana, the offering, the obedience to the guidance of the Divine, whether directly, if one has reached that stage, or through the psychic or to the guidance of the Guru. I may say that *prāyopaveśana* (fasting for a long time) has not anything to do with surrender: it is a form of tapasya of a very austere and, in my opinion, very excessive kind, often dangerous.

The core of the inner surrender is trust and confidence in the Divine. One takes the attitude: "I want the Divine and nothing else. I want to give myself entirely to him and since my soul wants that, it cannot be but that I shall meet and realise him. I ask nothing but that and his action in me to bring me to him, his action secret or open, veiled or manifest. I do not insist on my own time and way; let him do all in his own time and way; I shall believe in him, accept his will, aspire steadily for his light and presence and joy, go through all difficulties and delays, relying on him and never giving up. Let my mind be quiet and trust him and let him open it to his light; let my vital be quiet and turn to him alone and let him open it to his calm and joy. All for him and myself for him. Whatever happens, I will keep to this aspiration and self-giving and go on in perfect reliance that it will be done."

That is the attitude into which one must grow; for certainly it cannot be made perfect at once — mental and vital movements come across — but if one keeps the will to it, it will grow in the being. The rest is a matter of obedience to the guidance when it makes itself manifest, not allowing one's mental and vital movements to interfere.

It is not my intention to say that this way is the only way and sadhana cannot be done otherwise – there are so many others by which one can approach the Divine. But this is the only one I know by which the taking up of sadhana by the Divine becomes a sensible fact before the preparation of the nature is done. In other methods the Divine action may be felt from time to time, but it remains mostly behind the veil till all is ready. In some sadhanas the divine action is not recognised: all must be done by tapasya. In most there is a mixing of the two: the tapasya finally calling the direct help and intervention. The idea and experience of the Divine doing all belong to the yoga based on surrender. But whatever way is followed, the one thing to be done is to be faithful and go on to the end.

All can be done by the Divine, – the heart and nature purified, the inner consciousness awakened, the veils removed, – if one gives oneself to the Divine with trust and confidence and even if one cannot do so fully at once, yet the more one does so, the more the inner help and guidance come and the experience of the Divine grows within. If the questioning mind becomes less active and humility and the will to surrender grow, this ought to be perfectly possible. No other strength and tapasya are then needed, but this alone.

PERSONAL EFFORT AND SURRENDER

In the early part of the sadhana – and by early I do not mean a short part – effort is indispensable. Surrender of course, but surrender is not a thing that is done in a day. The mind has its ideas and it clings to them; the human vital resists surrender, for what it calls surrender in the early stages is a doubtful kind of self-giving with a demand in it; the physical consciousness is like a stone and what it calls surrender is often no more than inertia. It is only the psychic that knows

how to surrender and the psychic is usually very m h veiled
in the beginning. When the psychic awakes, it ca bring a
sudden and true surrender of the whole being, r the
difficulty of the rest is rapidly dealt with and disappe . But
till then effort is indispensable. Or else it is necessary l the
Force comes flooding down into the being from abov and
takes up the sadhana, does it for one more and more nd
leaves less and less to individual effort – but even the if
not effort, at least aspiration and vigilance are needed ll
the possession of mind, will, life and body by the Divi
Power is complete.

*

Yoga is an endeavour, a tapasya – it can cease to be so only
when one surrenders sincerely to a Higher Action and keeps
the surrender and makes it complete. It is not a fantasia
devoid of all reason and coherence or a mere miracle. It has
its laws and conditions and I do not see how you can demand
of the Divine to do everything by a violent miracle.

I have never said that this yoga is a safe one – no yoga is.
Each has its dangers as has every great attempt in human
life. But it can be carried through if one has a central
sincerity and a fidelity to the Divine. These are the two
necessary conditions.

*

The effort demanded of the Sadhak is that of aspiration,
rejection and surrender. If these three are done the rest is to
come of itself by the Grace of the Mother and the working of
her force in you. But of the three the most important is
surrender of which the first necessary form is trust and
confidence and patience in difficulty. There is no rule that
trust and confidence can only remain if aspiration is there.
On the contrary, when even aspiration is not there because
of the pressure of inertia, trust and confidence and patience
can remain. If trust and patience fail when aspiration is
quiescent, that would mean that the Sadhak is relying solely

on his own effort — it would mean, "Oh, my aspiration has failed, so there is no hope for me. My aspiration fails, so what can Mother do?" On the contrary, the Sadhak should feel, "Never mind, my aspiration will come back again. Meanwhile I know that the Mother is with me even when I do not feel her; she will carry me even through the darkest period." That is the fully right attitude you must have. To those who have it depression can do nothing; even if it comes it has to return baffled. That is not tamasic surrender. Tamasic surrender is when one says, "I won't do anything; let Mother do everything. Aspiration, rejection, surrender even are not necessary. Let her do all that in me." There is a great difference between the two attitudes. One is that of the shirker who won't do anything, the other is that of the Sadhak who does his best, but when he is reduced to quiescence for a time and things are adverse, keeps always his trust in the Mother's force and presence behind all and by that trust baffles the opposition force and calls back the activity of the Sadhana.

ASSENT

All the play in this world is based on a certain relative free will in the individual being. Even in the sadhana it remains and his consent is necessary at each step — even though it is by surrender to the Divine that he escapes from ignorance and separateness and ego, it must be at every step a free surrender.

*

The Divine Grace and Power can do everything, but with the full assent of the sadhak. To learn to give that full assent is the whole meaning of the sadhana. It may take time either because of ideas in the mind, desires in the vital or inertia in the physical consciousness, but these things have to be and can be removed with the aid or by calling in the action of the Divine Force.

*

You had written: "I need not bother about it — if peace is needed it will bring itself." Certainly, the main stress should be on the Force but the active assent of the sadhak is needed; in certain things his will also may be needed as an instrument of the Force.

WILL

So long as there is not a constant action of the Force from above or else of a deeper will from within, the mental will is necessary.

*

The Force also produces no definite and lasting fruit unless there is the will and resolution to achieve within the sadhak.

*

If there is a constant use of the will the rest of the being learns however slowly to obey the will and then the actions become in conformity with the will and not with the vital impulses and desires.

*

The will is a part of the consciousness and ought to be in human beings the chief agent in controlling the activities of the nature.

*

The energy which dictates the action or prevents a wrong action is the will.

*

There is only one way if you cannot exert your will – it is to call the Force; even the call only with the mind or the mental word is better than being extremely passive and submitted to the attack, – for although it may not succeed instantaneously, the mental call even ends by bringing the Force and opening up the consciousness again. For everything depends upon that. In the externalised consciousness obscurity and suffering can always be there; the more the internalised consciousness reigns, the more these things are pushed back and out, and with the full internalised consciousness they cannot remain – if they come, it is as outside touches unable to lodge themselves in the being.

*

Remind yourself always that the Divine Force is there, that you have felt it and that, even if you seem to lose consciousness of it for a time or it seems something distant, still it is there and is sure to prevail. For those whom the Force has touched and taken up, belong thenceforth to the Divine.

ASPIRATION

Personal aspiration is necessary until there is the condition in which all comes automatically and only a certain knowledge and assent is necessary for the development.

*

Aspiration is a call to the Divine, – will is the pressure of a conscious force on Nature.

*

Aspiration is to call the forces. When the forces have answered, there is a natural state of quiet receptivity concentrated but spontaneous.

*

Hardly anyone is strong enough to overcome by his own unaided aspiration and will the forces of the lower nature; even those who do it get only a certain kind of control, but not a complete mastery. Will and aspiration are needed to bring down the aid of the Divine Force and to keep the being on its side in its dealings with the lower powers. The Divine Force fulfilling the spiritual will and the heart's psychic aspiration can alone bring about the conquest.

*

It [the higher consciousness] may not come exactly according to the aspiration, but the aspiration is not ineffective. It keeps the consciousness open, prevents an inert state of acquiescence in all that comes and exercises a sort of pull on the sources of the higher consciousness.

*

Naturally, the more one-pointed the aspiration the swifter the progress. The difficulty comes when either the vital with its desires or the physical with its past habitual movements comes in — as they do with almost everyone. It is then that the dryness and difficulty of spontaneous aspiration come. This dryness is a well-known obstacle in all sadhana. But one has to persist and not be discouraged. If one keeps the will fixed even in these barren periods, they pass and after their passage a greater force of aspiration and experience becomes possible.

*

Yes, that is the way — the intensity of the aspiration brings the intensity of the experience and by repeated intensity of the experience, the change.

*

There is no need of words in aspiration. It can be expressed or unexpressed in words.

The aspiration need not be in the form of thought – it can be a feeling within that remains even when the mind is attending to the work.

DESIRE AND ASPIRATION

Pulling [down the higher consciousness] comes usually from a desire to get things for oneself – in aspiration there is a self-giving for the higher consciousness to descend and take possession – the more intense the call the greater the self-giving.

*

There is no doubt the mixture of desire in what you do, even in your endeavour of sadhana, that is the difficulty. The desire brings a movement of impatient effort and a reaction of disappointment and revolt when difficulty is felt and the immediate result is not there and other confusing and disturbing feelings. Aspiration should be not a form of desire, but the feeling of an inner soul's need, and a quiet settled will to turn towards the Divine and seek the Divine. It is certainly not easy to get rid of this mixture of desire entirely – not easy for anyone; but when one has the will to do it, this also can be effected by the help of the sustaining Force.

*

If there are good desires, bad desires will come also. There is a place for will and aspiration, not for desire. If there is desire there will be attachment, demand, craving, want of equanimity, sorrow at not getting, all that is unyogic.

*

One should be satisfied with what one gets and still aspire quietly without struggle, for more – till all has come. No desire, no struggle – aspiration, faith, openness – and the grace.

FAITH

Faith is a thing that precedes knowledge, not comes after knowledge. It is a glimpse of a truth which the mind has not yet seized as knowledge.

*

The faith in spiritual things that is asked of the sadhak is not an ignorant but a luminous faith, a faith in light and not in darkness. It is called blind by the sceptical intellect because it refuses to be guided by outer appearances or seeming facts, – for it looks for the truth behind, – and because it does not walk on the crutches of proof and evidence. It is an intuition, an intuition not only waiting for experience to justify it, but leading towards experience. If I believe in self-healing, I shall after a time find out the way to heal myself. If I have a faith in transformation, I can end by laying my hand on and unravelling the process of transformation. But if I begin with doubt and go on with more doubt, how far am I likely to go on the journey?

*

The phrase ["blind faith"] has no real meaning. I suppose they mean they will not believe without proof – but the conclusion formed after proof is not faith, it is knowledge or it is a mental opinion. Faith is something which one has before proof or knowledge and it helps you to arrive at knowledge or experience. There is no proof that God exists, but if I have faith in God, then I can arrive at the experience of the Divine.

*

Faith does not depend upon experience; it is something that is there before experience. When one starts the yoga, it is not usually on the strength of experience, but on the strength of faith. It is so not only in yoga and the spiritual life, but in ordinary life also. All men of action, discoverers, inventors, creators of knowledge proceed by faith and, until the proof is made or the thing done, they go on in spite of disappointment, failure, disproof, denial because of something in them that tells them that this is the truth, the thing that must be followed and done. Ramakrishna even went so far as to say, when asked whether blind faith was not wrong, that blind faith was the only kind to have, for faith is either blind or it is not faith but something else – reasoned inference, proved conviction or ascertained knowledge.

Faith is the soul's witness to something not yet manifested, achieved or realised, but which yet the Knower within us, even in the absence of all indications, feels to be true or supremely worth following or achieving. This thing within us can last even when there is no fixed belief in the mind, even when the vital struggles and revolts and refuses. Who is there that practises the yoga and has not his periods, long periods of disappointment and failure and disbelief and darkness? But there is something that sustains him and even goes on in spite of himself, because it feels that what it followed after was yet true and it more than feels, it knows. The fundamental faith in yoga is this, inherent in the soul, that the Divine exists and the Divine is the one thing to be followed after – nothing else in life is worth having in comparison with that. So long as a man has that faith, he is marked for the spiritual life and I will say that, even if his nature is full of obstacles and crammed with denials and difficulties, and even if he has many years of struggle, he is marked out for success in the spiritual life.

It is this faith that you need to develop – a faith which is in accordance with reason and common sense – that if the Divine exists and has called you to the Path, (as is evident), then there must be a Divine Guidance behind and through and in spite of all difficulties you will arrive. Not to listen to the hostile voices that suggest failure or to the voices of impatient, vital haste that echo them, not to believe that because great difficulties are there, there can be no success or that because the Divine has not yet shown himself he will never show himself, but to take the position that everyone takes when he fixes his mind on a great and difficult goal, "I will go on till I succeed — all difficulties notwithstanding." To which the believer in the Divine adds, "The Divine exists, my following after the Divine cannot fail. I will go on through everything till I find him."

*

One must say, "Since I want only the Divine, my success is sure, I have only to walk forward in all confidence and His own Hand will be there secretly leading me to Him by His own way and at His own time." That is what you must keep as your constant mantra. Anything else one may doubt but that he who desires only the Divine shall reach the Divine is a certitude and more certain than two and two make four. That is the faith every sadhak must have at the bottom of his heart, supporting him through every stumble and blow and ordeal. It is only false ideas still casting their shadows on your mind that prevent you from having it. Push them aside and the back of the difficulty will be broken.

*

The experience you had of the power of the Name and the protection is that of everyone who has used it with the same faith and reliance. To those who call from the heart for the protection, it cannot fail. Do not allow any outward circumstance to shake the faith in you; for nothing gives greater strength than this faith to go through and arrive at the goal. Knowledge and Tapasya, whatever their force, have a less sustaining power — faith is the strongest staff for the journey.

The protection is there over you and the watchful love of the Mother. Rely upon it and let your being open more and more to it — then it will repel attacks and always uphold you.

PATIENCE AND PERSEVERANCE

There are always difficulties and a hampered progress in the early stages and a delay in the opening of the inner doors until the being is ready. If you feel whenever you meditate the quiescence and the flashes of the inner Light and if the inward urge is growing so strong that the external hold is decreasing and the vital disturbances are losing their force, that is already a great progress. The road of yoga is long, every inch of ground has to be won against much resistance and no quality is more needed by the sadhak than patience and single-minded perseverance with a faith that remains firm through all difficulties, delays and apparent failures.

*

The power needed in yoga is the power to go through effort, difficulty or trouble without getting fatigued, depressed, discouraged or impatient and without breaking off the effort or giving up one's aim or resolution.

*

One who has not the courage to face patiently and firmly life and its difficulties will never be able to go through the still greater inner difficulties of the sadhana. The very first lesson in this yoga is to face life and its trials with a quiet mind, a firm courage and an entire reliance on the Divine Shakti.

*

"I will try again" is not sufficient; what is needed is to try always — steadily, with a heart free from despondency, as the Gita says, *anirvinnacetasā*. You speak of five and a half years as if it were a tremendous time for such an object, but a yogi who is able in that time to change radically his nature and get the concrete decisive experience of the Divine would have to be considered as one of the rare gallopers of the spiritual Way. Nobody has ever said that the spiritual change was an easy thing; all spiritual seekers will say that it is difficult but supremely worth doing. If one's desire for the Divine has become the master desire, then surely one can give one's whole life to it without repining and not grudge the time, difficulty or labour.

*

Impatience is always a mistake, it does not help but hinders. A quiet happy faith and confidence is the best foundation for sadhana; for the rest a constant opening wide of oneself to receive with an aspiration which may be intense, but must always be calm and steady. Full yogic realisation does not come all at once, it comes after a long preparation of the Adhar which may take a long time.

*

In a more deep and spiritual sense a concrete realisation is that which makes the thing realised more real, dynamic, intimately present to the consciousness than any physical thing can be. Such a realisation of the personal Divine or of the impersonal Brahman or of the Self does not usually come at the beginning of a sadhana or in the first years or for many years. It comes so to a very few. But to expect and demand it so soon would be taken in the eyes of any experienced yogi or sadhak as a rather rash and abnormal impatience. Most would say that a slow development is the best one can hope for in the first years and only when the nature is ready and fully concentrated towards the Divine can the definitive experience come. To some rapid preparatory experiences can come at a comparatively early stage, but even they cannot escape the labour of the consciousness which will make these experiences culminate in the realisation that is enduring and complete. It is not a question of liking or disliking, it is a matter of fact and truth and experience. It is the fact that people who are cheerful and ready to go step by step, even by slow steps, if need be, do actually march faster and more surely than those who are impatient and in haste. It is what I have always seen.

*

What I meant about the experiences was simply this that you have created your own ideas about what you want from the yoga and have always been measuring what began to come by that standard and because it was not according to expectations or up to that standard, telling yourself after a moment, "It is nothing, it is nothing". That dissatisfaction laid you open at every step to a reaction or a recoil which prevented any continuous development. The yogin who has experience knows that the small beginnings are of the greatest importance and have to be cherished and allowed with great patience to develop. He knows, for instance, that the neutral quiet so dissatisfying to the vital eagerness of the sadhak is the first step towards the peace that passeth all understanding, the small current or thrill of inner delight the first trickling of the ocean of Ananda, the play of lights or colours the key of the doors of the inner vision and experience, the descent that stiffens the body into a concentrated stillness the first touch of something at the end of which is the presence of the Divine. He is not impatient; he is rather careful not to disturb the evolution that is beginning. Certainly some sadhaks have strong and decisive experiences at the beginning, but these are followed by long labour in which there are many empty periods and periods of struggle.

SINCERITY

Sincerity means more than mere honesty. It means that you mean what you say, feel what you profess, are earnest in your will. As the sadhak aspires to be an instrument of the

Divine and one with the Divine, sincerity in him means that
he is really in earnest in his aspiration and refuses all other
will or impulse except the Divine's.

*

Sincere is simply an adjective meaning that the will must be
a true will. If you simply think "I aspire" and do things
inconsistent with the aspiration, or follow your desires or
open yourself to contrary influences, then it is not a sincere
will.

*

To be entirely sincere means to desire the divine Truth only,
to surrender yourself more and more to the Divine Mother,
to reject all personal demand and desire other than this one
aspiration, to offer every action in life to the Divine and do
it as the work given without bringing in the ego. This is the
basis of the divine life.

One cannot become altogether this at once, but if one
aspires at all times and calls in always the aid of the Divine
Shakti with a true heart and straightforward will, one grows
more and more into this consciousness.

*

Men are always mixed and there are qualities and defects
mingled together almost inextricably in their nature. What a
man wants to be or wants others to see in him or what he is
sometimes on one side of his nature or in some relations can
be very different from what he is in the actual fact or in other
relations or on another side of his nature. To be absolutely
sincere, straightforward, open, is not an easy achievement
for human nature. It is only by spiritual endeavour that one
can realise it — and to do it needs a severity of introspective
self-vision, an unsparing scrutiny of self-observation of
which many sadhaks and yogis even are not capable and it is
only by an illumining Grace that reveals the sadhak to
himself and transforms what is deficient in him that it can be

done. And even then only if he himself consents and lends himself wholly to the divine working.

*

The one condition of getting rid of things is an absolute central sincerity in all the parts of the being, and that means an absolute insistence on the Truth and nothing but the Truth. There will then be a readiness for unsparing self-criticism and vigilant openness to the light, an uneasiness when falsehood comes in, which will finally purify the whole being.

*

The most important thing for the purification of the heart is an absolute sincerity. No pretence with oneself, no concealment from the Divine, or oneself, or the Guru, a straight look at one's movements, a straight will to make them straight. It does not so much matter if it takes time: one must be prepared to make it one's whole life-task to seek the Divine. Purifying the heart means after all a pretty considerable achievement and it is no use getting despondent, despairful, etc., because one finds things in oneself that still need to be changed. If one keeps the true will and true attitude, then the intuitions or intimations from within will begin to grow, become clear, precise, unmistakable and the strength to follow them will grow also: and then before even you are satisfied with yourself, the Divine will be satisfied with you and begin to withdraw the veil by which he protects himself and his seekers against a premature and perilous grasping of the greatest thing to which humanity can aspire.

*

A sincere heart is worth all the extraordinary powers in the world.

QUIET, CALM, PEACE AND SILENCE

The words "peace, calm, quiet, silence" have each their own shade of meaning, but it is not easy to define them.

Peace – *śānti.*

Calm – *sthiratā.*

Quiet – *acañcalatā.*

Silence – *niścala-nīravatā.*

Quiet is a condition in which there is no restlessness or disturbance.

Calm is a still unmoved condition which no disturbance can affect – it is a less negative condition than quiet.

Peace is a still more positive condition; it carries with it a sense of settled and harmonious rest and deliverance.

Silence is a state in which either there is no movement of the mind or vital or else a great stillness which no surface movement can pierce or alter.

*

The first step is a quiet mind – silence is a further step, but quietude must be there; and by a quiet mind I mean a mental consciousness within which sees thoughts arrive to it and move about but does not itself feel that it is thinking or identifying itself with the thoughts or call them its own. Thoughts, mental movements may pass through it as way-farers appear and pass from elsewhere through a silent country – the quiet mind observes them or does not care to observe them, but, in either case, does not become active or lose its quietude. Silence is more than quietude; it can be gained by banishing thought altogether from the inner mind keeping it voiceless or quite outside; but more easily it is established by a descent from above – one feels it coming down, entering and occupying or surrounding the personal consciousness which then tends to merge itself in the vast impersonal silence.

*

Quietness is when the mind or vital is not troubled, restless, drawn about by or crowded with thoughts and feelings. Especially when either is detached and looks at these as a surface movement, we say that the mind or vital is quiet.

Calmness is a more positive condition, not merely an absence of restlessness, over-activity or trouble. When there is a clear or great or strong tranquillity which nothing troubles or can trouble, then we say that calm is established.

*

The difference between a vacant mind and a calm mind is this: that when the mind is vacant, there is no thought, no conception, no mental action of any kind, except an essential perception of things without the formed idea; but in the calm mind, it is the substance of the mental being that is still, so still that nothing disturbs it. If thoughts or activities come, they do not rise at all out of the mind, but they come from outside and cross the mind as a flight of birds crosses the sky in a windless air. It passes, disturbs nothing, leaving no trace. Even if a thousand images or the most violent events pass across it, the calm stillness remains as if the very texture of the mind were a substance of eternal and indestructible peace. A mind that has achieved this calmness can begin to act, even intensely and powerfully, but it will keep its fundamental stillness – originating nothing from itself but receiving from Above and giving it a mental form without adding anything of its own, calmly, dispassionately, though with the joy of the Truth and the happy power and light of its passage.

*

Peace is more positive than calm – there can be a negative calm which is merely an absence of disturbance or trouble, but peace is always something positive bringing not merely a release as calm does but a certain happiness or Ananda of itself.

There is also a positive calm, something that stands

against all things that seek to trouble, not thin and neutral like the negative calm, but strong and massive.

*

In peace there is besides the sense of stillness a harmony that gives a feeling of liberation and full satisfaction.

*

Of course. It is quite usual to feel an established peace in the inner being even if there is disturbance on the surface. In fact that is the usual condition of the yogi before he has attained the absolute *samatā* in all the being.

*

When the peace is fully established everywhere in the being, these things [reactions of the lower vital] will not be able to shake it. They may come first as ripples on the surface, then only as suggestions which one looks at or does not care to look at but in either case they don't get inside, affect or disturb at all.

It is difficult to explain, but it is something like a mountain at which one throws stones — if conscious all through the mountain may feel the touch of the stones, but the thing would be so slight and superficial that it would not be in the least affected. In the end even that reaction disappears.

*

When the mind is silent there is peace and in the peace all things that are divine can come. When there is not the mind, there is the Self which is greater than the mind.

*

It is not an undesirable thing for the mind to fall silent, to be free from thoughts and still — for it is oftenest when the mind falls silent that there is the full descent of a wide peace from above and in that wide tranquillity the realisation of the silent Self above the mind spread out in its vastness every-

where. Only, when there is the peace and the mental silence, the vital mind tries to rush in and occupy the place or
else the mechanical mind tries to raise up for the same
purpose its round of trivial habitual thoughts. What the
sadhak has to do is to be careful to reject and hush these
outsiders, so that during the meditation at least the peace
and quietude of the mind and vital may be complete. This
can be done best if you keep a strong and silent will. That
will is the will of the Purusha behind the mind; when the
mind is at peace, when it is silent one can become aware of
the Purusha, silent also, separate from the action of the
nature.

*

It is not possible for the spontaneous silent condition to last
always at once but that is what must grow in one till there is
a constant inner silence – a silence which cannot be disturbed by any outward activity or even by any attempt at
attack or disturbance.

The condition you describe shows precisely the growth of
this inner silence. It has to fix itself eventually as the basis of
all spiritual experience and activity. It does not matter if one
does not know what is going on within behind the silence.
For there are two conditions in the yoga, one in which all is
silent and there is no thought, feeling or movement even
though one is acting outwardly as others do – another in
which a new consciousness becomes active bringing knowledge, joy, love and other spiritual feelings and inner activities, but yet at the same time there is a fundamental silence
or quietude. Both are necessary in the development of the
inner being. The absolutely silent state, which is one of
lightness, voidness and release, prepares the other and
supports it when it comes.

*

Keep the quietude and do not mind if it is for a time an
empty quietude; the consciousness is often like a vessel

which has to be emptied of its mixed or undesirable contents; it has to be kept vacant for a while till it can be filled with things new and true, right and pure. The one thing to be avoided is the refilling of the cup with the old turbid contents. Meanwhile wait, open yourself upwards, call very quietly and steadily, not with a too restless eagerness, for the peace to come into the silence and, once the peace is there, for the joy and the presence.

*

Equanimity and peace in all conditions, in all parts of the being is the first foundation of the yogic status. Either Light (bringing with it Knowledge) or Force (bringing strength and dynamism of many kinds) or Ananda (bringing love and joy of existence) can come next according to the trend of the nature. But peace is the first condition without which nothing else can be stable.

WIDENESS

At last you have the true foundation of the sadhana. This calm, peace and surrender are the right atmosphere for all the rest to come, knowledge, strength, Ananda. Let it become complete.

It does not remain when engaged in work because it is still confined to the mind proper which has only just received the gift of silence. When the new consciousness is fully formed and has taken entire possession of the vital nature and the physical being (the vital as yet is only touched or dominated by the silence, not possessed by it), then this defect will disappear.

The quiet consciousness of peace you now have in the mind must become not only calm but wide. You must feel it everywhere, yourself in it and all in it. This also will help to bring the calm as a basis into the action.

The wider your consciousness becomes, the more you will be able to receive from above. The Shakti will be able to descend and bring strength and light as well as peace into the system. What you feel as narrow and limited in you is the physical mind; it can only widen if this wider consciousness and the light come down and possess the nature.

The physical inertia from which you suffer is likely to lessen and disappear only when strength from above descends into the system.

Remain quiet, open yourself and call the divine Shakti to confirm the calm and peace, to widen the consciousness and to bring into it as much light and power as it can at present receive and assimilate.

Take care not to be over-eager, as this may disturb again such quiet and balance as has been already established in the vital nature.

Have confidence in the final result and give time for the Power to do its work.

*

Yes, your experience was a very good one and your feeling about it was correct. When the consciousness is narrow and personal or shut in the body, it is difficult to receive from the Divine — the wider it expands, the more it can receive. A time comes when it feels as wide as the world and able to receive all the Divine into itself.

*

Wideness and calmness are the foundation of the yogic consciousness and the best condition for inner growth and experience. If a wide calm can be established in the physical consciousness, occupying and filling the very body and all its cells, that can become the basis for its transformation; in fact, without this wideness and calmness the transformation is hardly possible.

*

If you keep the wideness and calm and also the love for the Mother in the heart, then all is safe, for it means the double foundation of the yoga: the descent of the higher consciousness with its peace, freedom and serenity from above and the openness of the psychic which keeps all the effort or all the spontaneous movement turned towards the true goal.

EQUALITY

The passage through sattwa is the ordinary idea of yoga, it is the preparation and purification by the *yama-niyama* of Patanjali or by other means in other yogas, e.g., saintliness in the bhakti schools, the eightfold path in Buddhism, etc., etc. In our yoga the evolution through sattwa is replaced by the cultivation of equanimity, *samatā*, and by the psychic transformation.

*

Not to be disturbed by either joy or grief, pleasure or displeasure by what people say or do or by any outward things is called in yoga a state of *samatā*, equality to all things. It is of immense importance in sadhana to be able to reach this state. It helps the mental quietude and silence as well as the vital to come. It means indeed that the vital itself and the vital mind are already falling silent and becoming quiet. The thinking mind is sure to follow.

*

Equality is to remain unmoved within in all conditions.

*

Equality is the chief support of the true spiritual consciousness and it is this from which a sadhak deviates when he allows a vital movement to carry him away in feeling or

speech or action. Equality is not the same thing as forbearance, — though undoubtedly a settled equality immensely
extends, even illimitably, a man's power of endurance and
forbearance.

Equality means a quiet and unmoved mind and vital, it
means not to be touched or disturbed by things that happen
or things said or done to you, but to look at them with a
straight look, free from the distortions created by personal
feeling, and to try to understand what is behind them, why
they happen, what is to be learnt from them, what is it in
oneself which they are cast against and what inner profit or
progress one can make out of them; it means self-mastery
over the vital movements, — anger and sensitiveness and
pride as well as desire and the rest, — not to let them get hold
of the emotional being and disturb the inner peace, not to
speak and act in the rush and impulsion of these things,
always to act and speak out of a calm inner poise of the
spirit. It is not easy to have this equality in any full perfect
measure, but one should always try more and more to make
it the basis of one's inner state and outer movements.

Equality means another thing — to have an equal view of
men and their nature and acts and the forces that move
them; it helps one to see the truth about them by pushing
away from the mind all personal feeling in one's seeing and
judgment and even all the mental bias. Personal feeling
always distorts and makes one see in men's actions, not only
the actions themselves, but things behind them which, more
often than not, are not there. Misunderstanding, misjudg-
ment which could have been avoided are the result; things of
small consequence assume larger proportions. I have seen
that more than half of the untoward happenings of this kind
in life are due to this cause. But in ordinary life personal
feeling and sensitiveness are a constant part of human
nature and may be needed there for self-defence, although,
I think, even there, a strong, large and equal attitude towards men and things would be a much better line of

defence. But for a sadhak, to surmount them and live rather in the calm strength of the spirit is an essential part of his progress.

*

There can be no firm foundation in sadhana without equality, *samatā*. Whatever the unpleasantness of circumstances, however disagreeable the conduct of others, you must learn to receive them with a perfect calm and without any disturbing reaction. These things are the test of equality. It is easy to be calm and equal when things go well and people and circumstances are pleasant; it is when they are the opposite that the completeness of the calm, peace, equality can be tested, reinforced, made perfect.

*

Complete *samatā* takes long to establish and it is dependent on three things — the soul's self-giving to the Divine by an inner surrender, the descent of the spiritual calm and peace from above and the steady, long and persistent rejection of all egoistic, rajasic and other feelings that contradict *samatā*.

The first thing to do is to make the full consecration and offering of the heart — the increase of the spiritual calm and the surrender are the condition for the rejection of ego, *rajoguna*, etc. to be effective.

*

Samatā does not mean the absence of ego, but the absence of desire and attachment. The ego-sense may disappear or it may remain in a subtilised or dense form — it depends on the person.

*

To be free from all preference and receive joyfully whatever comes from the Divine Will is not possible at first for any human being. What one should have at first is the constant idea that what the Divine wills is always for the best even when the mind does not see how it is so, to accept with resignation what one cannot yet accept with gladness and so to arrive at a calm equality which is not shaken even when on the surface there may be passing movements of a momentary reaction to outward happenings. If that is once firmly founded, the rest can come.

*

The inner spiritual progress does not depend on outer conditions so much as in the way we react to them from within — that has always been the ultimate verdict of spiritual experience. It is why we insist on taking the right attitude and persisting in it, on an inner state not dependent on outer circumstances, a state of equality and calm, if it cannot be at once of inner happiness, on going more and more within and looking from within outwards instead of living in the surface mind which is always at the mercy of the shocks and blows of life. It is only from that inner state that one can be stronger than life and its disturbing forces and hope to conquer.

To remain quiet within, firm in the will to go through, refusing to be disturbed or discouraged by difficulties or fluctuations, that is one of the first things to be learned in the Path. To do otherwise is to encourage the instability of consciousness, the difficulty of keeping experience of which you complain. It is only if you keep quiet and steady within that the lines of experience can go on with some steadiness — though they are never without periods of interruption and fluctuation; but these, if properly treated, can then become periods of assimilation and exhaustion of difficulty rather than denials of sadhana.

A spiritual atmosphere is more important than outer conditions; if one can get that and also create one's own spiritual air to breathe in and live in it, that is the true condition of progress.

6

Sadhana through Work, Meditation, and Love and Devotion

SADHANA THROUGH WORK

THE MOTIVE FOR WORK IN YOGA

Men usually work and carry on their affairs from the ordinary motives of the vital being, need, desire of wealth or success or position or power or fame or the push to activity and the pleasure of manifesting their capacities, and they succeed or fail according to their capability, power of work and the good or bad fortune which is the result of their nature and their Karma. When one takes up the yoga and wishes to consecrate one's life to the Divine, these ordinary motives of the vital being have no longer their full and free play; they have to be replaced by another, a mainly psychic and spiritual motive, which will enable the sadhak to work with the same force as before, no longer for himself, but for the Divine.

*

The only work that spiritually purifies is that which is done without personal motives, without desire for fame or public recognition or worldly greatness, without insistence on one's own mental motives or vital lusts and demands or physical preferences, without vanity or crude self-assertion or claim for position or prestige, done for the sake of the Divine alone and at the command of the Divine. All work done in an egoistic spirit, however good for people in the world of the Ignorance, is of no avail to the seeker of the yoga.

*

Family, society, country are a larger ego – they are not the Divine. One can work for them and say that one is working for the Divine only if one is conscious of the Divine Adesh to act for that purpose or of the Divine Force working within one. Otherwise it is only an idea of the mind identifying country etc. with the Divine.

*

You used the Force for the work, and it supported you so long as you preferred to stick to that work. What is of first importance is not the religious or non-religious character of the work done, but the inner attitude in which it is done. If the attitude is vital and not psychic, then one throws oneself out in the work and loses the inner contact. If it is psychic, the inner contact remains, the Force is felt supporting or doing the work and the sadhana progresses.

*

All this insistence upon action is absurd if one has not the light by which to act. "Yoga must include life and not exclude it" does not mean that we are bound to accept life as it is with all its stumbling ignorance and misery and the obscure confusion of human will and reason and impulse and instinct which it expresses. The advocates of action think that by human intellect and energy making an always new rush, everything can be put right; the present state of the world after a development of the intellect and a stupendous output of energy for which there is no historical parallel is a signal proof of the emptiness of the illusion under which they labour. Yoga takes the stand that it is only by a change of consciousness that the true basis of life can be discovered; from within outward is indeed the rule. But within does not mean some quarter inch behind the surface. One must go deep and find the soul, the self, the Divine Reality within us and only then can life become a true expression of what we can be instead of a blind and always repeated confused blur of the inadequate and imperfect thing we were. The choice is between remaining in the old jumble and groping about in the hope of stumbling on some discovery or standing back and seeking the Light within till we discover and can build the Godhead within and without us.

*

I do not mean by work action done in the ego and the ignorance, for the satisfaction of the ego and in the drive of rajasic desire. There can be no Karmayoga without the will to get rid of ego, rajas and desire, which are the seals of ignorance.

I do not mean philanthropy or the service of humanity or all the rest of the things — moral or idealistic — which the mind of man substitutes for the deeper truth of works.

I mean by work action done for the Divine and more and more in union with the Divine — for the Divine alone and nothing else. Naturally that is not easy at the beginning, any more than deep meditation and luminous knowledge are easy or even true love and bhakti are easy. But like the others it has to be begun in the right spirit and attitude, with the right will in you, then all the rest will come.

Works done in this spirit are quite as effective as bhakti or contemplation. One gets by the rejection of desire, rajas and ego a quietude and purity into which the Peace ineffable can descend; one gets by the dedication of one's will to the Divine, by the merging of one's will in the Divine Will the death of ego and the enlarging into the cosmic consciousness or else the uplifting into what is above the cosmic; one experiences the separation of Purusha from Prakriti and is liberated from the shackles of the outer nature; one becomes aware of one's inner being and sees the outer as an instrument; one feels the universal Force doing one's works and the Self or Purusha watching or witness but free; one feels all one's works taken from one and done by the universal or supreme Mother or by the Divine Power controlling and acting from behind the heart. By constant referring of all one's will and works to the Divine, love and adoration grow, the psychic being comes forward. By the reference to the Power above, we can come to feel it above and its descent and the opening to an increasing consciousness and knowledge. Finally, works, bhakti and knowledge go together and self-perfection becomes possible – what we call the transformation of the nature.

These results certainly do not come all at once; they come more or less slowly, more or less completely according to the condition and growth of the being. There is no royal road to the divine realisation.

This is the Karmayoga laid down in the Gita as I have developed it for the integral spiritual life. It is founded not on speculation and reasoning but on experience. It does not exclude meditation and certainly does not exclude bhakti, for the self-offering to the Divine, the consecration of all oneself to the Divine which is the essence of this Karmayoga are essentially a movement of bhakti. Only it does exclude a life-fleeing exclusive meditation or an emotional bhakti shut up in its own inner dream taken as the whole movement of the yoga. One may have hours of pure absorbed meditation or of the inner motionless adoration and ecstasy, but they are not the whole of the integral yoga.

WORK AS PART OF THE YOGA

Work is part of the Yoga and it gives the best opportunity for calling down the Presence, the Light and the Power into the vital and its activities; it increases also the field and the opportunity of surrender.

*

Yoga through work is the easiest and most effective way to enter into the stream of this Sadhana.

*

... to quiet the mind and get the spiritual experience it is necessary first to purify and prepare the nature. This sometimes takes many years. Work done with the right attitude is the easiest means for that – i.e. work done without desire or ego, rejecting all movements of desire, demand or ego when they come, done as an offering to the Divine Mother, with the remembrance of her and prayer to her to manifest her force and take up the action so that there too and not only in inner silence you can feel her presence and working.

*

There should be not only a general attitude, but each work should be offered to the Mother so as to keep the attitude a living one all the time. There should be at the time of work no meditation, for that would withdraw the attention from the work, but there should be the constant memory of the One to whom you offer it. This is only a first process; for when you can have constantly the feeling of a calm being within concentrated in the sense of the Divine Presence while the surface mind does the work, or when you can begin to feel always that it is the Mother's force that is doing the work and you are only a channel or an instrument, then

in place of memory there will have begun the automatic
constant realisation of Yoga, divine union, in works.

*

It is not at first easy to remember the presence in work; but
if one revives the sense of the presence immediately after
the work is over it is all right. In time the sense of the
presence will become automatic even in work.

*

All the difficulties you describe are quite natural things
common to most people. It is easy for one, comparatively,
to remember and be conscious when one sits quiet in
meditation; it is difficult when one has to be busy with work.
The remembrance and consciousness in work have to come
by degrees, you must not expect to have it all at once;
nobody can get it all at once. It comes in two ways, – first, if
one practises remembering the Mother and offering the
work to her each time one does something (not all the time
one is doing, but at the beginning or whenever one can
remember,) then that slowly becomes easy and habitual to
the nature. Secondly, by the meditation an inner consciousness begins to develop which, after a time, not at once or
suddenly, becomes more and more automatically permanent. One feels this as a separate consciousness from that
outer which works. At first this separate consciousness is not
felt when one is working, but as soon as the work stops one
feels it was there all the time watching from behind; afterwards it begins to be felt during the work itself, as if there
were two parts of oneself – one watching and supporting
from behind and remembering the Mother and offering to
her and the other doing the work. When this happens, then
to work with the true consciousness becomes more and more
easy.

*

If you can't as yet remember the Divine all the time you are working, it does not greatly matter. To remember and dedicate at the beginning and give thanks at the end ought to be enough for the present. Or at the most to remember too when there is a pause. Your method seems to me rather painful and difficult, — you seem to be trying to remember and work with one and the same part of the mind. I don't know if that is possible. When people remember all the time during work (it can be done), it is usually with the back of their minds or else there is created gradually a faculty of double thought or else a double consciousness — one in front that works, and one within that witnesses and remembers. There is also another way which was mine for a long time — a condition in which the work takes place automatically and without intervention of personal thought or mental action, while the consciousness remains silent in the Divine. The thing, however, does not come so much by trying as by a very simple constant aspiration and will of consecration — or else by a movement of the consciousness separating the inner from the instrumental being. Aspiration and will of consecration calling down a greater Force to do the work is a method which brings great results, even if in some it takes a long time about it. That is a great secret of sadhana, to know how to get things done by the Power behind or above instead of doing all by the mind's effort. I don't mean to say that the mind's effort is unnecessary or has no result — only if it tries to do everything by itself, that becomes a laborious effort for all except the spiritual athletes. Nor do I mean that the other method is the longed-for short cut; the result may, as I have said, take a long time. Patience and firm resolution are necessary in every method of sadhana.

Strength is all right for the strong — but aspiration and the Grace answering to it are not altogether myths; they are great realities of the spiritual life.

*

One can both aspire and attend to the work and do many other things at the same time when the consciousness is developed by yoga.

*

All should be done quietly from within — working, speaking, reading, writing as part of the real consciousness — not with the dispersed and unquiet movement of the ordinary consciousness.

*

You must learn to act always from within — from your inner being which is in contact with the Divine. The outer should be a mere instrument and should not be allowed at all to compel or dictate your speech, thought or action.

DIFFICULTIES IN WORK

Yes, obviously, that is one great utility of work that it tests the nature and puts the sadhak in front of the defects of his outer being which might otherwise escape him.

*

For the sadhak outward struggles, troubles, calamities are only a means of surmounting ego and rajasic desire and attaining to complete surrender. So long as one insists on success, one is doing the work partly at least for the ego; difficulties and outward failures come to warn one that it is so and to bring complete equality. This does not mean that the power of victory is not to be acquired, but it is not success in the immediate work that is all-important; it is the power to receive and transmit a greater and greater correct vision and inner Force that has to be developed and this must be done quite coolly and patiently without being elated or disturbed by immediate victory or failure.

*

What you have to realise is that your success or failure depends, first and always, on your keeping in the right attitude and in the true psychic and spiritual atmosphere and allowing the Mother's force to act through you. . . .

If I can judge from your letters, you take its support too much for granted and lay the first stress on your own ideas and plans and words about the work; but these whether good or bad, right or mistaken, are bound to fail if they are not instruments of the true Force. . . . You have to be always concentrated, always referring all difficulties for solution to the force that is being sent from here, always letting it act and not substituting your own mind and separate vital will or impulse. . . .

Proceed with your work, never forgetting the condition of success. Do not lose yourself in the work or in your ideas or plans or forget to keep yourself in constant touch with the true source. Do not allow anybody's mind or vital influence or the influence of the surrounding atmosphere or the ordinary human mentality to come between you and the power and presence of the Mother.

*

The difficulty you find results very much from your always worrying with your mind about things, thinking "This is wrong, that is wrong in me or my work" and, as a result, "I am incompetent, I am bad, nothing can be done with me". Your embroidery work, your lampshades etc. have always been very good, and yet you are always thinking "this is bad work, that is wrong" and by doing so, confuse yourself and get into a muddle. Naturally, you make a mistake now and then, but more when you worry like that than when you do things simply and confidently.

It is better whether with work or with sadhana to go on quietly, allowing the Force to act and doing your best to let it work rightly, but without this self-tormenting and constant restless questioning at every point. Whatever defects there are would go much sooner, if you did not harp on them too much; for by dwelling on them so much you lose confidence in yourself and in your power of openness to the Force – which is there all the same – and put unnecessary difficulties in the way of its working.

*

Openness in work means the same thing as openness in the consciousness. The same Force that works in your consciousness in meditation and clears away the cloud and confusion whenever you open to it, can also take up your action and not only make you aware of the defects in it but keep you conscious of what is to be done and guide your mind and hands to do it. If you open to it in your work, you will begin to feel this guidance more and more until behind all your activities you will be aware of the Force of the Mother.

*

To be able to receive the Divine Power and let it act through you in the things of the outward life, there are three necessary conditions:

(i) Quietude, equality – not to be disturbed by anything that happens, to keep the mind still and firm, seeing the play of forces, but itself tranquil.

(ii) Absolute faith – faith that what is for the best will happen, but also that if one can make oneself a true instrument, the fruit will be that which one's will guided by the Divine Light sees as the thing to be done – *kartavyaṁ karma*.

(iii) Receptivity – the power to receive the Divine Force and to feel its presence and the presence of the Mother in it and allow it to work, guiding one's sight and will and action. If this power and presence can be felt and this plasticity made the habit of the consciousness in action, – but plasticity to the Divine force alone without bringing in any foreign element, – the eventual result is sure.

*

If you want the consciousness for true actions very much and aspire for it, it may come in one of several ways:

1. You may get the habit or faculty of watching your movements in such a way that you see the impulse to action coming and can see too its nature.

2. A consciousness may come which feels uneasy whenever a wrong thought or impulse to action or feeling is there.

3. Something within you may warn and stop you when you are going to do the wrong action.

STRAIN AND FATIGUE IN WORK

The first rule is – there must be sufficient sleep and rest, not in excess but not too little.

The body must be trained to work, but not strained beyond its utmost capacity.

The outer means without the inner is not effective. Up to a certain point by a *progressive* training the body may be made more capable of work. But the important thing is to bring down the force for work and the Rasa of work in the body. The body will then do what is asked of it without grudging or feeling fatigue.

Even so, even when the force and Rasa are there, one must keep one's sense of measure.

Work is a means of self-dedication to the Divine, but it must be done with the necessary inner consciousness in which the outer vital and physical also share.

A lazy body is certainly not a proper instrument for yoga – it must stop being lazy. But a fatigued and unwilling body also cannot receive properly or be a good instrument. The proper thing is to avoid either extreme.

*

Yes, it is a mistake to overstrain as there is a reaction afterwards. If there is energy, all must not be spent, some must be stored up so as to increase the permanent strength of the system.

*

When you feel tired, don't overstrain yourself but rest — doing only your ordinary work; restlessly doing something or other all the time is not the way to cure it. To be quiet without and within is what is needed when there is this sense of fatigue. There is always a strength near you which you can call in and will remove these things, but you must learn to be quiet in order to receive it.

*

During the course of the sadhana one can learn to draw upon the universal Life-Force and replenish the energies from it. But usually the best way is to learn to open oneself to the Mother's Force and become conscious of it supporting and moving or pouring into the system and giving the energy needed for the work whether it be mental, vital or physical.

There is naturally a higher Energy above the present universal forces and it is that which will transform the nature and take up the mental, vital, physical energies and change them into its own likeness.

*

Think of your work only when it is being done, not before and not after.

Do not let your mind go back on a work that is finished. It belongs to the past and all re-handling of it is a waste of power.

Do not let your mind labour in anticipation on a work that has to be done. The Power that acts in you will see to it at its own time.

These two habits of the mind belong to a past functioning that the transforming Force is pressing to remove and the physical mind's persistence in them is the cause of your strain and fatigue. If you can remember to let your mind

work only when its action is needed, the strain will lessen
and disappear. This is indeed the transitional movement
before the supramental working takes possession of the
physical mind and brings into it the spontaneous action of
the Light.

HARMONY AND ORGANISATION IN WORK

Orderly harmony and organisation in physical things is a
necessary part of efficiency and perfection and makes the
instrument fit for whatever work is given to it.

*

There can be no physical life without an order and rhythm.
When this order is changed, it must be in obedience to an
inner growth and not for the sake of external novelty. It is
only a certain part of the surface lower vital nature which
seeks always external change and novelty for its own sake.

It is by a constant inner growth that one can find a
constant newness and unfailing interest in life. There is no
other satisfying way.

*

A rule that can be varied by everyone at his pleasure is no
rule. In all countries in which organised work is successfully
done, (India is not one of them), rules exist and nobody
thinks of breaking them, for it is realised that work (or life
either) without discipline would soon become a confusion
and an anarchic failure. In the great days of India everything
was put under rule, even art and poetry, even yoga. Here in
fact rules are much less rigid than in any European organisation. Personal discretion can even in a frame of rules have
plenty of play − but discretion must be discreetly used,
otherwise it becomes something arbitrary or chaotic.

*

Yes, even in ordinary life there must be a control over the vital and the ego – otherwise life would be impossible. Even many animals, those who live in groups, have their strict rules imposing a control on the play of the ego and those who disobey will have a bad time of it. The Europeans especially understand this and even though they are full of ego, yet when there is a question of team work or group life, they are adepts at keeping it in leash, even if it growls inside; it is the secret of their success. But in yoga life of course it is a question not of controlling ego but of getting rid of it and rising to a higher principle, so demand is much more strongly and insistently discouraged.

*

Rules are indispensable for the orderly management of work; for without order and arrangement nothing can be properly done, all becomes clash, confusion and disorder.

In all such dealings with others, you should see not only your own side of the question but the other side also. There should be no anger, vehement reproach or menace, for these things only raise anger and retort on the other side. I write this because you are trying to rise above yourself and dominate your vital and when one wants to do that, one cannot be too strict with oneself in these things. It is best even to be severe with one's own mistakes and charitable to the mistakes of others.

*

To be impersonal generally is not to be ego-centric, not to regard things from the point of view of how they affect oneself, but to see what things are in themselves, to judge impartially, to do what is demanded by the purpose of things or by the will of the Master of things, not by one's own personal point of view or egoistic interest or ego-formed idea or feeling. In work it is to do what is best for the work, without regard to one's own prestige or convenience, not to regard the work as one's own but as the Mother's, to do it according to rule, discipline, impersonal arrangement, even if conditions are not favourable to do the best according to the conditions, etc., etc. The impersonal worker puts his best capacity, zeal, industry into the work, but not his personal ambitions, vanity, passions. He has always something in view that is greater than his little personality and his devotion or obedience to that dictates his conduct.

*

To be free from all egoistic motive, careful of truth in speech and action, void of self-will and self-assertion, watchful in all things, is the condition for being a flawless servant.

CARE OF MATERIAL THINGS

Material things are not to be despised – without them there can be no manifestation in the material world.

*

The rough handling and careless breaking or waste and misuse of physical things is a denial of the yogic consciousness and a great hindrance to the bringing down of the Divine Truth to the material plane.

*

Wanton waste, careless spoiling of physical things in an incredibly short time, loose disorder, misuse of service and materials due either to vital grasping or to tamasic inertia are baneful to prosperity and tend to drive away or discourage the Wealth-Power. These things have long been rampant in the society and, if that continues, an increase in our means might well mean a proportionate increase in the wastage and disorder and neutralise the material advantage. This must be remedied if there is to be any sound progress.

Asceticism for its own sake is not the ideal of this yoga,

but self-control in the vital and right order in the material are a very important part of it – and even an ascetic discipline is better for our purpose than a loose absence of true control. Mastery of the material does not mean having plenty and profusely throwing it out or spoiling it as fast as it comes or faster. Mastery implies in it the right and careful utilisation of things and also a self-control in their use.

*

It is very true that physical things have a consciousness within them which feels and responds to care and is sensitive to careless touch and rough handling. To know or feel that and learn to be careful of them is a great progress of consciousness.

WORK AND MEDITATION

Work for the Mother done with the right concentration on her is as much a Sadhana as meditation and inner experiences.

*

Those who do work for the Mother in all sincerity are prepared by the work itself for the right consciousness even if they do not sit down for meditation or follow any particular practice of Yoga. It is not necessary to tell you how to meditate; whatever is needful will come of itself, if in your work and at all times you are sincere and keep yourself open to the Mother.

*

I have always said that work done as sadhana – done, that is to say, as an outflow of energy from the Divine and offered to the Divine or work done for the sake of the Divine or work done in a spirit of devotion is a powerful means of sadhana and that such work is especially necessary in this yoga. Work, bhakti and meditation are the three supports of yoga. One can do with all three or two or one. There are people who can't meditate in the set way that one calls meditation, but they progress through work or through bhakti or through the two together. By work and bhakti one can develop a consciousness in which eventually a natural meditation and realisation becomes possible.

*

It is not our experience that by meditation alone it is possible to change the nature, nor has retirement from outward activity and work much profited those who have tried it; in many cases it has been harmful. A certain amount of concentration, an inner aspiration in the heart and an opening of the consciousness to the Mother's presence there and to the descent from above are needed. But without action, without work the nature does not really change; it is there and by contact with men that there is the test of the change in the nature. As for the work one does, there is no higher or lower work; all work is the same provided it is offered to the Mother and done for her and in her power.

*

It is not well to spend the whole time or the greater part of the time in meditation unless one is very strong in mind — for one gets into the habit of living in an inner world entirely and losing touch with external realities — this brings in a one-sided inharmonious movement and may lead to disturbance of balance. To do both meditation and work and dedicate both to the Mother is the best thing.

SADHANA THROUGH MEDITATION

Your questions cover the whole of a very wide field. It is therefore necessary to reply to them with some brevity, touching only on some principal points.

1. *What meditation exactly means.*

There are two words used in English to express the Indian idea of *dhyāna*, "meditation" and "contemplation". Meditation means properly the concentration of the mind on a single train of ideas which work out a single subject. Contemplation means regarding mentally a single object, image, idea so that the knowledge about the object, image or idea may arise naturally in the mind by force of the concentration. Both these things are forms of *dhyāna*, for the principle of *dhyāna* is mental concentration whether in thought, vision or knowledge.

There are other forms of *dhyāna*. There is a passage in which Vivekananda advises you to stand back from your thoughts, let them occur in your mind as they will and simply observe them and see what they are. This may be called concentration in self-observation.

This form leads to another, the emptying of all thought out of the mind so as to leave it a sort of pure vigilant blank on which the divine knowledge may come and imprint itself, undisturbed by the inferior thoughts of the ordinary human mind and with the clearness of a writing in white chalk on a blackboard. You will find that the Gita speaks of this rejection of all mental thought as one of the methods of yoga and even the method it seems to prefer. This may be called the *dhyāna* of liberation, as it frees the mind from slavery to the mechanical process of thinking and allows it to think or not to think, as it pleases and when it pleases, or to choose its own thoughts or else to go beyond thought to the pure perception of Truth called in our philosophy *Vijñāna*.

Meditation is the easiest process for the human mind, but the narrowest in its results; contemplation more difficult, but greater; self-observation and liberation from the chains of Thought the most difficult of all, but the widest and greatest in its fruits. One can choose any of them according to one's bent and capacity. The perfect method is to use them all, each in its own place and for its own object; but this would need a fixed faith and firm patience and a great energy of Will in the self-application to the yoga.

2. *What should be the object or ideas for meditation?*

Whatever is most consonant with your nature and highest aspirations. But if you ask me for an absolute answer, then I must say that Brahman is always the best object for meditation or contemplation and the idea on which the mind should fix is that of God in all, all in God and all as God. It does not matter essentially whether it is the Impersonal or the Personal God, or subjectively, the One Self. But this is the idea I have found the best, because it is the highest and embraces all other truths, whether truths of this world or of the other worlds or beyond all phenomenal existence, – "All this is the Brahman." . . .

3. *Conditions internal and external that are most essential for meditation.*

There are no *essential* external conditions, but solitude and seclusion at the time of meditation as well as stillness of the body are helpful, sometimes almost necessary to the beginner. But one should not be bound by external conditions. Once the habit of meditation is formed, it should be made possible to do it in all circumstances, lying, sitting, walking, alone, in company, in silence or in the midst of noise etc.

The first internal condition necessary is concentration of the will against the obstacles to meditation, i.e. wandering of the mind, forgetfulness, sleep, physical and nervous impatience and restlessness etc.

The second is an increasing purity and calm of the inner consciousness (*citta*) out of which thought and emotion arise, i.e. a freedom from all disturbing reactions, such as anger, grief, depression, anxiety about worldly happenings etc. Mental perfection and moral are always closely allied to each other.

*

If the difficulty in meditation is that thoughts of all kinds come in, that is not due to hostile forces but to the ordinary nature of the human mind. All sadhaks have this difficulty and with many it lasts for a very long time. There are several ways of getting rid of it. One of them is to look at the thoughts and observe what is the nature of the human mind as they show it but not to give any sanction and to let them run down till they come to a standstill – this is a way recommended by Vivekananda in his Rajayoga. Another is to look at the thoughts as not one's own, to stand back as the witness Purusha and refuse the sanction – the thoughts are regarded as things coming from outside, from Prakriti, and they must be felt as if they were passers-by crossing the mind-space with whom one has no connection and in whom one takes no interest. In this way it usually happens that after a time the mind divides into two, a part which is the mental witness watching and perfectly undisturbed and quiet and a part which is the object of observation, the Prakriti part in which the thoughts cross or wander. Afterwards one can proceed to silence or quiet the Prakriti part also. There is a third, an active method by which one looks to see where the thoughts come from and finds they come not from oneself, but from outside the head as it were; if one can detect them coming, then, before they enter, they have to be thrown away altogether. This is perhaps the most difficult way and not all can do it, but if it can be done it is the shortest and most powerful road to silence.

*

To silence the mind it is not enough to throw back each thought as it comes, that can only be a subordinate movement. One must get back from all thought and be separate from it, a silent consciousness observing the thoughts if they come, but not oneself thinking or identified with the thoughts. Thoughts must be felt as outside things altogether. It is then easier to reject thoughts or let them pass without their disturbing the quietude of the mind.

*

It is not easy to get into the Silence. That is only possible by throwing out all mental-vital activities. It is easier to let the Silence descend into you, i.e., to open yourself and let it descend. The way to do this and the way to call down the higher powers is the same. It is to remain quiet at the time of meditation, not fighting with the mind or making mental efforts to pull down the Power or the Silence but keeping only a silent will and aspiration for them. If the mind is active one has to learn to look at it, drawn back and not giving any sanction from within, until its habitual or mechanical activities begin to fall quiet for want of support from within. If it is too persistent, a steady rejection without strain or struggle is the one thing to be done.

MEDITATION AND CONCENTRATION
IN THE INTEGRAL YOGA

Then as to concentration. Ordinarily the consciousness is spread out everywhere, dispersed, running in this or that direction, after this subject and that object in multitude. When anything has to be done of a sustained nature the first thing one does is to draw back all this dispersed consciousness and concentrate. It is then, if one looks closely, bound to be concentrated in one place and on one occupation, subject or object — as when you are composing a poem or a botanist is studying a flower. The place is usually somewhere in the brain if it is the thought, in the heart if it is the feeling in which one is concentrated. The yogic concentration is simply an extension and intensification of the same thing. It may be on an object as when one does Tratak on a shining point — then one has to concentrate so that one sees only that point and has no other thought than that. It may be on an idea or a word or a name, the idea of the Divine, the word OM, the name Krishna, or a combination of idea and word or idea and name. But further in yoga one also concentrates in a particular place. There is the famous rule of concentrating between the eyebrows — the centre of the inner mind, of occult vision, of the will is there. What you do is to think firmly from there on whatever you make the object of your concentration or else try to see the image of it from there. If you succeed in this then after a time you feel that your whole consciousness is centred there in that place — of course for the time being. After doing it for some time and often it becomes easy and normal.

I hope this is clear. Well, in this yoga, you do the same, not necessarily at that particular spot between the eyebrows, but anywhere in the head or at the centre of the chest where the physiologists have fixed the cardiac centre. Instead of concentrating on an object, you concentrate in the head in a will, a call for the descent of the peace above or, as some do, an opening of the unseen lid and an ascent of the consciousness above. In the heart centre one concentrates in an aspiration, for an opening, for the presence of the living image of the Divine there or whatever else is the object. There may be Japa of a name but, if so, there must also be a concentration on it and the name must repeat itself there in the heart centre.

It may be asked what becomes of the rest of the consciousness when there is this local concentration? Well, it either falls silent as in any concentration or, if it does not, then thoughts or other things may move about, as if outside, but the concentrated part does not attend to them or notice. That is when the concentration is reasonably successful.

One has not to fatigue oneself at first by long concentration if one is not accustomed, for then in a jaded mind it loses its power and value. One can relax and meditate instead of concentrating. It is only as the concentration becomes normal that one can go on for a longer and longer time.

*

Concentration, for our yoga, means when the consciousness is fixed in a particular state (e.g. peace) or movement (e.g. aspiration, will, coming into contact with the Mother, taking the Mother's name); meditation is when the inner mind is looking at things to get the right knowledge.

*

Concentration is a gathering together of the consciousness and either centralising at one point or turning on a single object, e.g., the Divine; there can also be a gathered condition throughout the whole being, not at a point. In meditation it is not indispensable to gather like this, one can simply remain with a quiet mind thinking of one subject or observing what comes in the consciousness and dealing with it.

*

You have asked what is the discipline to be followed in order to convert the mental seeking into a living spiritual experience. The first necessity is the practice of concentration of your consciousness within yourself. The ordinary human mind has an activity on the surface which veils the real Self. But there is another, a hidden consciousness within behind the surface one in which we can become aware of the real Self and of a larger deeper truth of nature, can realise the Self and liberate and transform the nature. To quiet the surface mind and begin to live within is the object of this concentration. Of this true consciousness other than the superficial there are two main centres, one in the heart (not the physical heart, but the cardiac centre in the middle of the chest), one in the head. The concentration in the heart opens within and by following this inward opening and going deep one becomes aware of the soul or psychic being, the divine element in the individual. This being unveiled begins to come forward, to govern the nature, to turn it and all its movements towards the Truth, towards the Divine, and to call down into it all that is above. It brings the consciousness of the Presence, the dedication of the being to the Highest and invites the descent into our nature of a greater Force and Consciousness which is waiting above us. To concentrate in the heart centre with the offering of oneself to the Divine and the aspiration for this inward opening and for the Presence in the heart is the first way and, if it can be done, the natural beginning; for its result once obtained makes the spiritual path far more easy and safe than if one begins the other way.

That other way is the concentration in the head, in the mental centre. This, if it brings about the silence of the surface mind, opens up an inner, larger, deeper mind within which is more capable of receiving spiritual experience and spiritual knowledge. But once concentrated here one must open the silent mental consciousness upward to all that is above mind. After a time one feels the consciousness rising upward and in the end it rises beyond the lid which has so long kept it tied in the body and finds a centre above the head where it is liberated into the Infinite. There it begins to come into contact with the universal Self, the Divine Peace, Light, Power, Knowledge, Bliss, to enter into that and become that, to feel the descent of these things into the nature. To concentrate in the head with the aspiration for quietude in the mind and the realisation of the Self and Divine above is the second way of concentration. It is important, however, to remember that the concentration of the consciousness in the head is only a preparation for its rising to the centre above; otherwise, one may get shut up in one's own mind and its experiences or at best attain only to a reflection of the Truth above instead of rising into the spiritual transcendence to live there. For some the mental concentration is easier, for some the concentration in the

heart centre; some are capable of doing both alternately —
but to begin with the heart centre, if one can do it, is the
more desirable.

SAMADHI

In samadhi it is the inner mental, vital, physical which are
separated from the outer, no longer covered by it — therefore they can fully have inner experiences. The outer mind is
either quiescent or in some way reflects or shares the experience. As for the central consciousness being separated
from all mentality that would mean a complete trance
without any recorded experiences.

*

Chit is the pure consciousness, as in Sat-Chit-Ananda.

Chitta is the stuff of mixed mental-vital-physical consciousness out of which arise the movements of thought,
emotion, sensation, impulse, etc. It is these that in the
Patanjali system have to be stilled altogether so that the
consciousness may be immobile and go into Samadhi.

Our yoga has a different function. The movements of the
ordinary consciousness have to be quieted and into the
quietude there has to be brought down a higher consciousness and its powers which will transform the nature.

*

The experience you had is of course the going inside of the
consciousness which is usually called trance or samadhi. The
most important part of it however is the silence of the mind
and vital which is fully extended to the body also. To get the
capacity of this silence and peace is a most important step in
the sadhana. It comes at first in meditation and may throw
the consciousness inward in trance, but it has to come
afterwards in the waking state and establish itself as a

permanent basis for all the life and action. It is the condition
for the realisation of the Self and the spiritual transformation of the nature.

*

On the contrary, it is in the waking state that this realisation
must come and endure in order to be a reality of the life. If
experienced in trance it would be a superconscient state true
for some part of the inner being, but not real to the whole
consciousness. Experiences in trance have their utility for
opening the being and preparing it, but it is only when the
realisation is constant in the waking state that it is truly
possessed. Therefore in this yoga most value is given to the
waking realisation and experience.

To work in the calm ever-widening consciousness is at
once a sadhana and a siddhi.

*

Samadhi is not a thing to be shunned – only it has to be
made more and more conscious.

*

It is not necessary to be in samadhi to be in contact with the
Divine.

PRACTICAL ADVICE ABOUT MEDITATION

What do you call meditation? Shutting the eyes and concentrating? It is only one method for calling down the true
consciousness. To join with the true consciousness or feel its
descent is the only thing important and if it comes without
the orthodox method, as it always did with me, so much the
better. Meditation is only a means or device, the true movement is when even walking, working or speaking one is still
in sadhana.

*

The sitting motionless posture is the natural posture for concentrated meditation — walking and standing are active conditions. It is only when one has gained the enduring rest and passivity of the consciousness that it is easy to concentrate and receive when walking or doing anything. A fundamental passive condition of the consciousness gathered into itself is the proper poise for concentration and a seated gathered immobility in the body is the best position for that. It can be done also lying down, but that position is too passive, tending to be inert rather than gathered. This is the reason why yogis always sit in an *asana*. One can accustom oneself to meditate walking, standing, lying but sitting is the first natural position.

*

There is no harm in concentrating sometimes in the heart and sometimes above the head. But concentration in either place does not mean keeping the attention fixed on a particular spot; you have to take your station of consciousness in either place and concentrate there not on the place, but on the Divine. This can be done with eyes shut or with eyes open, according as it best suits you.

You can concentrate on the sun, but to concentrate on the Divine is better than to concentrate on the sun.

*

At the top of the head or above it is the right place for yogic concentration in reading or thinking.

*

It is quite natural to want to meditate while reading yogic literature — that is not the laziness.

The laziness of the mind consists in not meditating, when the consciousness wants to do so.

*

It is not a fact that when there is obscurity or inertia, one cannot concentrate or meditate. If one has in the inner being the steady will to do it, it can be done.

       *

Effort means straining endeavour. There can be an action with a will in it in which there is no strain or effort.

 Straining and concentration are not the same thing. Straining implies an over-eagerness and violence of effort, while concentration is in its nature quiet and steady. If there is restlessness or over-eagerness, then that is not concentration.

       *

It is certainly much better to remain silent and collected for a time after the meditation. It is a mistake to take the meditation lightly — by doing that one fails to receive or spills what is received or most of it.

       *

The best help for concentration is to receive the Mother's calm and peace into your mind. It is there above you — only the mind and its centres have to open to it.

SADHANA THROUGH LOVE AND DEVOTION

DIVINE LOVE, UNIVERSAL LOVE AND PSYCHIC LOVE

To bring the Divine Love and Beauty and Ananda into the world is, indeed, the whole crown and essence of our yoga. But it has always seemed to me impossible unless there comes as its support and foundation and guard the Divine Truth — what I call the supramental — and its Divine Power. Otherwise Love itself blinded by the confusions of this present consciousness may stumble in its human receptacles and, even otherwise, may find itself unrecognised, rejected or rapidly degenerating and lost in the frailty of man's inferior nature. But when it comes in the divine truth and power, Divine Love descends first as something transcendent and universal and out of that transcendence and universality it applies itself to persons according to the Divine Truth and Will, creating a vaster, greater, purer personal love than any the human mind or heart can now imagine. It is when one has felt this descent that one can be really an instrument for the birth and action of the Divine Love in the world.

*

The Divine Love may not be able yet to manifest on the physical plane, humanity being what it is, as fully and freely as it would otherwise do, but that does not make it less close or intense than the human. It is there waiting to be understood and accepted and meanwhile giving all the help you can receive to raise and widen you into the consciousness in which it will be no longer possible for these difficulties and these misunderstandings to recur — the state in which there is possible the full and perfect union.

*

And let me say also that, as regards human love and divine Love, I admitted the first as that from which we have to proceed and to arrive at the other, intensifying and transforming into itself, not eliminating, human love. Divine Love, in my view of it, is again not something ethereal, cold and far, but a love absolutely intense, intimate and full of unity, closeness and rapture using all the nature for its expression. Certainly, it is without the confusions and disorders of the present lower vital nature which it will change into something entirely warm, deep and intense; but that is no reason for supposing that it will lose anything that is true and happy in the elements of love.

*

The Divine's love is that which comes from above poured down from the Divine Oneness and its Ananda on the being – psychic love is a form taken by divine love in the human being according to the need and possibilities of the human consciousness.

*

The psychic love is pure and full of self-giving without egoistic demands, but it is human and can err and suffer. The Divine Love is something much vaster and deeper and full of light and Ananda.

*

The love that belongs to the spiritual planes is of a different kind – the psychic has its own more personal love, bhakti, surrender. Love in the higher or spiritual mind is more universal and impersonal. The two must go together to make the highest divine love.

*

Universal love is the spiritual founded on the sense of the One and the Divine everywhere and the change of the personal into a wide universal consciousness, free from attachment and ignorance.

*

Cosmic love depends on the realisation of oneness of self with all. Psychic love or feeling for all can exist without this realisation.

BHAKTI

There is always the personal and the impersonal side of the Divine and the Truth and it is a mistake to think the impersonal alone to be true or important, for that leads to a void incompleteness in part of the being, while only one side

is given satisfaction. Impersonality belongs to the intellectual mind and the static self, personality to the soul and
heart and dynamic being. Those who disregard the personal
Divine ignore something which is profound and essential.

In following the heart in its purer impulses one follows
something that is at least as precious as the mind's loyalty to
its own conceptions of what the Truth may be.

*

The nature of Bhakti is adoration, worship, self-offering to
what is greater than oneself; the nature of love is a feeling or
a seeking for closeness and union. Self-giving is the character of both; both are necessary in the yoga and each gets its
full force when supported by the other.

*

Bhakti is not an experience, it is a state of the heart and
soul. It is a state which comes when the psychic being is
awake and prominent.

*

The ordinary Bhakta is not a lion heart. The lion hearts get
experiences comparatively soon but the ordinary Bhakta has
often to feed on his own love or yearning for years and years
— and he does it.

*

Your whole-hearted acceptance of the Vaishnava idea and
Bhakti becomes rather bewildering when it is coupled with
an insistence that love cannot be given to the Divine until
one has experience of the Divine. For what is more common
in the Vaishnava attitude than the joy of Bhakti for its own
sake? "Give me Bhakti," it cries, "whatever else you may
keep from me. Even if it is long before I can meet you, even
if you delay to manifest yourself, let my Bhakti, my seeking
for you, my cry, my love, my adoration be always there."
How constantly the Bhakta has sung, "All my life I have

been seeking you and still you are not there, but still I seek and cannot cease to seek and love and adore." If it were really impossible to love God unless you first experience him, how could this be? In fact, your mind seems to be putting the cart before the horse. One seeks after God first with persistence or with passion, one finds him afterwards, some sooner than others, but most after a long seeking. One does not find him first, then seek after him. Even a glimpse often comes only after long or fervent seeking. One has the love of God or at any rate some heart's desire for him and afterwards one becomes aware of God's love, its reply to the heart's desire, its response of the supreme joy and Ananda. One does not say to God, "Show your love from the first, shower on me the experience of yourself, satisfy my demand, then I will see whether I can love you so long as you deserve it." It is surely the seeker who must seek and love first, follow the quest, become impassioned for the Sought — then only does the veil move aside and the Light appear and the Face manifest that alone can satisfy the soul after its long sojourn in the desert.

Then again you may say, "Yes, but whether I love or not, I want, I have always wanted and now I want more and more, but I get nothing." Yes, but wanting is not all. As you now begin to see, there are conditions that have to be met — like the purification of the heart. Your thesis was, "Once I want God, God must manifest to me, come to me, at least give glimpses of himself to me, the real, solid, concrete experience, not mere vague things which I can't understand or value. God's Grace must answer my call for it, whether I yet deserve it or not — or else there is no Grace." God's Grace may indeed do that in certain cases, but where does the "must" come in? If God must do it, it is no longer God's Grace, but God's duty or an obligation or a contract or a treaty. The Divine looks into the heart and removes the veil at the moment which he knows to be the right moment to do it. You have laid stress on the Bhakti theory that one has only to call his name and he must reply, he must at once be there. Perhaps, but for whom is this true? For a certain kind of Bhakta surely who feels the power of the Name, who has the passion of the Name and puts it into his cry. If one is like that, then there may be the immediate reply – if not, one has to become like that, then there will be the reply. But some go on using the Name for years, before there is an answer. Ramakrishna himself got it after a few months, but what months! and what a condition he had to pass through before he got it! Still he succeeded quickly because he had a pure heart already – and that divine passion in it.

It is not surely the Bhakta but the man of knowledge who demands experience first. He can say, "How can I know without experience?" but he too goes on seeking like Tota Puri even though for thirty years, striving for the decisive realisation. It is really the man of intellect, the rationalist who says, "Let God, if he exists, prove himself to me first, then I will believe, then I will make some serious and prolonged effort to explore him and see what he is like."

All this does not mean that experience is irrelevant to sadhana – I certainly cannot have said such a stupid thing. What I have said is that the love and seeking of the Divine can be and ordinarily is there before the experience comes – it is an instinct, an inherent longing in the soul and it comes up as soon as certain coverings of the soul disappear or begin to disappear. The next thing I have said is that it is better to get the nature ready first (the purified heart and all that) before the "experiences" begin rather than the other way round and I base that on the many cases there have been of the danger of experiences before the heart and vital are ready for the true experience. Of course, in many cases there is a true experience first, a touch of the Grace, but it is not something that lasts and is always there but rather something that touches and withdraws and waits for the nature to get ready. But this is not in every case, not even in the majority of cases, I believe. One has to begin with the soul's inherent longing, then the struggle with the nature to get the temple ready, then the unveiling of the Image, the permanent Presence in the sanctuary.

*

The Divine Love, unlike the human, is deep and vast and silent; one must become quiet and wide to be aware of it and reply to it. He must make it his whole object to be surrendered so that he may become a vessel and instrument – leaving it to the Divine Wisdom and Love to fill him with what is needed. Let him also fix this in the mind not to insist that in a given time he must progress, develop, get realisation; whatever time it takes, he must be prepared to wait and persevere and make his whole life an aspiration and an opening for the one thing only, the Divine. To give oneself is the secret of sadhana, not to demand and acquire. The more one gives oneself, the more the power to receive will grow. But for that all impatience and revolt must go; all suggestions of not getting, not being helped, not being loved, going away, of abandoning life or the spiritual endeavour must be rejected.

THE EMOTIONS

When the love goes towards the Divine, there is still this ordinary human element in it. There is the call for a return and if the return does not seem to come, the love may sink; there is the self-interest, the demand for the Divine as a giver of all that the human being wants and, if the demands are not acceded to, *abhimāna* against the Divine, loss of faith, loss of fervour, etc. etc. But the true love for the Divine is in its fundamental nature not of this kind, but psychic and spiritual. The psychic element is the need of the inmost being for self-giving, love, adoration, union which can only be fully satisfied by the Divine. The spiritual element is the need of the being for contact, merging, union with its own highest and whole self and source of being and consciousness and bliss, the Divine. These two are two sides of the same thing. The mind, vital, physical can be the supports and recipients of this love, but they can be fully that only when they become remoulded in harmony with the psychic and spiritual elements of the being and no longer bring in the lower insistences of the ego.

*

As for the heart, the movement of longing for the Divine, weeping, sorrowing, yearning is not essential in this yoga. A strong aspiration there must be, an intense longing there may very well be, an ardent love and will for union; but there need be no sorrow or disturbance.

*

Emotion is necessary in the yoga and it is only the excessive emotional sensitiveness which makes one enter into despondency over small things that has to be overcome. The very basis of this yoga is bhakti and if one kills one's emotional being, there can be no bhakti. So there can be no possibility of emotion being excluded from the yoga.

*

It is no part of this yoga to dry up the heart; but the emotions must be turned towards the Divine. There may be short periods in which the heart is quiescent, turned away from the ordinary feelings and waiting for the inflow from above; but such states are not states of dryness but of silence and peace. The heart in this yoga should in fact be the main centre of concentration until the consciousness rises above.

*

If one does not encourage the devotion of the emotional being merely because the lower vital is not yet under control and acts differently, then how is the devotion to grow and how is the lower vital to change? Until the final clarification and harmonising of the nature there are always contradictions in the being, but that is not a reason for in any way suppressing the play of the better movements – on the contrary it is these that should be cultivated and made to increase.

WORSHIP

There is no restriction in this yoga to inward worship and meditation only. As it is a yoga for the whole being, not for the inner being only, no such restriction could be intended. Old forms of the different religions may fall away, but absence of all forms is not the rule of the sadhana.

*

These are exaggerations made by the mind taking one side of Truth and ignoring the other sides. The inner bhakti is the main thing and without it the external becomes a form and mere ritual, but the external has its place and use when it is straightforward and sincere.

*

What is meant by *bāhyapūjā* [external worship]? If it is purely external, then of course it is the lowest form; but if done with the true consciousness, it can bring the greatest possible completeness to the adoration by allowing the body and the most external consciousness to share in the spirit and act of worship.

MANTRA AND JAPA

The word is a sound expression of the idea. In the supra-physical plane when an idea has to be realised, one can by repeating the word-expression of it, produce vibrations which prepare the mind for the realisation of the idea. That is the principle of the Mantras and of Japa. One repeats the name of the Divine and the vibrations created in the consciousness prepare the realisation of the Divine. It is the same idea that is expressed in the Bible: "God said, Let there be Light, and there was Light". It is creation by the Word.

*

OM is the mantra, the expressive sound-symbol of the Brahman Consciousness in its four domains from the Turiya to the external or material plane. The function of a mantra is to create vibrations in the inner consciousness that will prepare it for the realisation of what the mantra symbolises and is supposed indeed to carry within itself. The mantra OM should therefore lead towards the opening of the consciousness to the sight and feeling of the One Consciousness in all material things, in the inner being and in the supra-physical worlds, in the causal plane above now supercon-scient to us and, finally, the supreme liberated transcendence above all cosmic existence. The last is usually the main preoccupation with those who use the mantra.

In this yoga there is no fixed mantra, no stress is laid on mantras, although sadhaks can use one if they find it helpful or so long as they find it helpful. The stress is rather on an aspiration in the consciousness and a concentration of the mind, heart, will, all the being. If a mantra is found helpful for that, one uses it. OM if rightly used (not mechanically) might very well help the opening upwards and outwards (cosmic consciousness) as well as the descent.

*

The name of the Divine is usually called in for protection, for adoration, for increase of bhakti, for the opening up of the inner consciousness, for the realisation of the Divine in that aspect. As far as it is necessary to work in the sub-conscious for that, the Name must be effective there.

*

The japa is usually successful only on one of two conditions – if it is repeated with a sense of its significance, a dwelling of something in the mind on the nature, power, beauty, attraction of the Godhead it signifies and is to bring into the consciousness, – that is the mental way; or if it comes up from the heart or rings in it with a certain sense or feeling of bhakti making it alive, – that is the emotional way. Either the mind or the vital has to give it support or sustenance. But if it makes the mind dry and the vital restless, it must be missing that support and sustenance. There is, of course, a third way, the reliance on the power of the mantra or name in itself; but then one has to go on till that power has sufficiently impressed its vibration on the inner being to make it at a given moment suddenly open to the Presence or the Touch. But if there is a struggling or insistence for the result, then this effect which needs a quiet receptivity in the mind is impeded. That is why I insisted so much on mental quietude and not on too much straining or effort, to give time to allow the psychic and the mind to develop the necessary condition of receptivity – a receptivity as natural as when one receives an inspiration for poetry and music. It is also why I do not want you to discontinue your poetry – it helps and does not hinder the preparation, because it is a means of developing the right position of receptivity and bringing out the bhakti which is there in the inner being. To spend all the energy in japa or meditation is a strain which even those who are accustomed to successful meditation find it difficult to maintain – unless in periods when there is an uninterrupted flow of experiences from above.

*

Prayer and meditation count for so much in yoga. But the prayer must well up from the heart on a crest of emotion or aspiration, the Japa or meditation come in a live push carrying the joy or the light of the thing in it. If done mechanically and merely as a thing that ought to be done (stern grim duty!), it must tend towards want of interest and dryness and so be ineffective. . . . You were doing Japa too much as a means for bringing about a result, I meant too much as a device, a process laid down for getting the thing done. That was why I wanted the psychological conditions in you to develop, the psychic, the mental, for when the psychic is forward, there is no lack of life and joy in the prayer, the aspiration, the seeking, no difficulty in having the constant stream of bhakti and when the mind is quiet and inturned and upturned there is no difficulty or want of interest in meditation. Meditation, by the way, is a process leading towards knowledge and through knowledge, it is a thing of the head and not of the heart, so if you want *dhyāna*, you can't have an aversion to knowledge. Concentration in the heart is not meditation, it is a call on the Divine, on the Beloved. This yoga too is not a yoga of knowledge alone, knowledge is one of its means, but its base being self-offering, surrender, bhakti, it is based in the heart and nothing can be eventually done without this base. There are plenty of people here who do or have done Japa and base themselves on bhakti, very few comparatively who have done the "head" meditation; love and bhakti and works are usually the base; how many can proceed by knowledge? Only the few.

*

To know about the sadhana with the mind is not indispensable. If one has bhakti and aspires in the heart's silence, if there is the true love for the Divine, then the nature will open of itself, there will be the true experience and the Mother's power working within you, and the necessary knowledge will come.

BHAKTI AND THE INTEGRAL YOGA

As regards X's question – this is not a yoga of bhakti alone; it is or at least it claims to be an integral yoga, that is, a turning of all the being in all its parts to the Divine. It follows that there must be knowledge and works as well as bhakti, and in addition, it includes a total change of the nature, a seeking for perfection, so that the nature also may become one with the nature of the Divine. It is not only the heart that has to turn to the Divine and change, but the mind also – so knowledge is necessary, and the will and power of action and creation also – so works too are necessary. In this yoga the methods of other yogas are taken up – like this of Purusha-Prakriti, but with a difference in the final object. Purusha separates from Prakriti, not in order to abandon her, but in order to know himself and her and to be no longer her plaything, but the knower, lord and upholder of the nature; but having become so or even in becoming so, one offers all that to the Divine. One may begin with knowledge or with works or with bhakti or with Tapasya of self-purification for perfection (change of nature) and develop the rest as a subsequent movement or one may combine all in one movement. There is no single rule for all, it depends on the personality and the nature. Surrender is the main power of the yoga, but the surrender is bound to be progressive; a complete surrender is not possible in the beginning, but only a will in the being for that completeness, – in fact it takes time; yet it is only when the surrender is complete that the full flood of the sadhana is possible. Till then there must be the personal effort with an increasing reality of surrender. One calls in the power of the Divine Shakti and once that begins to come into the being, it at first supports the personal endeavour, then progressively takes up the whole action, although the consent of the sadhak continues to be always necessary. As the Force works, it brings in the different processes that are necessary for the sadhak, processes of knowledge, of bhakti, of spiritualised action, of transformation of the nature. The idea that they cannot be combined is an error.

7

Experiences and Realisations

SPIRITUAL EXPERIENCE AND REALISATION

As there is a category of facts to which our senses are our best available but very imperfect guides, as there is a category of truths which we seek by the keen but still imperfect light of our reason, so according to the mystic, there is a category of more subtle truths which surpass the reach both of the senses and the reason but can be ascertained by an inner direct knowledge and direct experience. These truths are supersensuous, but not the less real for that: they have immense results upon the consciousness changing its substance and movement, bringing especially deep peace and abiding joy, a great light of vision and knowledge, a possibility of the overcoming of the lower animal nature, vistas of a spiritual self-development which without them do not exist. A new outlook on things arises which brings with it, if fully pursued into its consequences, a great liberation, inner harmony, unification − many other possibilities besides. These things have been experienced, it is true, by a small minority of the human race, but still there has been a host of independent witnesses to them in all times, climes and conditions and numbered among them are some of the greatest intelligences of the past, some of the world's most remarkable figures. Must these possibilities be immediately condemned as chimeras because they are not only beyond the average man in the street but also not easily seizable even by many cultivated intellects or because their method is more difficult than that of the ordinary sense or reason? If there is any truth in them, is not this possibility opened by them worth pursuing as disclosing a highest range of self-discovery and world discovery by the human soul? At its best, taken as true, it must be that — at its lowest taken as only a possibility, as all things attained by man have been only a possibility in their earlier stages, it is a great and may well be a most fruitful adventure.

*

It is spirituality when you begin to become aware of another consciousness than the ego and begin to live in it or under its influence more and more. It is that consciousness wide, infinite, self-existent, pure of ego etc. which is called Spirit (Self, Brahman, Divine), so this necessarily must be the meaning of spirituality. Realisation is this and all else that the experience and growth of this greater consciousness brings with it.

*

There are two classes of things that happen in yoga, realisations and experiences. Realisations are the reception in the consciousness and the establishment there of the fundamental truths of the Divine, of the Higher or Divine Nature, of the world-consciousness and the play of its forces, of one's own self and real nature and the inner nature of things, the power of these things growing in one till they are a part of one's inner life and existence. . . . These things also are often called experiences when they only come in flashes, snatches or rare visitations; they are spoken of as full realisations only when they become very positive or frequent or continuous or normal.

*

An experience of a truth in the substance of mind, in the vital or the physical, wherever it may be, is the beginning of realisation. When I experience peace, I begin to realise what it is. Repetition of the experience leads to a fuller and more permanent realisation. When it is settled anywhere, that is the full realisation of it in that place or that part of the being.

*

The yogi is one who is already established in realisation — the sadhak is one who is getting or still trying to get realisation.

*

There is no law that a feeling cannot be an experience; experiences are of all kinds and take all forms in the consciousness. When the consciousness undergoes, sees or feels anything spiritual or psychic or even occult, that is an experience — in the technical yogic sense, for there are of course all sorts of experiences that are not of that character. The feelings themselves are of many kinds. The word feeling is often used for an emotion, and there can be psychic or spiritual emotions which are numbered among yogic experiences, such as a wave of *śuddha bhakti* or the rising of love towards the Divine. A feeling also means a perception of something felt — a perception in the vital or psychic or in the essential substance of the consciousness. I find even often a mental perception when it is very vivid described as a feeling. If you exclude all these feelings and kindred ones and say that they are feelings, not experiences, then there is very little room left for experiences at all. Feeling and vision are the main forms of spiritual experience. One sees and feels the Brahman everywhere; one feels a force enter or go out from one; one feels or sees the presence of the Divine within or around one; one feels or sees the descent of Light; one feels the descent of Peace or Ananda. Kick out all that on the ground that it is only a feeling and you make a clean sweep of most of the things that we call experience. Again, we feel a change in the substance of the consciousness or the state of consciousness. We feel ourselves spreading in wideness and the body as a small thing in the wideness (this can be seen also); we feel the heart-consciousness being wide instead of narrow, soft instead of hard, illumined instead of obscure, the head-consciousness also, the vital, even the physical; we feel thousands of things of all kinds and why are we not to call them experience? Of course it is an inner sight, an inner feeling, subtle feeling, not material, like the feeling of a cold wind or a stone or any other object, but as the inner consciousness deepens it is not less vivid or concrete, it is even more so.

THE INWARD MOVEMENT

You must gather yourself within more firmly. If you disperse yourself constantly, go out of the inner circle, you will constantly move about in the pettiness of the ordinary outer nature and under the influences to which it is open. Learn to live within, to act always from within, from a constant communion with the Mother. It may be difficult at first to do it always and completely, but it can be done if one sticks to it – and it is at that price, by learning to do that, that one can have the siddhi in the yoga.

*

What you say about the outer being is correct, it must change and manifest what is within in the inner nature. But for that one must have experiences in the inner nature and through these the power of the inner nature grows till it can influence wholly and possess the outer being. To change the outer consciousness entirely without developing this inner consciousness would be too difficult. That is why these inner experiences are going on to prepare the growth of the inner consciousness. There is an inner mind, an inner vital, an inner physical consciousness which can more easily than the outer receive the higher consciousness above and put itself into harmony with the psychic being; when that is done the outer nature is felt as only a fringe on the surface, not as oneself, and is more easily transformed altogether.

*

The outer being can grow in faith, fidelity to the Divine, reverence, love, worship and adoration, great things in themselves, – though in fact these things too come from within, – but realisation can only take place when the inner being is awake with its vision and feeling of things unseen. Till then, one can feel the results of the divine help and, if one has faith, know that they are the work of the Divine; but it is only then that one can feel clearly the Force at work, the divine Presence, the direct communion.

*

The piercing of the veil between the outer consciousness and the inner being is one of the crucial movements in yoga. For yoga means union with the Divine, but it also means awaking first to your inner self and then to your higher self, – a movement inward and a movement upward. It is, in fact, only through the awakening and coming to the front of the inner being that you can get into union with the Divine. The outer physical man is only an instrumental personality and by himself he cannot arrive at this union, – he can only get occasional touches, religious feelings, imperfect intimations. And even these come not from the outer consciousness but from what is within us.

There are two mutually complementary movements; in one the inner being comes to the front and impresses its own normal motions on the outer consciousness to which they are unusual and abnormal; the other is to draw back from the outer consciousness, to go inside into the inner planes, enter the world of your inner self and wake in the hidden parts of your being. When that plunge has once been taken, you are marked for the yogic, the spiritual life and nothing can efface the seal that has been put upon you.

This inward movement takes place in many different ways and there is sometimes a complex experience combining all the signs of the complete plunge. There is a sense of going in or deep down, a feeling of the movement towards inner depths; there is often a stillness, a pleasant numbness, a stiffness of the limbs. This is the sign of the consciousness retiring from the body inwards under the pressure of a force from above, – that pressure stabilising the body into an immobile support of the inner life, in a kind of strong and still spontaneous *āsana*. There is a feeling of waves surging up, mounting to the head, which brings an outer unconsciousness and an inner waking. It is the ascending of the lower consciousness in the Adhara to meet the greater consciousness above. It is a movement analogous to that on which so much stress is laid in the Tantric process, the awakening of the Kundalini, the Energy coiled up and latent in the body and its mounting through the spinal cord and the centres (*cakras*) and the Brahmarandhra to meet the Divine above. In our yoga it is not a specialised process, but a spontaneous uprush of the whole lower consciousness sometimes in currents or waves, sometimes in a less concrete motion, and on the other side a descent of the Divine Consciousness and its Force into the body. This descent is felt as a pouring in of calm and peace, of force and power, of light, of joy and ecstasy, of wideness and freedom and knowledge, of a Divine Being or a Presence – sometimes one of these, sometimes several of them or all together. The movement of ascension has different results; it may liberate the consciousness so that one feels no longer in the body, but above it or else spread in wideness with the body either almost non-existent or only a point in one's free expanse. It may enable the being or some part of the being to go out from the body and move elsewhere, and this action is usually accompanied by some kind of partial *samādhi* or else a complete trance. Or, it may result in empowering the consciousness, no longer limited by the body and the habits of the external nature, to go within, to enter the inner mental depths, the inner vital, the inner (subtle) physical, the psychic, to become aware of its inmost psychic self or its inner mental, vital and subtle physical being and, it may be, to move and live in the domains, the planes, the worlds that correspond to these parts of the nature. It is the repeated and constant ascent of the lower consciousness that enables the mind, the vital, the physical to come into touch with the higher planes up to the supramental and get impregnated with their light and power and influence. And it is the repeated and constant descent of the Divine Consciousness and its Force that is the means for the transformation of the whole being and the whole nature. Once this descent becomes habitual, the Divine Force, the Power of the Mother, begins to work, no longer from above only or from behind the veil, but consciously in the Adhara itself, and deals with its difficulties and possibilities and carries on the yoga.

Last comes the crossing of the border. It is not a falling asleep or a loss of consciousness, for the consciousness is there all the time; only it shifts from the outer and physical, becomes closed to external things and recedes into the inner psychic and vital part of the being. There it passes through many experiences and of these some can and should be felt in the waking state also; for both movements are necessary, the coming out of the inner being to the front as well as the going in of the consciousness to become aware of the inner self and nature. But for many purposes the ingoing movement is indispensable. Its effect is to break or at least to open and pass the barrier between this outer instrumental consciousness and that inner being which it very partially strives to express, and to make possible in future a conscious awareness of all the endless riches of possibility and experience and new being and new life that lie untapped behind the veil of this small and very blind and limited material personality which men erroneously think to be the whole of themselves. It is the beginning and constant enlarging of this deeper and fuller and richer awareness that is accomplished between the inward plunge and the return from this inner world to the waking state.

The sadhak must understand that these experiences are not mere imaginations or dreams but actual happenings, for even when, as often occurs, they are formations only of a wrong or misleading or adverse kind, they have still their power as formations and must be understood before they can be rejected and abolished. Each inner experience is perfectly real in its own way, although the values of different experiences differ greatly, but it is real with the reality of the inner self and the inner planes. It is a mistake to think that we live physically only, with the outer mind and life. We are all the time living and acting on other planes of consciousness, meeting others there and acting upon them, and what we do and feel and think there, the forces we gather, the results we prepare have an incalculable importance and effect, unknown to us, upon our outer life. Not all of it comes through, and what comes through takes another form in the physical – though sometimes there is an exact correspondence; but this little is at the basis of our outward existence. All that we become and do and bear in the physical life is prepared behind the veil within us. It is therefore of immense importance for a yoga which aims at the transformation of life to grow conscious of what goes on within these domains, to be master there and be able to feel, know and deal with the secret forces that determine our destiny and our internal and external growth or decline.

It is equally important for those who want that union with the Divine without which the transformation is impossible. The aspiration could not be realised if you remained bound by your external self, tied to the physical mind and its petty movements. It is not the outer being which is the source of the spiritual urge; the outer being only undergoes the inner drive from behind the veil. It is the inner psychic being in you that is the bhakta, the seeker after the union and the Ananda, and what is impossible for the outer nature left to itself becomes perfectly possible when the barrier is down and the inner self in the front. For, the moment this comes strongly to the front or draws the consciousness powerfully into itself, peace, ecstasy, freedom, wideness, the opening to light and a higher knowledge begin to become natural, spontaneous, often immediate in their emergence.

THE WITNESS CONSCIOUSNESS

It is not possible to distinguish the psychic being at first. What has to be done is to grow conscious of an inner being which is separate from the external personality and nature — a consciousness or Purusha calm and detached from the outer actions of the Prakriti.

*

There is a stage in the sadhana in which the inner being begins to awake. Often the first result is the condition made up of the following elements:

1. A sort of witness attitude in which the inner consciousness looks at all that happens as a spectator or observer, observing things but taking no active interest or pleasure in them.

2. A state of neutral equanimity in which there is neither joy nor sorrow, only quietude.

3. A sense of being something separate from all that happens, observing it but not part of it.

4. An absence of attachment to things, people or events.

*

The condition in which all movements become superficial and empty with no connection with the soul is a stage in the withdrawal from the surface consciousness to the inner consciousness. When one goes into the inner consciousness, it is felt as a calm, pure existence without any movement, but eternally tranquil, unmoved and separate from the outer nature. This comes as a result of detaching oneself from the movements, standing back from them and is a very important movement of the sadhana. The first result of it is an entire quietude but afterwards that quietude begins (without the quietude ceasing) to fill with the psychic and other inner movements which create a true inner and spiritual life behind the outer life and nature. It is then easier to govern and change the latter.

*

The consciousness you speak of would be described in the Gita as the witness Purusha. The Purusha or basic consciousness is the true being or at least, in whatever plane it manifests, represents the true being. But in the ordinary nature of man it is covered up by the ego and the ignorant play of the Prakriti and remains veiled behind as the unseen Witness supporting the play of the Ignorance. When it emerges, you feel it as a consciousness behind, calm, central, unidentified with the play which depends upon it. It may be covered over, but it is always there. The emergence of the Purusha is the beginning of liberation. But it can also become slowly the Master — slowly because the whole habit of the ego and the play of the lower forces is against that. Still it can dictate what higher play is to replace the lower movement and then there is the process of that replacement, the higher coming, the lower struggling to remain and push away the higher movement. You say rightly that the offering to the Divine shortens the whole thing and is more effective, but usually it cannot be done completely at once owing to the past habit and the two methods continue together until the complete surrender is possible.

*

The witness attitude is not meant as a convenient means for disowning responsibility of one's defects and thereby refusing to mend them. It is meant for self-knowledge and, in our yoga, as a convenient station (detached and uninvolved, therefore not subject to Prakriti) from which one can act on the wrong movements by refusal of assent and by substituting for them the action of the true consciousness from within or above.

*

The inner being is composed of the inner mental, the inner vital, the inner physical. The psychic is the inmost supporting all the others. Usually it is in the inner mental that this separation first happens and it is the inner mental Purusha who remains silent, observing the Prakriti as separate from himself. But it may also be the inner vital Purusha or inner physical or else without location simply the whole Purusha consciousness separate from the whole Prakriti. Sometimes it is felt above the head, but then it is usually spoken of as the Atman and the realisation is that of the silent Self.

THE CONSCIOUSNESS OF THE SELF

It is an experience of the extension of consciousness. In yoga experience the consciousness widens in every direction, around, below, above, in each direction stretching to infinity. When the consciousness of the yogi becomes liberated, it is not in the body, but in this infinite height, depth, and wideness that he lives always. Its basis is an infinite void or silence, but in that all can manifest – Peace, Freedom, Power, Light, Knowledge, Ananda. This consciousness is usually called the consciousness of the Self or Atman, for it is a pure existence or self that is the source of all things and contains all things.

*

The Self is being, not a being. By Self is meant the conscious essential existence, one in all.

*

Everything acts in the self. The whole play of Nature takes place in the self, in the Divine. The self contains the universe.

*

The Self or Atman is inactive; Nature (Prakriti) or Shakti acts. When the Self is felt it is first an infinite existence, silence, freedom, peace that is felt — that is called Atman or Self. What action takes place in it is according to the realisation either felt as forces of Nature working in that wideness, as the Divine Shakti working or as the cosmic Divine or various powers of them working. It is not felt that the Self is acting.

*

The self is felt either as universal, one in all, or as universalised individual the same in essence as others, extended everywhere from each being but centred here. Of course centre is a way of speaking, because no physical centre is usually felt — only all the actions take place around the individual.

*

You must dismiss the fear of the concentration. The emptiness you feel coming on you is the silence of the great peace in which you become aware of your self, not as the small ego shut up in the body, but as the spiritual self wide as the universe. Consciousness is not dissolved; it is the limits of the consciousness that are dissolved. In that silence thoughts may cease for a time, there may be nothing but a great limitless freedom and wideness, but into that silence, that empty wideness descends the vast peace from above, light, bliss, knowledge, the higher Consciousness in which you feel the oneness of the Divine. It is the beginning of the transformation and there is nothing in it to fear.

*

The vastness, the overwhelming calm and silence in which you feel merged is what is called the Atman or the silent Brahman. It is the whole aim of many yogas to get this realisation of Atman or silent Brahman and live in it. In our yoga it is only the first stage of the realisation of the Divine and of that growing of the being into the higher or divine Consciousness which we call transformation.

*

The realisation of the Spirit comes long before the development of overmind or supermind; hundreds of sadhaks in all times have had the realisation of the Atman in the higher mental planes, *buddheh paratah*, but the supramental realisation was not theirs. One can get *partial* realisations of the Self or Spirit or the Divine on any plane, mental, vital, physical even, and when one rises above the ordinary mental plane of man into a higher and larger mind, the Self begins to appear in all its conscious wideness.

It is by full entry into this wideness of the Self that cessation of mental activity becomes possible; one gets the inner Silence. After that this inner Silence can remain even when there is activity of any kind; the being remains silent within, the action goes on in the instruments, and one receives all the necessary initiations and execution of action whether mental, vital or physical from a higher source without the fundamental peace and calm of the Spirit being troubled.

The overmind and supermind states are something yet higher than this; but before one can understand them, one must first have the self-realisation, the full action of the spiritualised mind and heart, the psychic awakening, the liberation of the imprisoned consciousness, the purification and entire opening of the Adhar. Do not think now of those ultimate things (overmind, supermind), but get first these foundations in the liberated nature.

*

Liberation is the first necessity, to live in the peace, silence, purity, freedom of the self. Along with that or afterwards if one wakens to the cosmic consciousness, then one can be free, yet one with all things.

To have the cosmic consciousness without liberation is possible, but then there is no freedom anywhere in the being from the lower nature and one may become in one's extended consciousness the playground of all kinds of forces without being able to be either free or master.

On the other hand, if there has been Self-realisation, there is one part of the being that remains untouched amid the play of the cosmic forces — while if the peace and purity of the self has been established in the whole inner consciousness, then the outer touches of the lower nature can't come in or overpower. This is the advantage of Self-realisation preceding the cosmic consciousness and supporting it.

THE COSMIC CONSCIOUSNESS

Man is shut up at present in his surface individual consciousness and knows the world (or rather the surface of it) only through his outward mind and senses and by interpreting their contacts with the world. By yoga there can open in him a consciousness which becomes one with that of the world; he becomes directly aware of a universal Being, universal states, universal Force and Power, universal Mind, Life, Matter and lives in conscious relations with these things. He is then said to have cosmic consciousness.

*

The cosmic consciousness is that in which the limits of ego, personal mind and body disappear and one becomes aware of a cosmic vastness which is or filled by a cosmic spirit and aware also of the direct play of cosmic forces, universal mind forces, universal life forces, universal energies of Matter, universal overmind forces. But one does not become aware of all these together; the opening of the cosmic consciousness is usually progressive. It is not that the ego, the body, the personal mind disappear, but one feels them as only a small part of oneself. One begins to feel others too as part of oneself or varied repetitions of oneself, the same self modified by Nature in other bodies. Or, at the least, as living in the larger universal self which is henceforth one's own greater reality. All things in fact begin to change their nature and appearance; one's whole experience of the world is radically different from that of those who are shut up in their personal selves. One begins to know things by a different kind of experience, more direct, not depending on the external mind and the senses. It is not that the possibility of error disappears, for that cannot be so long as mind of any kind is one's instrument for transcribing knowledge, but there is a new, vast and deep way of experiencing, seeing, knowing, contacting things; and the confines of knowledge can be rolled back to an almost unmeasurable degree. The thing one has to be on guard against in the cosmic consciousness is the play of a magnified ego, the vaster attacks of the hostile forces − for they too are part of the cosmic consciousness − and the attempt of the cosmic Illusion (Ignorance, Avidya) to prevent the growth of the soul into the cosmic Truth. These are things that one has to learn from experience; mental teaching or explanation is quite insufficient. To enter safely into the cosmic consciousness and to pass safely through it, it is necessary to have a strong central unegoistic sincerity and to have the psychic being, with its divination of truth and unfaltering orientation towards the Divine, already in front in the nature.

*

When one has the cosmic consciousness, one can feel the cosmic Self as one's own self, one can feel one with other beings in the cosmos, one can feel all the forces of Nature as moving in oneself, all selves as one's own self.

There is no why except that it is so, since all is the One.

*

In the cosmic consciousness the personal "I" disappears into the one Self of all. The "I" which alone exists is not that of the person, the individualised "I", but the universalised "I" identical with all and with the cosmic Self (Atman).

*

The overmind is the basis of the total cosmic consciousness, but the cosmic consciousness itself can be felt on any plane, not only above mind, but in mind, life, matter.

*

The cosmic consciousness has many levels – the cosmic physical, the cosmic vital, the cosmic Mind, and above the higher planes of cosmic Mind there is the Intuition and above that the overmind and still above that the supermind where the Transcendental begins. In order to live in the Intuition plane (not merely to receive intuitions), one has to live in the cosmic consciousness because there the cosmic and individual run into each other as it were, and the mental separation between them is already broken down, so nobody can reach there who is still in the separative ego.

A reflected static realisation of Sachchidananda is possible on any of the cosmic planes, but the full entering into it, the entire union with the Supreme Divine dynamic as well as static, comes with the transcendence.

*

There are in the cosmic consciousness two sides – one the contact with and perception of the ordinary cosmic forces and the beings behind these forces, that is what I call the cosmic Ignorance – the other is the perception of the cosmic Truths, the realisation of the one universal, the one universal Force, all the Vedantic truths of the One in all and all in one, all the various aspects of the Divine in the cosmic and a host of other things can come which do help to realisation and knowledge – provided they are taken in the right way. However all that can be best dealt with when it actually comes. It does not always come as soon as there is the widening – many pass through the widening of the consciousness to what is beyond the cosmic and take the cosmic in detail afterwards – and it is perhaps the safest order.

THE INTERMEDIATE ZONE

It [the breaking of the veil] comes of itself with the pressure of the sadhana. It can also be brought about by specific concentration and effort.

It is certainly better if the psychic is conscious and active before there is the removing of the veil or screen between the individual and the universal consciousness which comes when the inner being is brought forward in all its wideness. For then there is much less danger of the difficulties of what I have called the Intermediate Zone.

*

I mean by it [the intermediate zone] that when the sadhak gets beyond the barriers of his own embodied personal mind he enters into a wide range of experiences which are not the limited solid physical truth of things and not yet either the spiritual truth of things. It is a zone of formations, mental, vital, subtle physical, and whatever one forms or is formed by the forces of these worlds in us becomes for the sadhak for a time the truth – unless he is guided and listens to his guide. Afterwards if he gets through he discovers what it was and passes on into the subtle truth of things. It is a border-land where all the worlds meet, mental, vital, subtle physical, pseudo-spiritual – but there is no order or firm foothold – a passage between the physical and the true spiritual realms.

*

The intermediate zone means simply a confused condition or passage in which one is getting out of the personal consciousness and opening into the cosmic (cosmic Mind, cosmic vital, cosmic physical, something perhaps of the cosmic higher Mind) without having yet transcended the human mind levels. One is not in possession of or direct contact with the divine Truth *on its own levels*, but one can receive something from them, even from the overmind, indirectly. Only, as one is still immersed in the cosmic Ignorance, all that comes from above can be mixed, perverted, taken hold of for their purposes by lower, even by hostile Powers.

It is not necessary for everyone to struggle through the intermediate zone. If one has purified oneself, if there is no abnormal vanity, egoism, ambition or other strong misleading element, or if one is vigilant and on one's guard, or if the psychic is in front, one can either pass rapidly and directly or with a minimum of trouble into the higher zones of consciousness where one is in direct contact with the Divine Truth.

On the other hand the passage through the higher zones – higher Mind, illumined Mind, Intuition, overmind is obligatory – they are the true Intermediaries between the present consciousness and the supermind.

*

Do not be over-eager for experiences; for experiences you can always get, having once broken the barrier between the physical mind and the subtle planes. What you have to aspire for most is the improved quality of the recipient consciousness in you, discrimination in the mind, the unattached impersonal Witness look on all that goes on in you and around you, purity in the vital, calm equanimity, enduring patience, absence of pride and the sense of greatness — and more especially, the development of the psychic being in you — surrender, self-giving, psychic humility, devotion. It is a consciousness made up of these things, cast in this mould, that can bear without breaking, stumbling or deviation into error the rush of lights, power and experiences from the supraphysical planes. An entire perfection in these respects is hardly possible until the whole nature from the higher mind to the subconscient physical is made one in the light that is greater than the mind, but a sufficient foundation and a consciousness always self-observant, vigilant and growing in these things is indispensable — for perfect purification is the basis of the perfect Siddhi.

SUPRAPHYSICAL VISION, AUDITION, SENSATION

No, it was neither optical illusion nor hallucination nor coincidence nor auto-suggestion nor any of the other ponderous and vacant polysyllables by which physical science tries to explain away or rather avoid explaining the scientifically inexplicable. In these matters the scientist is always doing what he is always blaming the layman for doing when the latter lays down the law on things about which he is profoundly ignorant without investigation or experiment, without ascertained knowledge — simply by evolving a theory or *a priori* idea out of his own mind and plastering it as a label on the unexplained phenomena.

There is, as I have told you, a whole range or many inexhaustible ranges of sensory phenomena other than the outward physical which one can become conscious of, see, hear, feel, smell, touch, mentally contact — to use the new established Americanism — either in trance or sleep or an inward state miscalled sleep or simply and easily in the waking state. This faculty of sensing supraphysical things internally or externalising them, so to speak, so that they become visible, audible, sensible to the outward eye, ear, even touch, just as are gross physical objects, this power or gift is not a freak or an abnormality; it is a universal faculty present in all human beings, but latent in most, in some rarely or intermittently active, occurring as if by accident in others, frequent or normally active in a few. But just as anyone can, with some training, learn science and do things which would have seemed miracles to his forefathers, so almost anyone, if he wants, can with a little concentration and training develop the faculty of supraphysical vision. When one starts yoga, this power is often, though not invariably – for some find it difficult – one of the first to come out from its latent condition and manifest itself, most often without any effort, intention or previous knowledge on the part of the sadhak. It comes more easily with the eyes shut than with the eyes open, but it does come in both ways. The first sign of its opening in the externalised way is very often that seeing of "sparkles" or small luminous dots, shapes, etc., which was your first introduction to the matter; a second is, often enough, most easily, round luminous objects like a star; seeing of colours is a third initial experience – but they do not always come in that order. The yogis in India very often in order to develop the power use the method of *trāṭak*, concentrating the vision on a single point or object – preferably a luminous object. Your looking at the star was precisely an exercise in *trāṭak* and had the effect which any yogi in India would have told you is normal. For all this is not fancy or delusion, it is part of an occult science which has been practised throughout the historic and prehistoric ages in all countries and it has always been known to be not merely auto-suggestive or hallucinatory in its results, but, if one can get the key, veridical and verifiable.

*

I remember when I first began to see inwardly (and outwardly also with the open eye), a scientific friend of mine began to talk of after-images — "these are only after-images"! I asked him whether after-images remained before the eye for two minutes at a time — he said, "no", to his knowledge only for a few seconds; I also asked him whether one could get after-images of things not around one or even not existing upon this earth, since they had other shapes, another character, other hues, contours and a very different dynamism, life-movements and values — he could not reply in the affirmative. That is how these so-called scientific explanations break down as soon as you pull them out of their cloudland of mental theory and face them with the actual phenomena they pretend to decipher.

*

Subjective visions can be as real as objective sight — the only difference is that one is of real things in material space, while the others are of real things belonging to other planes down to the subtle physical; even symbolic visions are real in so far as they are symbols of realities. Even dreams can have a reality in the subtle domain. Visions are unreal only when these are merely imaginative mental formations, not representing anything that is true or was true or is going to be true.

This power of vision is sometimes inborn and habitual even without any effort of development, sometimes it wakes up of itself and becomes abundant or needs only a little practice to develop; it is not necessarily a sign of spiritual attainment, but usually when by practice of yoga one begins to go inside or live within, the power of subtle vision awakes to a greater or less extent; but this does not always happen easily, especially if one has been habituated to live much in the intellect or in an outward vital consciousness.

*

Visions do not come from the spiritual plane – they come from the subtle physical, the vital, the mental, the psychic or from the planes above the Mind. What comes from the spiritual plane are experiences of the Divine, e.g. the experience of self everywhere, of the Divine in all, etc.

*

All visions have a significance of one kind or another. This power of vision is very important for the yoga and should not be rejected although it is not the most important thing – for the most important thing is the change of the consciousness. All other powers like this of vision should be developed without attachment as parts and aids of the yoga.

*

The utility of psychic experiences and knowledge of the invisible worlds as of other yogic experiences is not to be measured by our narrow human notions of what may be useful for the present physical life of man. In the first place these things are necessary for the fulness of the consciousness and the completeness of the being. In the second place these other worlds are actually working upon us. And if you know and can enter into them then instead of being the victims and puppets of these powers we can consciously deal with, control and use them. Thirdly, in my yoga, the yoga of the supramental, the opening of the psychic consciousness to which these experiences belong is quite indispensable. For it is only through the psychic opening that the supramental can fully descend with a strong and concrete grasp and transform the mental, vital and physical being.

*

The spiritual realisation is of primary importance and indispensable. I would consider it best to have the spiritual and psychic development first and have it with the same fullness before entering the occult regions. Those who enter the latter first may find their spiritual realisation much delayed – others fall into the mazy traps of the occult and do not come out in this life. Some no doubt can carry on both together, the occult and the spiritual, and make them help each other; but the process I suggest is the safer.

The governing factors for us must be the spirit and the psychic being united with the Divine – the occult laws and phenomena have to be known but only as an instrumentation, not as the governing principles. The occult is a vast field and complicated and not without its dangers. It need not be abandoned but it should not be given the first place.

*

The stumbling-block of X was ambition, pride, vanity – the desire to be a big yogi with occult powers. To try to bring down occult powers into an unpurified mind, heart and body – well, you can do it if you want to dance on the edge of a precipice. Or you can do it if your aim is not to be spiritual but to be an occultist, for then you can follow the necessary methods and get the help of the occult powers. On the other hand, the true occult spiritual forces and mysteries can be called down or can come down without calling, but this must be made secondary to the one true thing, the seeking for the Divine, and if it is part of the Divine plan in you. Occult powers can only be for the spiritual man an instrumentation of the Divine Power that uses him: they cannot be made the aim or an aim of his sadhana.

SYMBOLS, LIGHTS, COLOURS, SOUNDS

It depends on the nature of the symbolic vision whether it is merely representative, presenting to the inner vision and nature (even though the outer mind has not the understanding, the inner can receive its effect) the thing symbolised in its figure or whether it is dynamic. The Sun symbol, for instance, is usually dynamic. Again, among the dynamic symbols some may bring simply the influence of the thing symbolised, some indicate what is being done but not yet finished, some a formative experience that visits the consciousness, some a prophecy of something that may or will or is soon about to happen. There are others that are not merely symbols but present actualities seen by the vision in a symbolic figure.

*

These things [seeing Buddha, Ramakrishna, Vivekananda, Shankara frequently in vision] are the result of past thoughts and influences. They are of various kinds – sometimes merely thought-forms created by one's own thought-force to act as a vehicle for some mental realisation – sometimes Powers of different planes that take these forms as a support for their work through the individual, – but sometimes one is actually in communion with that which had the name and form and personality of Buddha or Ramakrishna or Vivekananda or Shankara.

It is not necessary to have an element akin to these personalities – a thought, an aspiration, a formation of the mind or vital are enough to create the connection – it is sufficient for a vibration of response anywhere to what these Powers represent.

*

Fire, lights, sun, moon are usual symbols and seen by most in sadhana. They indicate movement or action of inner forces. The Sun means the inner truth.

*

Lights are of all kinds, supramental, mental, vital, physical, divine or Asuric – one has to watch, grow in experience and learn to know one from another. The true lights however are by their clarity and beauty not difficult to recognise.

*

In interpreting these phenomena [colours seen in vision] you must remember that all depends on the order of things which the colours indicate in any particular case. There is an order of significances in which they indicate various psychological dynamisms, e.g., faith, love, protection, etc. There is another order of significances in which they indicate the aura or the activity of divine beings, Krishna, Mahakali, Radha or else of other superhuman beings; there is another in which they indicate the aura around objects or living persons — and that does not exhaust the list of possibilities. A certain knowledge, experiences, growing intuition are necessary to perceive in each case the true significance. Observation and exact description are also very necessary; for sometimes people say, for instance, yellow when they mean gold or *vice versa*; there are besides different possible meanings for different shades of the same colour. Again, if you see colour near or round a person or by looking at him or her, it does not necessarily indicate that person's aura; it may be something else near him or around him. In some cases it may have nothing to do with the person or object you look at, which may serve merely the purpose of a background or a point of concentration — as when you see colours on a wall or by looking at a bright object.

*

The sounds or voices you hear are like the sights (persons, objects) you see. As there is an inner sight other than the physical, so there is an inner hearing other than that of the external ear, and it can listen to voices and sounds and words of other worlds, other times and places, or those which come from supraphysical beings. But here you must be careful. If conflicting voices try to tell you what to do or not to do, you should not listen to them or reply.

*

The sounds of bells and the seeing of lights and colours are signs of the opening of the inner consciousness which brings

with it an opening also to sights and sounds of other planes
than the physical. Some of these things like the sound of
bells, crickets, etc. seem even to help the opening. The
Upanishad speaks of them as *brahmavyaktikarāni yoge*.

The lights represent forces — or sometimes a formed light
like that you saw may be the light of a being of the supraphysical planes.

EXPERIENCES IN DREAM

In sleep we leave the physical body, only a subconscient
residue remaining, and enter all planes and all sorts of
worlds. In each we see scenes, meet beings, share in happenings, come across formations, influences, suggestions
which belong to these planes. Even when we are awake, part
of us moves in these planes, but their activity goes on behind
the veil; our waking minds are not aware of it. Dreams are
often only incoherent constructions of our subconscient, but
others are records (often much mixed and distorted) or
transcripts of experiences in these supraphysical planes.
When we do sadhana, this kind of dream becomes very
common; then subconscious dreams cease to predominate.

*

It is the subconscient that is active in the ordinary dreams.
But in the dreams in which one goes out into other planes of
consciousness, mental, vital, subtle physical, it is part of the
inner being, inner mental or vital or physical that is usually
active.

*

Your second experience is a first movement of the awakening of the inner being in sleep. Ordinarily when one sleeps
a complex phenomenon happens. The waking consciousness
is no longer there, for all has been withdrawn within into the

inner realms of which we are not aware when we are awake, though they exist; for then all that is put behind a veil by the waking mind and nothing remains except the surface self and the outward world — much as the veil of the sunlight hides from us the vast worlds of the stars that are behind it. Sleep is a going inward in which the surface self and the outside world are put away from our sense and vision. But in ordinary sleep we do not become aware of the worlds within; the being seems submerged in a deep subconscience. On the surface of this subconscience floats an obscure layer in which dreams take place, as it seems to us, but, more correctly it may be said, are recorded. When we go very deeply asleep, we have what appears to us as a dreamless slumber; but, in fact, dreams are going on, but they are either too deep down to reach the recording surface or are forgotten, all recollection of their having existed even is wiped out in the transition to the waking consciousness. Ordinary dreams are for the most part or seem to be incoherent, because they are either woven by the subconscient out of deep-lying impressions left in it by our past inner and outer life, woven in a fantastic way which does not easily yield any clue of meaning to the waking mind's remembrance, or are fragmentary records, mostly distorted, of experiences which are going on behind the veil of sleep — very largely indeed these two elements get mixed up together. For, in fact, a large part of our consciousness in sleep does not get sunk into this subconscious state; it passes beyond the veil into other planes of being which are connected with our own inner planes, planes of supraphysical existence, worlds of a larger life, mind or psyche which are there behind and whose influences come to us without our knowledge. Occasionally we get a dream from these planes, something more than a dream, — a dream experience which is a record direct or symbolic of what happens to us or around us there. As the inner consciousness grows by sadhana, these dream experiences increase in number, clearness, coherence, accuracy and after some growth of experi-

ence and consciousness, we can, if we observe, come to
understand them and their significance to our inner life.
Even we can by training become so conscious as to follow
our own passage, usually veiled to our awareness and
memory, through many realms and the process of the return
to the waking state. At a certain pitch of this inner wake-
fulness this kind of sleep, a sleep of experiences, can replace
the ordinary subconscious slumber. . . .

When this growth of the inner sleep consciousness begins,
there is often a pull to go inside and pursue the development
even when there is no fatigue or need of sleep. Another
cause aids this pull. It is usually the vital part of the inner
being that first wakes in sleep and the first dream experiences (as opposed to ordinary dreams) are usually, in the
great mass, experiences of the vital plane, a world of supraphysical life, full of variety and interest, with many pro-
vinces, luminous or obscure, beautiful or perilous, often
extremely attractive, where we can get much knowledge too
both of our concealed parts of nature and of things happening to us behind the veil and of others which are of
concern for the development of our parts of nature. The
vital being in us then may get very much attracted to this
range of experience, may want to live more in it and less in
the outer life. This would be the source of that wanting to
get back to something interesting and enthralling which
accompanies the desire to fall into sleep. But this must not
be encouraged in waking hours, it should be kept for hours
set apart for sleep where it gets its natural field. Otherwise
there may be an unbalancing, a tendency to live more and
too much in the visions of the supraphysical realms and a
decrease of the hold on outer realities. The knowledge, the
enlargement of our consciousness of these fields of inner
nature is very desirable, but it must be kept in its own place
and limits.

*

What you say about the different vital worlds is no doubt interesting and has a certain truth, but you must remember that these worlds, which are different from the true or divine vital, are full of enchantments and illusions and they present appearances of beauty which allure only to mislead or destroy. They are worlds of 'Rakshasimaya' and their heavens are more dangerous than their hells. They have to be known and their powers met when need be but not accepted; our business is with the supramental and with the vital only when it is supramentalised and until then we have always to be on our guard against any lures from that other quarter.

EXTERIORISATION

When the vital being goes out [of the body], it moves on the vital plane and in the vital consciousness and, even if it is aware of physical scenes and things, it is not with a physical vision. It is possible for one who has trained his faculties to enter into touch with physical things although he is moving about in the vital body, to see and sense them accurately, even to act on them and physically move them. But the ordinary sadhak who has no knowledge or organised experience or training in these things cannot do it. He must understand that the vital plane is different from the physical and that things that happen there are not physical happenings, though, if they are of the right kind and properly understood and used, they may have a meaning and value for the earth life. But also the vital consciousness is full of false formations and many confusions and it is not safe to move among them without knowledge and without a direct protection and guidance.

*

Your three experiences related in your letter mean that you are going out in your vital body into the vital worlds and meeting the beings and formations of these worlds. The old man of the temple and the girls you saw are hostile beings of the vital plane.

It is better not to go in this way unless one has the protection of someone (physically present) who has knowledge and power on the vital world. As there is no one there who can do this for you, you should draw back from this movement. Aspire for perfect surrender, calm, peace, light, consciousness and strength in the mind and the heart. When the mental being and the psychic being are thus open, luminous and surrendered, then the vital can open and receive the same illumination. Till then premature adventures on the vital plane are not advisable.

8

The Triple Transformation:
Psychic, Spiritual and Supramental

THE MEANING OF TRANSFORMATION

If one can remain always in the higher consciousness, so much the better. But why does not one remain always there? Because the lower is still part of the nature and it pulls you down towards itself. If on the other hand the lower is transformed, it becomes of one kind with the higher and there is nothing lower to pull downward.

Transformation means that the higher consciousness or nature is brought down into the mind, vital and body and takes the place of the lower. There is a higher consciousness of the true self, which is spiritual, but it is above; if one rises above into it, then one is free as long as one remains there, but if one comes down into or uses mind, vital or body – and if one keeps any connection with life, one has to do so, either to come down and act from the ordinary consciousness or else to be in the self but use mind, life and body, then the imperfections of these instruments have to be faced and mended – they can only be mended by transformation.

*

By transformation I do not mean some change of the nature – I do not mean, for instance, sainthood or ethical perfection or yogic siddhis (like the Tantrik's) or a transcendental (*cinmaya*) body. I use transformation in a special sense, a change of consciousness radical and complete and of a certain specific kind which is so conceived as to bring about a strong and assured step forward in the spiritual evolution of the being of a greater and higher kind and of a larger sweep and completeness than what took place when a mentalised being first appeared in a vital and material animal world. If anything short of that takes place or at least if a real beginning is not made on that basis, a fundamental progress towards this fulfilment, then my object is not accomplished. A partial realisation, something mixed and inconclusive, does not meet the demand I make on life and yoga.

Light of realisation is not the same thing as Descent. Realisation by itself does not necessarily transform the being as a whole; it may bring only an opening or heightening or widening of the consciousness at the top so as to realise something in the Purusha part without any radical change in the parts of Prakriti. One may have some light of realisation at the spiritual summit of the consciousness but the parts below remain what they were. I have seen any number of instances of that. There must be a descent of the light not merely into the mind or part of it but into all the being down to the physical and below before a real transformation can take place. A light in the mind may spiritualise or otherwise change the mind or part of it in one way or another, but it need not change the vital nature; a light in the vital may purify and enlarge the vital movements or else silence and immobilise the vital being, but leave the body and the physical consciousness as it was, or even leave it inert or shake its balance. And the descent of Light is not enough, it must be the descent of the whole higher consciousness, its Peace, Power, Knowledge, Love, Ananda. Moreover, the descent may be enough to liberate, but not to perfect, or it may be enough to make a great change in the inner being, while the outer remains an imperfect instrument, clumsy, sick or unexpressive. Finally, transformation effected by the sadhana cannot be complete unless it is a supramentalisation of the being. Psychicisation is not enough, it is only a beginning; spiritualisation and the descent of the higher consciousness is not enough, it is only a middle term; the ultimate achievement needs the action of the supramental Consciousness and Force. Something less than that may very well be considered enough by the individual, but it is not enough for the earth-consciousness to take the definitive stride forward it must take at one time or another.

THE PSYCHIC TRANSFORMATION

The psychic is the first of two transformations necessary – if you have the psychic transformation it facilitates immensely the other, i.e., the transformation of the ordinary human into the higher spiritual consciousness – otherwise one is likely to have either a slow and dull or exciting but perilous journey.

*

I have read your account of your sadhana. There is nothing to say, I think, – for it is all right – except that the most important thing for you is to develop the psychic fire in the heart and the aspiration for the psychic being to come forward as the leader of the sadhana. When the psychic does so, it will show you the "undetected ego-knots" of which you speak and loosen them or burn them in the psychic fire. This psychic development and the psychic change of mind, vital and physical consciousness is of the utmost importance because it makes safe and easy the descent of the higher consciousness and the spiritual transformation without which the supramental must always remain far distant. Powers etc. have their place, but a very minor one so long as this is not done.

*

Purification and consecration are two great necessities of sadhana. Those who have experiences before purification run a great risk: it is much better to have the heart pure first, for then the way becomes safe. That is why I advocate the psychic change of the nature first — for that means the purification of the heart: the turning of it wholly to the Divine, the subjection of the mind and the vital to the control of the inner being, the soul. Always, when the soul is in front, one gets the right guidance from within as to what is to be done, what avoided, what is the wrong thing or the true thing in thought, feeling, action. But this inner intimation emerges in proportion as the consciousness grows more and more pure.

*

As for experiences, they are all right but the trouble is that they do not seem to change the nature, they only enrich the consciousness — even the realisation, on the mind level, of the Brahman seems to leave the nature almost where it was, except for a few. That is why we insist on the psychic transformation as the first necessity — for that does change the nature — and its chief instrument is bhakti, surrender, etc.

*

The soul, the psychic being is in direct touch with the divine Truth, but it is hidden in man by the mind, the vital being and the physical nature. One may practise yoga and get illuminations in the mind and the reason; one may conquer power and luxuriate in all kinds of experiences in the vital; one may establish even surprising physical Siddhis; but if the true soul-power behind does not manifest, if the psychic nature does not come into the front, nothing genuine has been done. In this yoga the psychic being is that which opens the rest of the nature to the true supramental light and finally to the supreme Ananda. Mind can open by itself to its own higher reaches; it can still itself and widen into the Impersonal; it may too spiritualise itself in some kind of static liberation or Nirvana; but the supramental cannot find a sufficient base in a spiritualised mind alone. If the inmost soul is awakened, if there is a new birth out of the mere mental, vital and physical into the psychic consciousness, then this yoga can be done; otherwise (by the sole power of the mind or any other part) it is impossible. . . . If there is a refusal of the psychic new birth, a refusal to become the child new born from the Mother, owing to attachment to intellectual knowledge or mental ideas or to some vital desire, then there will be a failure in the sadhana.

*

In the psychic transformation there are three main elements: (1) the opening of the occult inner mind, inner vital, inner physical, so that one becomes aware of all that lies behind the surface mind, life and body – (2) the opening of the psychic being or soul by which it comes forward and governs the mind, life and body turning all to the Divine – (3) the opening of the whole lower being to the spiritual truth – this last may be called the psycho-spiritual part of the change. It is quite possible for the psychic transformation to take one beyond the individual into the cosmic. Even the occult opening establishes a connection with the cosmic mind, cosmic vital, cosmic physical. The psychic realises the contact with all-existence, the oneness of the Self, the universal love and other realisations which lead to the cosmic consciousness.

THE PSYCHIC OPENING

The psychic being emerges slowly in most men, even after taking up sadhana. There is so much in the mind and vital that has to change and readjust itself before the psychic can be entirely free. One has to wait till the necessary process has gone far enough before it can burst its agelong veil and come in front to control the nature. It is true that nothing can give so much inner happiness and joy – though peace can come by the mental and vital liberation or through the growth of a strong *samatā* in the being.

*

The psychic being is in the heart centre in the middle of the chest (not in the physical heart, for all the centres are in the middle of the body), but it is deep behind. When one is going away from the vital into the psychic, it is felt as if one is going deep deep down till one reaches that central place of the psychic. The surface of the heart centre is the place of the emotional being; from there one goes deep to find the psychic. The more one goes, the more intense becomes the psychic happiness which you describe.

*

What is meant by [the psychic's] coming to the front is simply this. The psychic ordinarily is deep within. Very few people are aware of their souls — when they speak of their soul, they usually mean the vital + mental being or else the (false) soul of desire. The psychic remains behind and acts only through the mind, vital and physical wherever it can. For this reason the psychic being except where it is very much developed has only a small and partial, concealed and mixed or diluted influence on the life of most men. By coming forward is meant that it comes from behind the veil, its presence is felt already in the waking daily consciousness, its influence fills, dominates, transforms the mind and vital and their movements, even the physical. One is aware of one's soul, feels the psychic to be one's true being, the mind and the rest begin to be only instruments of the inmost within us.

*

When the psychic being comes in front, there is an auto-matic perception of the true and untrue, the divine and the undivine, the spiritual right and wrong of things, and the false vital and mental movements and attacks are immediately exposed and fall away and can do nothing; gradually the vital and physical as well as the mind get full of this psychic light and truth and sound feeling and purity, and such violent attacks as you have are impossible.

*

When the psychic is in the front, the sadhana becomes natural and easy and it is only a question of time and natural development. When the mind or the vital or the physical consciousness is on the top, then the sadhana is a tapasya and a struggle.

*

It is the psychic being in you that has come forward – and when the psychic being comes forward all is happiness, the right attitude, the right vision of things. Of course in one sense it is the same I that puts forward different parts of itself. But when these different parts are all under the control of the psychic and turned by it towards the reception of the higher consciousness, then there begins the harmonisation of all the parts and their progressive recasting into moulds of the higher consciousness growing in peace, light, force, love, knowledge, Ananda which is what we call the transformation.

CONDITIONS OF THE PSYCHIC OPENING

The realisation of the psychic being, its awakening and the bringing of it in front depend mainly on the extent to which one can develop a personal relation with the Divine, a relation of Bhakti, love, reliance, self-giving, rejection of the insistences of the separating and self-asserting mental, vital and physical ego.

*

Then only can the psychic being fully open when the sadhak has got rid of the mixture of vital motives with his sadhana and is capable of a simple and sincere self-offering to the Mother. If there is any kind of egoistic turn or insincerity of motive, if the yoga is done under a pressure of vital demands, or partly or wholly to satisfy some spiritual or other ambition, pride, vanity or seeking after power, position or influence over others or with any push towards satisfying any vital desire with the help of the yogic force, then the psychic cannot open, or opens only partially or only at times and shuts again because it is veiled by the vital activities; the psychic fire fails in the strangling vital smoke. Also, if the mind takes the leading part in the yoga and puts the inner soul into the background, or if the bhakti or other movements of the sadhana take more of a vital than of a psychic form, there is the same inability. Purity, simple sincerity and the capacity of an unegoistic unmixed self-offering without pretension or demand are the condition of an entire opening of the psychic being.

*

For the opening of the psychic being, concentration on the Mother and self-offering to her are the direct way. The growth of Bhakti which you feel is the first sign of the psychic development. A sense of the Mother's presence or force or the remembrance of her supporting and strengthening you is the next sign. Eventually, the soul within begins to be active in aspiration and psychic perception guiding the mind to the right thoughts, the vital to the right movements and feelings, showing and rejecting all that has to be put away and turning the whole being in all its movements to the Divine alone.

*

If desire is rejected and no longer governs the thought, feeling or action and there is a steady aspiration of an entirely sincere self-giving, the psychic usually after a time opens of itself.

*

Aspiration, constant and sincere, and the will to turn to the Divine alone are the best means to bring forward the psychic.

*

That is one part of the psychic experience – the other is a complete self-giving, absence of demand, a prominence of the psychic being by which all that is false, wrong, egoistic, contrary to the Divine Truth, Divine Will, Divine Purity and Light is shown, falls away, cannot prevail in the nature. With all that the increase of the psychic qualities, gratitude, obedience, unselfishness, fidelity to the true perception, true impulse etc. that comes from the Mother or leads to the Mother. When this side grows, then the other, the Presence, Love, Joy, Beauty can develop and be permanently there.

THE SPIRITUAL TRANSFORMATION

Psychicisation means the change of the lower nature bringing right vision into the mind, right impulse and feeling into the vital, right movement and habit into the physical – all turned towards the Divine, all based on love, adoration, bhakti – finally, the vision and sense of the Mother everywhere in all as well as in the heart, her Force working in the being, faith, consecration, surrender.

The spiritual change is the established descent of the peace, light, knowledge, power, bliss from above, the awareness of the Self and the Divine and of a higher cosmic consciousness and the change of the whole consciousness to that.

*

Between psychicisation and spiritualisation there is a difference. The spiritual is the change that descends from above, the psychic is the change that comes from within by the psychic dominating the mind, vital and physical.

*

The two feelings are both of them right – they indicate the two necessities of the sadhana. One is to go inward and open fully the connection between the psychic being and the outer nature. The other is to open upward to the Divine Peace, Force, Light, Ananda above, to rise up into it and bring it down into the nature and the body. Neither of these two movements, the psychic and the spiritual, is complete without the other. If the spiritual ascent and descent are not made, the spiritual transformation of the nature cannot happen; if the full psychic opening and connection is not made, the transformation cannot be complete.

There is no incompatibility between the two movements; some begin the psychic first, others the spiritual first, some carry on both together. The best way is to aspire for both and let the Mother's Force work it out according to the need and turn of the nature.

*

The action of the higher consciousness does not usually begin by changing the outer nature – it works on the inner being, prepares that and then goes outward. Before that, whatever change is done in the outer nature has to be done by the psychic.

*

"Transformation" is a word that I have brought in myself (like "supermind") to express certain spiritual concepts and spiritual facts of the integral yoga. People are now taking them up and using them in senses which have nothing to do with the significance which I put into them. Purification of the nature by the "influence" of the Spirit is not what I mean by transformation; purification is only part of a psychic change or a psycho-spiritual change – the word besides has many senses and is very often given a moral or ethical meaning which is foreign to my purpose. What I mean by the spiritual transformation is something dynamic (not merely liberation of the Self or realisation of the One which can very well be attained without any descent). It is a putting on of the spiritual consciousness, dynamic as well as static, in every part of the being down to the subconscient. That cannot be done by the influence of the Self leaving the consciousness fundamentally as it is with only purification, enlightenment of the mind and heart and quiescence of the vital. It means a bringing down of the Divine Consciousness static and dynamic into all these parts and the entire re-placement of the present consciousness by that. This we find unveiled and unmixed above mind, life and body. It is a matter of the undeniable experience of many that this can descend and it is my experience that nothing short of its *full* descent can thoroughly remove the veil and mixture and effect the full spiritual transformation. No metaphysical or logical reasoning in the void as to what the Atman "must" do or can do or needs or needs not to do is relevant here or of any value. I may add that transformation is not the central object of other paths as it is of this yoga – only so much purification and change is demanded by them as will lead to liberation and the beyond-life. The influence of the Atman can no doubt do that – a full descent of a new consciousness into the whole nature from top to bottom to transform life here is not needed at all for the spiritual escape from life.

THE CENTRAL PROCESS OF THE YOGA

I have said that the most decisive way for the Peace or the Silence to come is by a descent from above. In fact, in reality though not always in appearance, that is how they always come; — not in appearance always, because the sadhak is not always conscious of the process; he feels the peace settling in him or at least manifesting, but he has not been conscious how and whence it came. Yet it is the truth that all that belongs to the higher consciousness comes from above, not only the spiritual peace and silence, but the Light, the Power, the Knowledge, the higher seeing and thought, the Ananda come from above. It is also possible that up to a certain point they may come from within, but this is because the psychic being is open to them directly and they come first there and then reveal themselves in the rest of the being from the psychic or by its coming into the front. A disclosure from within or a descent from above, these are the two sovereign ways of the Yoga-siddhi. An effort of the external surface mind or emotions, a Tapasya of some kind may seem to build up some of these things, but the results are usually uncertain and fragmentary, compared to the result of the two radical ways. That is why in this yoga we insist always on an "opening" — an opening inwards of the inner mind, vital, physical to the inmost part of us, the psychic, and an opening upwards to what is above the mind — as indispensable for the fruits of the sadhana.

The underlying reason for this is that this little mind, vital and body which we call ourselves is only a surface movement and not our "self" at all. It is an external bit of personality put forward for one brief life, for the play of the Ignorance. It is equipped with an ignorant mind stumbling about in search of fragments of truth, an ignorant vital rushing about in search of fragments of pleasure, an obscure and mostly subconscious physical receiving the impacts of things and suffering rather than possessing a resultant pain or pleasure. All that is accepted until the mind gets disgusted and starts looking about for the real Truth of itself and things, the vital gets disgusted and begins wondering whether there is not such a thing as real bliss and the physical gets tired and wants liberation from itself and its pains and pleasures. Then it is possible for the little ignorant bit of personality to get back to its real Self and with it to these greater things – or else to extinction of itself, Nirvana.

The real Self is not anywhere on the surface but deep within and above. Within is the soul supporting an inner mind, inner vital, inner physical in which there is a capacity for universal wideness and with it for the things now asked for – direct contact with the truth of self and things, taste of a universal bliss, liberation from the imprisoned smallness and sufferings of the gross physical body. Even in Europe the existence of something behind the surface is now very frequently admitted, but its nature is mistaken and it is called subconscient or subliminal, while really it is very conscious in its own way and not subliminal but only behind the veil. It is, according to our psychology, connected with the small outer personality by certain centres of consciousness of which we become aware by yoga. Only a little of the inner being escapes through these centres into the outer life, but that little is the best part of ourselves and responsible for our art, poetry, philosophy, ideals, religious aspirations, efforts at knowledge and perfection. But the inner centres are for the most part closed or asleep – to open them and make them awake and active is one aim of yoga. As they open, the powers and possibilities of the inner being also are aroused in us; we awake first to a larger consciousness and then to a cosmic consciousness; we are no longer little separate personalities with limited lives but centres of a universal action and in direct contact with cosmic forces. Moreover, instead of being unwillingly playthings of the latter, as is the surface person, we can become to a certain extent conscious and masters of the play of nature – how far this goes depending on the development of the inner being and its opening upward to the higher spiritual levels. At the same time the opening of the heart centre releases the psychic being which proceeds to make us aware of the Divine within us and of the higher Truth above us.

For the highest spiritual Self is not even behind our personality and bodily existence but is above it and altogether exceeds it. The highest of the inner centres is in the head, just as the deepest is the heart; but the centre which opens directly to the Self is above the head, altogether outside the physical body, in what is called the subtle body, *sūkṣma śarīra*. This Self has two aspects and the results of realising it correspond to these two aspects. One is static, a condition of wide peace, freedom, silence: the silent Self is unaffected by any action or experience; it impartially supports them but does not seem to originate them at all, rather to stand back detached or unconcerned, *udāsīna*. The other aspect is dynamic and that is experienced as a cosmic Self or Spirit which not only supports but originates and contains the whole cosmic action – not only that part of it which concerns our physical selves but also all that is beyond it – this world and all other worlds, the supraphysical as well as the physical ranges of the universe. Moreover, we feel the Self as one in all; but also we feel it as above all, transcendent, surpassing all individual birth or cosmic existence. To get into the universal Self – one in all – is to be liberated from ego; ego either becomes a small instrumental circumstance in the consciousness or even disappears from our consciousness altogether. That is the extinction or Nirvana of the ego. To get into the transcendent self above all makes us capable of transcending altogether even cosmic consciousness and action – it can be the way to that complete liberation from the world-existence which is called also extinction, *laya, mokṣa, nirvāṇa*.

It must be noted however that the opening upward does not necessarily lead to peace, silence and Nirvana only. The sadhak becomes aware not only of a great, eventually an infinite peace, silence, wideness above us, above the head as it were and extending into all physical and supraphysical space, but also he can become aware of other things – a vast Force in which is all power, a vast Light in which is all knowledge, a vast Ananda in which is all bliss and rapture. At first they appear as something essential, indeterminate, absolute, simple, *kevala*: a Nirvana into any of these things seems possible. But we can come to see too that this Force contains all forces, this Light all lights, this Ananda all joy and bliss possible. And all this can descend into us. Any of them and all of them can come down, not peace alone; only the safest is to bring down first an absolute calm and peace, for that makes the descent of the rest more secure; otherwise it may be difficult for the external nature to contain or bear so much Force, Light, Knowledge or Ananda. All these things together make what we call the higher spiritual or Divine Consciousness. The psychic opening through the heart puts us primarily into connection with the individual Divine, the Divine in his inner relation with us; it is especially the source of love and bhakti. This upward opening puts us into direct relation with the whole Divine and can create in us the divine consciousness and a new birth or births of the spirit.

When the Peace is established, this higher or Divine Force from above can descend and work in us. It descends usually first into the head and liberates the inner mind centres, then into the heart centre and liberates fully the psychic and emotional being, then into the navel and other vital centres and liberates the inner vital, then into the Muladhara and below and liberates the inner physical being. It works at the same time for perfection as well as liberation; it takes up the whole nature part by part and deals with it, rejecting what has to be rejected, sublimating what has to be sublimated, creating what has to be created. It integrates, harmonises, establishes a new rhythm in the nature. It can bring down too a higher and yet higher force and range of the higher nature until, if that be the aim of the sadhana, it becomes possible to bring down the supramental force and existence. All this is prepared, assisted, farthered by the work of the psychic being in the heart centre; the more it is open, in front, active, the quicker, safer, easier the working of the Force can be. The more love and bhakti and surrender grow in the heart, the more rapid and perfect becomes the evolution of the sadhana. For the descent and transformation imply at the same time an increasing contact and union with the Divine.

That is the fundamental rationale of the sadhana. It will be evident that the two most important things here are the opening of the heart centre and the opening of the mind centres to all that is behind and above them. For the heart opens to the psychic being and the mind centres open to the higher consciousness and the nexus between the psychic being and the higher consciousness is the principal means of the siddhi. The first opening is effected by a concentration in the heart, a call to the Divine to manifest within us and through the psychic to take up and lead the whole nature. Aspiration, prayer, bhakti, love, surrender are the main supports of this part of the sadhana — accompanied by a rejection of all that stands in the way of what we aspire for. The second opening is effected by a concentration of the consciousness in the head (afterwards, above it) and an aspiration and call and a sustained will for the descent of the divine Peace, Power, Light, Knowledge, Ananda into the being — the Peace first or the Peace and Force together. Some indeed receive Light first or Ananda first or some sudden pouring down of knowledge. With some there is first an opening which reveals to them a vast infinite Silence, Force, Light or Bliss above them and afterwards either they ascend to that or these things begin to descend into the lower nature. With others there is either the descent, first into the head, then down to the heart level, then to the navel and below and through the whole body, or else an inexplicable opening — without any sense of descent — of peace, light, wideness or power, or else a horizontal opening into the cosmic consciousness or in a suddenly widened mind an outburst of knowledge. Whatever comes has to be welcomed — for there is no absolute rule for all — but if the peace has not come first, care must be taken not to swell oneself in exultation or lose the balance. The capital movement however is when the Divine Force or Shakti, the power of the Mother comes down and takes hold, for then the organisation of the consciousness begins and the larger foundation of the yoga.

The result of the concentration is not usually immediate – though to some there comes a swift and sudden outflowering; but with most there is a time longer or shorter of adaptation or preparation, especially if the nature has not been prepared already to some extent by aspiration and Tapasya. The coming of the result can sometimes be aided by associating with the concentration one of the processes of the old yoga. There is the Adwaita process of the way of knowledge – one rejects from oneself the identification with the mind, vital, body, saying continually "I am not the mind", "I am not the vital" , "I am not the body", seeing these things as separate from one's real self – and after a time one feels all the mental, vital, physical processes and the very sense of mind, vital, body becoming externalised, an outer action, while within and detached from them there grows the sense of a separate self-existent being which opens into the realisation of the cosmic and transcendent spirit. There is also the method – a very powerful method – of the Sankhyas, the separation of the Purusha and the Prakriti. One enforces on the mind the position of the Witness – all action of mind, vital, physical becomes an outer play which is not myself or mind, but belongs to Nature and has been enforced on an outer me. I am the witness Purusha; I am silent, detached, not bound by any of these things. There grows up in consequence a division in the being; the sadhak feels within him the growth of a calm silent separate consciousness which feels itself quite apart from the surface play of the mind and the vital and physical Nature. Usually when this takes place, it is possible very rapidly to bring down the peace of the higher consciousness and the action of the higher Force and the full march of the yoga. But often the Force itself comes down first in response to the concentration and call and then, if these things are necessary, it does them and uses any other means or process that is helpful or indispensable.

One thing more. In this process of the descent from above and the working it is most important not to rely entirely on oneself, but to rely on the guidance of the Guru and to refer all that happens to his judgment and arbitration and decision. For it often happens that the forces of the lower nature are stimulated and excited by the descent and want to mix with it and turn it to their profit. It often happens too that some Power or Powers undivine in their nature present themselves as the Supreme Lord or as the Divine Mother and claim the being's service and surrender. If these things are accepted, there will be an extremely disastrous consequence. If indeed there is the assent of the sadhak to the Divine working alone and the submission or surrender to that guidance, then all can go smoothly. This assent and a rejection of all egoistic force or forces that appeal to the ego are the safeguard throughout the sadhana. But the ways of nature are full of snares, the disguises of the ego are innumerable, the illusions of the Powers of Darkness, Rakshasi Maya, are extraordinarily skilful; the reason is an insufficient guide and often turns traitor; vital desire is always with us tempting to follow any alluring call. This is the reason why in this yoga we insist so much on what we call Samarpana — rather inadequately rendered by the English word surrender. If the heart centre is fully opened and the psychic is always in control, then there is no question; all is safe. But the psychic can at any moment be veiled by a lower upsurge. It is only a few who are exempt from these dangers and it is precisely those to whom surrender is easily possible. The guidance of one who himself is by identity or represents the Divine is in this difficult endeavour imperative and indispensable.

What I have written may help you to get some clear idea of what I mean by the central process of the yoga. I have written at some length but, naturally, could cover only the fundamental things. Whatever belongs to circumstance and detail must arise as one works out the method, or rather as it works itself out — for the last is what usually happens when there is an effective beginning of the action of the sadhana.

ASCENT AND DESCENT

The practice of this yoga is double – one side is of an ascent of the consciousness to the higher planes, the other is that of a descent of the power of the higher planes into the earth-consciousness so as to drive out the Power of darkness and ignorance and transform the nature.

*

It is the aim of the sadhana that the consciousness should rise out of the body and take its station above, – spreading in the wideness everywhere, not limited to the body. Thus liberated one opens to all that is above this station, above the ordinary mind, receives there all that descends from the heights, observes from there all that is below. Thus it is possible to witness in all freedom and to control all that is below and to be a recipient or a channel for all that comes down and presses into the body, which it will prepare to be an instrument of a higher manifestation, remoulded into a higher consciousness and nature.

*

An ascension of the consciousness to a position which is no longer in the body but above it. The consciousness can thus ascend and rise higher and higher with the awareness of entering regions above the ordinary mind; usually it does not go very far at first but acquires the capacity to go always higher in repetitions of this experience. At the close of the experience it returns to the body. But also there comes a definitive rise by which the consciousness permanently takes its station above. It is no longer in the body or limited by it; it feels itself not only above it but extended in space; the body is below its high station and enveloped in its extended consciousness. Sometimes indeed the extension is felt only above on the higher level and the enveloping extension below comes only afterwards as a later experience. But the nature of it is to be definitive, it is not merely an experience but a realisation, a permanent change. This brings a liberation from identification with the body which becomes only a circumstance in the largeness of the being, an instrumental part of it; or it is felt as something very small or even non-existent, nothing seems to be felt but a wide practically infinite consciousness which is oneself – or if not at once infinite, yet what is now called a boundless finite.

This new consciousness is open to all knowledge from above, but it does not think with the brain as does the ordinary mind – it has other and larger means of awareness than thought. No methodical opening of the centres is necessary – the centres are in fact open, otherwise there could not be this ascent. In this yoga their opening comes automatically – what we call opening is not that, but an ability of the consciousness itself on the various levels to receive the descent of the Higher Consciousness above. By the ascent one can indeed bring down knowledge from above. But the larger movement is to receive it from above and let it flow through into the lower mental and other levels. I may add that on all these levels, in mind, heart and below there comes a liberation from the physical limitation, a wideness which no longer allows an identification with the body.

THE YOGA-SHAKTI AND THE PROCESS OF
ASCENT AND DESCENT

I do not see what is your difficulty. That there is a divine force asleep or veiled by Inconscience in Matter and that the Higher Force has to descend and awaken it with the Light and Truth is a thing that is well known; it is at the very base of this yoga.

*

There is a force which accompanies the growth of the new consciousness and at once grows with it and helps it to come about and to perfect itself. This force is the Yoga-Shakti. It is here coiled up and asleep in all the centres of our inner being (Chakras) and is at the base what is called in the Tantras the Kundalini Shakti. But it is also above us, above our head as the Divine Force — not there coiled up, involved, asleep, but awake, scient, potent, extended and wide; it is there waiting for manifestation and to this Force we have to open ourselves — to the power of the Mother. In the mind it manifests itself as a divine mind-force or a universal mind-force and it can do everything that the personal mind cannot do; it is then the yogic mind-force. When it manifests and acts in the vital or the physical in the same way, it is there apparent as a yogic life-force or a yogic body-force. It can awake in all these forms, bursting outwards and upwards, extending itself into wideness from below; or it can descend and become there a definite power for things; it can pour downwards into the body, working, establishing its reign, extending into wideness from above, link the lowest in us with the highest above us, release the individual into a cosmic universality or into absoluteness and transcendence.

*

The sensation in the spine and on both sides of it is a sign of the awakening of the Kundalini Power. It is felt as a descending and an ascending current. There are two main nerve-channels for the currents, one on each side of the central channel in the spine. The descending current is the energy from the above coming down to touch the sleeping Power in the lowest nerve-centre at the bottom of the spine; the ascending current is the release of the energy going up from the awakened Kundalini. This movement as it proceeds opens up the six centres of the subtle nervous system and by the opening one escapes from the limitations of the surface consciousness bound to the gross body and great ranges of experiences proper to the subliminal self, mental, vital, subtle physical are shown to the sadhak. When the Kundalini meets the higher Consciousness as it ascends through the summit of the head, there is an opening of the higher superconscient reaches above the normal mind. It is by ascending through these in our consciousness and receiving a descent of their energies that it is possible ultimately to reach the supermind. This is the method of the Tantra. In our yoga it is not necessary to go through the systematised method. It takes place spontaneously according to the need by the force of the aspiration. As soon as there is an opening the Divine Power descends and conducts the necessary working, does what is needed, each thing in its time, and the yogic Consciousness begins to be born in the sadhak.

*

In [this] yoga there may be an occasional current in the spine as in other nerve channels or different parts of the body, but no awakening of the Kundalini in this particular and powerful fashion. There is only a quiet uprising of the consciousness from the lower centres to join the spiritual consciousness above and a descent of the Divine Force from above which does its own work in the mind and body – the manner and stages varying in each sadhak.

THE DESCENT OF PEACE, POWER, LIGHT, ANANDA

The descent of Peace, the descent of Force or Power, the descent of Light, the descent of Ananda, these are the four things that transform the nature.

*

Your description of the solid cool block of peace pressing on the body and making it immobile makes it certain that it is what we call in this yoga the descent of the higher consciousness. A deep, intense or massive substance of peace and stillness is very commonly the first of its powers that descends and many experience it in that way. At first it comes and stays only during meditation or, without the sense of physical inertness or immobility, a little while longer and afterwards is lost; but if the sadhana follows its normal course, it comes more and more, lasting longer and in the end as an enduring deep peace and inner stillness and release becomes a normal character of the consciousness, the foundation indeed of a new consciousness, calm and liberated.

*

Quiet, quiet and more quiet, calm strength, calm gladness are what are needed in mind and nerves and body as a basis for the siddhi – precisely because the Force, the Light, the Ananda that come down are extremely intense and need a great stillness in the body to bear and support.

*

It is the universal experience of sadhaks that force or consciousness or Ananda like this first comes from above – or around – and presses on or surrounds the head, then it pierces the skull as it were and fills first the brain and forehead and then the whole head and descends occupying each centre till the whole system is full and replete. Of course there are, or can be, preliminary rushes occupying the whole body for a time or some part of the system most open and least resistant to the influence.

*

It is possible that there may have been too much haste in this attempt to open the navel and the lower centre. In this yoga the movement is downward – first the two head centres, then the heart, then the navel and then the two others. If the higher experience is first fully established with its higher consciousness, knowledge and will in the three upper centres, then it is easier to open the three lower ones without too much disturbance.

*

These are some of the effects of the descent of higher Consciousness into the most physical. It brings light, consciousness, force, Ananda into the cells and all the physical movements. The body becomes conscious and vigilant and performs the right movements, obeying the higher will or else automatically by the force of the consciousness that has come into it. It becomes more possible to control the functions of the body and set right anything that is wrong, to deal with illness and pain, etc. A greater control comes over the actions of the body and even over happenings to it from outside, e.g., minimising of accidents and small mishaps. The body becomes a more effective instrument for work. It becomes possible to minimise fatigue. Peace, happiness, strength, lightness come in the whole physical system. These are the more obvious and normal results which grow as the consciousness grows but there are as many others that are possible. There is also the unity with the earth-consciousness, the constant sense of the Divine in the physical, etc. . . .

It is, of course, not easy to make the physical entirely conscious in this way — for it is the seat of unconsciousness and obscurity and inertia — but a partial and sufficiently effective introduction of the higher Consciousness can be established as a basis and the rest of the ground conquered as its force increases on the body.

DIFFICULTIES IN THE PROCESS OF DESCENT

The descent is that of the powers of the higher consciousness which is above the head. It usually descends from centre to centre till it has occupied the whole being. But at the beginning the action is very variable. It is only when the Peace from above has not only descended but established itself in the whole system that there is a continuous action. The descent comes in order to transform the consciousness but the transformation takes time. It is not done all in a moment.

*

The Power does not descend with the object of raising up the lower forces, but in the way it has to work at present, that uprising comes in as a reaction to the working. What is needed is the establishment of the calm and wide consciousness at the base of the whole Nature, so that when the lower nature appears it will not be as an attack or struggle but as if a Master of forces were there seeing the defects of the present machinery and doing step by step what is necessary to remedy and change it.

*

Headaches "produced by a pressure from above", as you put it, are not due to the pressure or produced by it, but produced by a resistance.

*

The pressure does not "bring" a resistance. "If there were no resistance there would be no headache" is the proper knowledge, not the reverse. So long as you think that it is the pressure that brings the resistance, the very idea will create the resistance.

*

Probably the accumulated Force became more than the physical being could receive. When that happens the right thing to do is to widen oneself (one can do it by a little practice). If the consciousness is in a state of wideness then it can receive any amount of force without inconvenience.

*

That [shaking of the body] sometimes happens when the force is coming down. It must be allowed to pass off as the body becomes more quiet and assimilative.

*

The quiet flow is necessary for permeating the lower parts. The big descents open the way and bring constant reinforcement and the culminating force at the end — but the quiet flow is also needed.

ASSIMILATION OF THE FORCE

As regards your own sadhana and those of others . . . I think it necessary to make two or three observations. First, I have for some time had the impression that there is a too constant activity and pressure for rapidity of progress and a multitude of experiences. These things are all right in themselves, but there must be certain safeguards. First there should be sufficient periods of rest and silence, even of relaxation, in which there can be a quiet assimilation. Assimilation is very important and periods necessary for it should not be regarded with impatience as stoppages of the yoga. Care should be taken to make calm and quiet strength and inner silence the basic condition for all activity. There should be no excessive strain; any fatigue, disturbance, or inordinate sensitiveness of the nervous and physical parts, of which you mention certain symptoms in your letters, should be quieted and removed, as they are often signs of overstrain or too great an activity or rapidity in the yoga. It must also be remembered that experiences are only valuable as indications and openings and the main thing always is the steady harmonious and increasingly organised opening and change of the different parts of the consciousness and the being.

*

It is quite usual to have such periods in the day. The consciousness needs time for rest and assimilation, it cannot be at the same pitch of intensity at all times. During the assimilation a calm quietude is the proper condition.

*

One can assimilate in sleep also. Remaining awake like that is not good, as in the end it strains the nerves and the system receives wrongly in an excited way or else gets too tired to receive.

ALTERNATIONS IN THE INTENSITY OF THE FORCE

It is somewhat like that. That is to say, there are always alternations in the intensity of the Force at its work. It comes with great power and effects something that has to be done; then it is either concealed or retires a little or is felt but from behind a screen as you say, while something comes up that has to be prepared for illumination and then it comes in front again and does what has to be done there. But formerly while the support, help, even the deeper consciousness was always there, as you now rightly feel, yet when a veil fell, then it was all forgotten and you felt as if there was nothing but darkness and confusion. This happens to most sadhaks in the earlier stages. It is a great progress, a decisive advance if, at the time the Force is acting behind the screen, you feel that it is there, that the help and support, the more enlightened consciousness is there still. This is the second stage in the sadhana. There is a third when there is no screen and the Force and all else are always felt whether actively working or pausing during a transition.

*

The length of your period of dullness is also no sufficient reason for losing belief in your capacity or your spiritual destiny. I believe that alternations of bright and dark periods are almost a universal experience of yogis, and the exceptions are very rare. If one inquires into the reasons of this phenomenon, — very unpleasant to our impatient human nature, — it will be found, I think, that they are in the main two. The first is that the human consciousness either cannot bear a constant descent of the Light or Power or Ananda, or cannot at once receive and absorb it; it needs periods of assimilation; but this assimilation goes on behind the veil of the surface consciousness; the experience or the realisation that has descended retires behind the veil and leaves this outer or surface consciousness to lie fallow and become ready for a new descent. In the more developed stages of the yoga these dark or dull periods become shorter, less trying as well as uplifted by the sense of the greater consciousness which, though not acting for immediate progress, yet remains and sustains the outer nature. The second cause is some resistance, something in the human nature that has not felt the former descent, is not ready, is perhaps unwilling to change, — often it is some strong habitual formation of the mind or the vital or some temporary inertia of the physical consciousness and not exactly a part of the nature, — and this, whether showing or concealing itself, thrusts up the obstacle. If one can detect the cause in oneself, acknowledge it, see its workings and call down the Power for its removal, then the periods of obscurity can be greatly shortened and their acuity becomes less. But in any case the Divine Power is working always behind and one day, perhaps when one least expects it, the obstacle breaks, the clouds vanish and there is again the light and the sunshine. The best thing in these cases is, if one can manage it, not to fret, not to despond, but to insist quietly and keep oneself open, spread to the Light and waiting in faith for it to come; that I have found shortens these ordeals. Afterwards, when the obstacle disappears, one finds that a great progress has been made and that the consciousness is far more capable of receiving and retaining than before. There is a return for all the trials and ordeals of the spiritual life.

THE SUPRAMENTAL TRANSFORMATION

There are different statuses (*avasthā*) of the Divine Consciousness. There are also different statuses of transformation. First is the psychic transformation, in which all is in contact with the Divine through the individual psychic consciousness. Next is the spiritual transformation in which all is merged in the Divine in the cosmic consciousness. Third is the supramental transformation in which all becomes supramentalised in the divine gnostic consciousness. It is only with the last that there can begin the *complete* transformation of mind, life and body — in my sense of completeness.

You are mistaken in two respects. First, the endeavour towards this achievement is not new and some yogis have achieved it, I believe — but not in the way I want it. They achieved it as a personal siddhi maintained by yoga-siddhi — not a dharma of the nature. Secondly, the supramental transformation is not the same as the spiritual-mental. It is a change of mind, life and body which the mental or overmental-spiritual cannot achieve.

*

Spiritualisation means the descent of the higher peace, force, light, knowledge, purity, Ananda, etc., which belong to any of the higher planes from Higher Mind to overmind, for in any of these the Self can be realised. It brings about a

subjective transformation; the instrumental Nature is only
so far transformed that it becomes an instrument for the
Cosmic Divine to get some work done, but the self within
remains calm and free and united with the Divine. But this is
an incomplete individual transformation — the full transformation of the instrumental Nature can only come when
the supramental change takes place. Till then the nature
remains full of many imperfections, but the Self in the
higher planes does not mind them, as it is itself free and
unaffected. The inner being down to the inner physical can
also become free and unaffected. The overmind is subject to
limitations in the working of the effective Knowledge, limitations in the working of the Power, subject to a partial and
limited Truth, etc. It is only in the supermind that the full
Truth-Consciousness comes into being.

*

If spiritual and supramental were the same thing, as you say
my readers imagine, then all the sages and devotees and
yogis and sadhaks throughout the ages would have been
supramental beings and all I have written about the supermind would be so much superfluous stuff, useless and otiose.
Anybody who had spiritual experiences would then be a
supramental being; the Ashram would be chock-full of
supramental beings and every other Ashram in India also.
Spiritual experiences can fix themselves in the inner consciousness and alter it, transform it, if you like; one can
realise the Divine everywhere, the Self in all and all in the
Self, the universal Shakti doing all things; one can feel
merged in the Cosmic Self or full of ecstatic bhakti or
Ananda. But one may and usually does still go on in the
outer parts of Nature thinking with the intellect or at best
the intuitive mind, willing with a mental will, feeling joy and
sorrow on the vital surface, undergoing physical afflictions
and suffering from the struggle of life in the body with death
and disease. The change then only will be that the inner self

will watch all that without getting disturbed or bewildered, with a perfect equality, taking it as an inevitable part of Nature, inevitable at least so long as one does not withdraw to the Self out of Nature. That is not the transformation I envisage. It is quite another power of knowledge, another kind of will, another luminous nature of emotion and aesthesis, another constitution of the physical consciousness that must come in by the supramental change.

PREPARATION FOR THE SUPRAMENTAL CHANGE

All should understand that the true direct supramental does not come at the beginning but much later on in the sadhana. First the opening up and illumination of the mental, vital and physical beings; secondly, the making intuitive of the mind, through will etc. and the development of the hidden soul consciousness progressively replacing the surface consciousness; thirdly, the supramentalising of the changed mental, vital and physical beings and finally the descent of the true supramental and the rising into the supramental plane.

This is the natural order of the yoga. These stages may overlap and intermix, there may be many variations, but the last two can only come in an advanced state of the progress. Of course the supramental Divine guides this yoga throughout but it is first through many intermediary planes; and it cannot easily be said of anything that comes in the earlier periods that it is the direct or full supramental. To think so when it is not so may well be a hindrance to progress.

*

One has to know about overmind and supermind but there should be no ambition to reach them – it should be regarded as a natural end of the sadhana which will come of itself. The concentration should be all on the immediate step – whatever is being done at the time. So have the working of the Power and let it work all out step by step.

*

Certainly, the overmind descent is necessary for those who want the supramental change. Unless the overmind opens, there can be no direct supramental opening of the consciousness. If one remains in the mind, even illumined mind or the intuition, one can have indirect messages or an influence from the supramental, but not a direct supramental control of the consciousness or the supramental change.

*

The supramental creation, since it is to be a creation upon earth, must be not only an inner change but a physical and external manifestation also. And it is precisely for this part of the work, the most difficult of all, that surrender is most needful; for this reason, that it is the actual descent of the supramental Divine into Matter and the working of the Divine Presence and Power there that can alone make the physical and external change possible. Even the most powerful self-assertion of human will and endeavour is impotent to bring it about; as for egoistic insistence and vital revolt, they are, so long as they last, insuperable obstacles to the descent. Only a calm, pure and surrendered physical consciousness, full of the psychic aspiration, can be its field; this alone can make an effective opening of the material being to the Light and Power and the supramental change a thing actual and practicable.

*

Get the psychic being in front and keep it there, putting its power on the mind, vital and physical, so that it shall communicate to them its force of single-minded aspiration, trust, faith, surrender, direct and immediate detection of whatever is wrong in the nature and turned towards ego and error, away from Light and Truth.

Eliminate egoism in all its forms; eliminate it from every movement of your consciousness.

Develop the cosmic consciousness — let the ego-centric outlook disappear in wideness, impersonality, the sense of the Cosmic Divine, the perception of universal forces, the realisation and understanding of the cosmic manifestation, the play.

Find in place of ego the true being — a portion of the Divine, issued from the World-Mother and an instrument of the manifestation. This sense of being a portion of the Divine and an instrument should be free from all pride, sense or claim of ego or assertion of superiority, demand or desire. For if these elements are there, then it is not the true thing.

Most in doing yoga live in the mind, vital, physical, lit up occasionally or to some extent by the higher mind and by the illumined mind; but to prepare for the supramental change it is necessary (as soon as, personally, the time has come) to open up to the Intuition and the overmind, so that these may make the whole being and the whole nature ready for the supramental change. Allow the consciousness quietly to develop and widen and the knowledge of these things will progressively come.

Calm, discrimination, detachment (but not indifference) are all very important, for their opposites impede very much the transforming action. Intensity of aspiration should be there, but it must go along with these. No hurry, nor inertia, neither rajasic over-eagerness nor tamasic discouragement — a steady and persistent but quiet call and working. No snatching or clutching at realisation, but allowing realisation to come from within and above and observing accurately its field, its nature, its limits.

Let the power of the Mother work in you, but be careful to avoid any mixture or substitution, in its place, of either a magnified ego-working or a force of Ignorance presenting itself as Truth. Aspire especially for the elimination of all obscurity and unconsciousness in the nature.

These are the main conditions of preparation for the supramental change; but none of them is easy, and they must be complete before the nature can be said to be ready. If the true attitude (psychic, unegoistic, open only to the Divine Force) can be established, then the process can go on much more quickly. To take and keep the true attitude, to further the change in oneself, is the help that can be given, the one thing asked to assist the general change.

TRANSFORMATION OF THE BODY

The object of supramentalisation is a body fitted to embody and express the physical consciousness on earth so long as one remains in the physical life. It is a step in the spiritual evolution on the earth, not a step in the passage towards a supraphysical world. The supramentalisation is the most difficult part of the change arrived at by the supramental yoga, and all depends on whether a sufficient change can be achieved in the consciousness at present to make such a step possible. . . . One has first of all to supramentalise sufficiently the mind and vital and physical consciousness generally – afterwards one can think of supramentalisation of the body. The psychic and spiritual transformation must come first, only afterwards would it be practical or useful to discuss the supramentalisation of the whole being down to the body.

*

It is quite impossible for the supramental to take up the body before there has been the full supramental change in the mind and the vital. X and others seem always to expect some kind of unintelligible miracle – they do not understand that it is a concentrated evolution, swift but following the law of creation that has to take place. A miracle can be a moment's wonder. A change according to the Divine Law can alone endure.

*

The change of the consciousness is the necessary thing and without it there can be no physical siddhi. But the fullness of the supramental change is not possible, if the body remains as it is, a slave of death, disease, decay, pain, unconsciousness and all the other results of the ignorance. If these are to remain the descent of the supramental is hardly necessary — for a change of consciousness which would bring mental-spiritual union with the Divine, the overmind is sufficient, even the Higher Mind is sufficient. The supramental descent is necessary for a dynamic action of the Truth in mind, vital and body. This would imply as a final result the disappearance of the unconsciousness of the body; it would no longer be subject to decay and disease. That would mean that it would not be subject to the ordinary processes by which death comes. If a change of body had to be made, it would have to be by the will of the inhabitant. This (not an obligation to live 3000 years, for that too would be a bondage) would be the essence of physical immortality. Still, if one wanted to live 1000 years or more, then supposing one had the complete siddhi, it should not be impossible.

*

There can be no immortality of the body without supramentalisation; the potentiality is there in the yogic force and yogis can live for 200 or 300 years or more, but there can be no real principle of it without the supramental.

Even Science believes that one day death may be conquered by physical means and its reasonings are perfectly sound. There is no reason why the supramental Force should not do it. Forms on earth do not last (they do in other planes) because these forms are too rigid to grow expressing the progress of the spirit. If they become plastic enough to do that there is no reason why they should not last.

*

Death is there because the being in the body is not yet developed enough to go on growing in the same body without the need of change and the body itself is not sufficiently conscious. If the mind and vital and the body itself were more conscious and plastic, death would not be necessary.

*

As for conquest of death, it is only one of the sequelae of supramentalisation – and I am not aware that I have forsworn my views about the supramental descent. But I never said or thought that the supramental descent would automatically make everybody immortal. The supramental can only make the best conditions for anybody who can open up to it then or thereafter attaining to the supramental consciousness and its consequences. But it could not dispense with the necessity of sadhana. If it did, the logical consequence would be that the whole earth, men, dogs and worms would suddenly wake up to find themselves supramental. There would be no need of an Ashram or of yoga.

Why vital? What is vital is the supramental change of consciousness – conquest of death is something minor and, as I have always said, the last physical result of it, not the first result of all or the most important – a thing to be added to complete the whole, not the one thing needed and essential. To put it first is to reverse all spiritual values – it would mean that the seeker was actuated, not by any high spiritual aim but by a vital clinging to life or a selfish and timid seeking for the security of the body – such a spirit could not bring the supramental change.

*

To merge the consciousness in the Divine and to keep the psychic being controlling and changing all the nature and keeping it turned to the Divine till the whole being can live in the Divine is the transformation we seek. There is further the supramentalisation, but this only carries the transformation to its own highest and largest possibilities – it does not alter its essential nature.

Immortality is one of the possible results of supramentalisation, but it is not an obligatory result and it does not mean that there will be an eternal or indefinite prolongation of life as it is. That is what many think it will be, that they will remain what they are with all their human desires and the only difference will be that they will satisfy them endlessly; but such an immortality would not be worth having and it would not be long before people are tired of it. To live in the Divine and have the divine Consciousness is itself immortality and to be able to divinise the body also and make it a fit instrument for divine works and divine life would be its material expression only.

9

Transformation of the Nature

EXPERIENCES AND TRANSFORMATION

The difficulty of the yoga is not in getting experiences or a subjective realisation of the Truth; it is in objectivising the Truth, that is in making the outer consciousness down to the material an expression of the inner Truth. So long as that is not done the attacks of the lower Nature can always intervene.

*

Experiences and descents are very good for preparation, but change of the consciousness is the thing wanted — it is the proof that the experiences and descents have had an effect. Descents of peace are good, but an increasingly stable quietude and silence of the mind is something more valuable. When that is there, then other things can come — usually one at a time, light or strength and force or knowledge or Ananda. It is not necessary to go on forever always having the same preparatory experiences — a time comes when the consciousness begins to take a new poise and another state.

*

Merely to have experiences of the higher consciousness will not change the nature. Either the higher consciousness has to make a dynamic descent into the whole being and change it; or it must establish itself in the inner being down to the inner physical so that the latter feels itself separate from the outer and is able to act freely upon it; or the psychic must come forward and change the nature; or the inner will must awake and force the nature to change. These are the four ways in which change can be brought about.

TRANSFORMATION OF THE MIND

THE THINKING MIND

To have a developed intellect is always helpful if one can enlighten it from above and turn it to a divine use.

*

The intellect can be as great an obstacle as the vital when it chooses to prefer its own constructions to the Truth.

*

The intellect of most men is extremely imperfect, ill-trained, half-developed — therefore in most the conclusions of the intellect are hasty, ill-founded and erroneous or, if right, right more by chance than by merit or right working. The conclusions are formed without knowing the facts or the correct or sufficient data, merely by a rapid inference and the process by which it comes from the premises to the conclusions is usually illogical or faulty — the process being unsound by which the conclusion is arrived at, the conclusion is also likely to be fallacious. At the same time the intellect is usually arrogant and presumptuous, confidently asserting its imperfect conclusions as the truth and setting down as mistaken, stupid or foolish those who differ from them. Even when fully trained and developed, the intellect cannot arrive at absolute certitude or complete truth, but it can arrive at one aspect or side of it and make a reasonable

or probable affirmation; but untrained, it is a quite insufficient instrument, at once hasty and peremptory and unsafe
and unreliable.

*

Its [the intellect's] function is to reason from the perceptions
of the mind and senses, to form conclusions and to put
things in logical relation with each other. A well-trained
intellect is a good preparation of the mind for greater
knowledge, but it cannot itself give the yogic knowledge or
know the Divine – it can only have ideas about the Divine,
but having ideas is not knowledge. In the course of the
sadhana intellect has to be transformed into the higher mind
which is itself a passage towards the true knowledge.

*

There is no reason why one should not receive through the
thinking mind, as one receives through the vital, the emotional and the body. The thinking mind is as capable of
receiving as these are, and, since it has to be transformed as
well as the rest, it must be trained to receive, otherwise no
transformation of it could take place.

It is the ordinary unenlightened activity of the intellect
that is an obstacle to spiritual experience, just as the ordinary unregenerated activity of the vital or the obscure
stupidly obstructive consciousness of the body is an obstacle.
What the sadhak has to be specially warned against in the
wrong processes of the intellect is, first, any mistaking of
mental ideas and impressions or intellectual conclusions for
realisation; secondly, the restless activity of the mere mind
which disturbs the spontaneous accuracy of psychic and
spiritual experience and gives no room for the descent of the
true illuminating knowledge or else deforms it as soon as it
touches or even before it fully touches the human mental
plane. There are also of course the usual vices of the intellect, – its leaning towards sterile doubt instead of luminous
reception and calm enlightened discrimination; its arrogance

claiming to judge things that are beyond it, unknown to it, too deep for it by standards drawn from its own limited experience; its attempts to explain the supraphysical by the physical or its demand for the proof of higher and occult things by the criteria proper to Matter and mind in Matter; others also too many to enumerate here. Always it is substituting its own representations and constructions and opinions for the true knowledge. But if the intellect is surrendered, open, quiet, receptive, there is no reason why it should not be a means of reception of the Light or an aid to the experience of spiritual states and to the fullness of an inner change.

*

The thinking mind has to learn how to be entirely silent. It is only then that true knowledge can come.

*

The turmoil of mental (intellectual) activity has also to be silenced like the vital activity of desire in order that the calm and peace may be complete. Knowledge has to come but from above. In this calm the ordinary mental activities like the ordinary vital activities become surface movements with which the silent inner self is not connected. It is the liberation necessary in order that the true knowledge and the true life-activity may replace or transform the activities of the Ignorance.

*

To think and question about an experience when it is happening is the wrong thing to do; it stops it or diminishes it. Let the experience have its full play — if it is something like this "new life force" or peace or Force or anything else helpful. When it is over, you can think about it — not while it is proceeding. For these experiences are spiritual and not mental and the mind has to be quiet and not interfere.

THE VITAL MIND

The thinking mind does not lead men, does not influence them the most – it is the vital propensities and the vital mind that predominate. The thinking mind with most men is, in matters of life, only an instrument of the vital.

*

There is a part of the nature which I have called the vital mind; the function of this mind is not to think and reason, to perceive, consider and find out or value things, for that is the function of the thinking mind proper, *buddhi*, – but to plan or dream or imagine what can be done. It makes formations for the future which the will can try to carry out if opportunity and circumstances become favourable or even it can work to make them favourable. In men of action this faculty is prominent and a leader of their nature; great men of action always have it in a very high measure. But even if one is not a man of action or practical realisation or if circumstances are not favourable or one can do only small and ordinary things, this vital mind is there. It acts in them on a small scale, or if it needs some sense of largeness, what it does very often is to plan in the void, knowing that it cannot realise its plans or else to imagine big things, stories, adventures, great doings in which oneself is the hero or the creator. What you describe as happening in you is the rush of this vital mind or imagination making its formations; its action is not peculiar to you but works pretty much in the same way in most people – but in each according to his turn of fancy, interest, favourite ideas or desires. You have to become master of its action and not to allow it to seize your mind and carry it away when and where it wants. In sadhana when the experiences begin to come, it is exceedingly important not to allow this power to do what it likes with you; for it then creates false experiences according to its nature and persuades the sadhak that these experiences are true or it builds unreal formations and persuades him that this is what he has to do. Some have been taken away by this misleading force used by powers of Falsehood who persuaded them through it that they had a great spiritual, political or social work to do in the world and led them away to disappointment and failure. It is rising in you in order that you may understand what it is and reject it.

THE PHYSICAL MIND

Of course most men live in their physical mind and vital, except a few saints and a rather larger number of intellectuals. That is why, as it is now discovered, humanity has made little progress in the last three thousand years, except in information and material equipment. A little less cruelty and brutality perhaps, more plasticity of the intellect in the elite, a quicker habit of change in forms, that is all.

*

The physical mind is that which is fixed on physical objects and happenings, sees and understands these only, and deals with them according to their own nature, but can with difficulty respond to the higher forces. Left to itself, it is sceptical of the existence of supraphysical things, of which it has no direct experience and to which it can find no clue; even when it has spiritual experiences, it forgets them easily, loses the impression and result and finds it difficult to believe. To enlighten the physical mind by the consciousness of the higher spiritual and supramental planes is one object of this yoga, just as to enlighten it by the power of the higher vital and higher mental elements of the being is the greatest part of human self-development, civilisation and culture.

*

It [the physical mind] is the instrument of understanding and ordered action on physical things. Only instead of being obscure and ignorant and fumbling as now or else guided only by an external knowledge it has to become conscious of the Divine and to act in accordance with an inner light, will and knowledge putting itself into contact and an understanding unity with the physical world.

*

What you have now seen and describe in your letter is the ordinary activity of the physical mind which is full of ordinary habitual and constantly recurrent thoughts and is always busy with external objects and activities. What used to trouble you before was the vital mind which is different, — for that is always occupied with emotions, passions, desires, reactions of all kinds to the contacts of life and the behaviour of others. The physical mind also can be responsive with these things but in a different way – its nature is less that of desire than of habitual activity, small common interests, pains and pleasures. If one tries to control or suppress it, it becomes more active.

To deal with this mind two things are necessary, (1) not so much to try to control or fight with or suppress it as to stand back from it: one looks at it and sees what it is but refuses to follow its thoughts or run about among the objects it pursues, remaining at the back of the mind quiet and separate; (2) to practise quietude and concentration in this separateness, until the habit of quiet takes hold of the physical mind and replaces the habit of these small activities. This of course takes time and can only come by practice.

*

It is the nature of the physical mind not to believe or accept anything that is supraphysical unless it is enlightened and compelled by the light to do it. Do not identify yourself with this mind, do not consider it as yourself but only as an obscure functioning of Nature. Call down the light into it until it is compelled to believe.

TRANSFORMATION OF THE VITAL

Our evolution has brought the being up out of inconscient Matter into the Ignorance of mind, life and body tempered by an imperfect knowledge and is trying to lead us into the light of the Spirit, to lift us into that light and to bring the light down into us, into body and life as well as mind and heart and to fill with it all that we are. This and its consequences, of which the greatest is the union with the Divine and life in the divine consciousness, is the meaning of the integral transformation. Mind is our present topmost faculty; it is through the thinking mind and the heart with the soul, the psychic being behind them that we have to grow into the Spirit, for what the Force first tries to bring about is to fix the mind in the right central idea, faith or mental attitude and the right aspiration and poise of the heart and to make these sufficiently strong and firm to last in spite of other things in the mind and heart which are other than or in conflict with them. Along with this it brings whatever experiences, realisations or descent or growth of knowledge the mind of the individual is ready for at the time or as much of it, however small, as is necessary for its further progress: sometimes these realisations and experiences are very great and abundant, sometimes few and small or negligible; in some there seems to be in this first stage nothing much of these things or nothing decisive – the Force seems to concentrate on a preparation of the mind only. In many cases the sadhana seems to begin and proceed with experiences in the vital; but in reality this can hardly take place without some mental preparation, even if it is nothing more than a turning of the mind or some kind of opening which makes the vital experiences possible. In any case, to begin with the vital is a hazardous affair; the difficulties there are more numerous and more violent than on the mental plane and the pitfalls are innumerable. The access to the soul, the psychic being is less easy because it is covered up with a thick veil of ego, passion and desire. One is apt to be swallowed up in a maze of vital experiences, not always reliable, the temptation of small siddhis, the appeal of the powers of darkness to the ego. One has to struggle through these densities to the psychic being behind and bring it forward; then only can the sadhana on the vital plane be safe.

However that be, the descent of the sadhana, of the action of the Force into the vital plane of our being becomes after some time necessary. The Force does not make a wholesale change of the mental being and nature, still less an integral transformation before it takes this step: if that could be done, the rest of the sadhana would be comparatively secure and easy. But the vital is there and always pressing on the mind and heart, disturbing and endangering the sadhana and it cannot be left to itself for too long. The ego and desires of the vital, its disturbances and upheavals have to be dealt with and if not at once expelled, at least dominated and prepared for a gradual if not a rapid modification, change, illumination. This can only be done on the vital plane itself by descending to that level. The vital ego itself must become conscious of its own defects and willing to get rid of them; it must decide to throw away its vanities, ambitions, lusts and longings, its rancours and revolts and all the rest of the impure stuff and unclean movements within it. This is the time of the greatest difficulties, revolts and dangers. The vital ego hates being opposed in its desires, resents disappointment, is furious against wounds to its pride and vanity; it does not like the process of purification and it may very well declare Satyagraha against it, refuse to co-operate, justify its own demands and inclinations, offer passive resistance of many kinds, withdraw the vital support which is necessary both to the life and the sadhana and try to withdraw the being from the path of spiritual endeavour. All this has to be faced and overcome, for the temple of the being has to be swept clean if the Lord of our being is to take his place and receive our worship there.

VITAL DISSATISFACTION

Disappointed vital desire must bring about suffering. Pain and suffering are necessary results of the Ignorance in which we live; men grow by all kinds of experience, pain and suffering as well as their opposites, joy and happiness and ecstasy. One can get strength from them if one meets them in the right way. Many take a joy in pain and suffering when associated with struggle or endeavour or adventure, but that is more because of the exhilaration and excitement of the struggle than because of suffering for its own sake. There is, however, something in the vital which takes joy in the whole of life, its dark as well as its bright sides. There is also something perverse in the vital which takes a kind of dramatic pleasure in its own misery and tragedy, even in degradation or in illness.

*

The thing in you which enjoys the suffering and wants it is part of the human vital – it is these things that we describe as the insincerity and perverse twist of the vital; it cries out against sorrow and trouble and accuses the Divine and life and everybody else of torturing it, but for the most part the sorrow and the trouble come and remain because the perverse something in the vital wants them! That element in the vital has to be got rid of altogether.

*

Yes, it is so. Even there is something in the vital consciousness that would not feel at home if there were no suffering in life. It is the physical that fears and abhors suffering, but the vital takes it as part of the play of life.

*

The vital can be all right when things are going on swimmingly, but when difficulties become strong, it sinks and lies supine. Also if a bait is held out to the vital ego, then it can become enthusiastic and active.

*

It is an oscillation due to something in the resistant part (not the whole of it) being still dissatisfied at the call to change. When any vital element is disappointed, dissatisfied, called or compelled to change but not yet willing, it has the tendency to create non-response or non-co-operation of the vital, leaving the physical dull or insensible without the vital push. With the psychic pressure this remnant of resistance will pass.

*

The feeling of the desert comes because of the resistance of the vital which wants life to be governed by desire. If that is not allowed, it regards existence as a desert and puts that impression on the mind.

*

The ordinary freshness, energy, enthusiasm of the nature comes either from the vital, direct when it is satisfying its own instincts and impulses, indirect when it co-operates with or assents to the mental, physical or spiritual activities. If the vital resents, there is revolt and struggles. If the vital no longer insists on its own impulses and instincts but does not co-operate there is either dryness or a neutral state. Dryness comes in when the vital is quiescent but passively unwilling, not interested, the neutral state when it neither assents nor is unwilling, − simply quiescent, passive. This, however, the neutral state can deepen into positive calm and peace by a greater influx from above which keeps the vital not only quiescent but at least passively acquiescent. With the active interest and consent of the vital the peace becomes a glad or joyful peace or a strong peace supporting and entering into action or active experience.

*

There are some who are solid and tenacious in their vital, it is they who can be steady — others are more mercurial and easily moved by impulses, it is these who are sometimes enthusiastic, sometimes drop into fatigue. It is a matter of temperament. On the other hand the mercurial people are often capable of a quicker ardour, so that they can progress fast if they want in their own way. In any case the remedy for all that is to find one's true self above mind and vital and so not bound by temperament.

PURIFICATION OF THE VITAL

The vital is an indispensable instrument — no creation or strong action is possible without it. It is simply a question of mastering it and of converting it into the true vital which is at once strong and calm and capable of great intensity and free from ego.

*

It is through a change in the vital that the deliverance from the blind vital energy must come — by the emergence of the true vital which is strong, wide, at peace, a willing instrument of the Divine and of the Divine alone.

*

The human vital is almost always of that nature, but that is no reason why one should accept it as an unchangeable fact and allow a restless vital to drive one as it likes. Even apart from yoga, in ordinary life, only those are considered to have full manhood or are likely to succeed in their life, their ideals or their undertakings who take in hand this restless vital, concentrate and control it and subject it to discipline. It is by the use of the mental will that they discipline it, compelling it to do not what it wants but what the reason or the will sees to be right or desirable. In yoga one uses the

inner will and compels the vital to submit itself to tapasya so
that it may become calm, strong, obedient – or else one calls
down the calm from above obliging the vital to renounce
desire and become quiet and receptive. The vital is a good
instrument but a bad master. If you allow it to follow its likes
and dislikes, its fancies, its desires, its bad habits, it becomes
your master and peace and happiness are no longer possible.
It becomes not your instrument or the instrument of the
Divine Shakti, but of any force of the Ignorance or even any
hostile force that is able to seize and use it.

*

In the ordinary life people accept the vital movements,
anger, desire, greed, sex, etc. as natural, allowable and
legitimate things, part of the human nature. Only so far as
society discourages them or insists to keep them within fixed
limits or subject to a decent restraint or measure, people try
to control them so as to conform to the social standard of
morality or rule of conduct. Here, on the contrary, as in all
spiritual life, the conquest and complete mastery of these
things is demanded. That is why the struggle is more felt, not
because these things rise more strongly in sadhaks than in
ordinary men, but because of the intensity of the struggle
between the spiritual mind which demands control and the
vital movements which rebel and want to continue in the
new as they did in the old life. As for the idea that the
sadhana raises up things of the kind, the only truth in that is
this that, first, there are many things in the ordinary man of
which he is not conscious, because the vital hides them from
the mind and gratifies them without the mind realising what
is the force that is moving the action – thus things that are
done under the plea of altruism, philanthropy, service, etc.
are largely moved by ego which hides itself behind these
justifications; in yoga the secret motive has to be pulled out
from behind the veil, exposed and got rid of. Secondly,
some things are suppressed in the ordinary life and remain
lying in the nature, suppressed but not eliminated; they may

rise up any day or they may express themselves in various nervous forms or other disorders of the mind or vital or body without it being evident what is their real cause. This has been recently discovered by European psychologists and much emphasised, even exaggerated in a new science called psycho-analysis. Here again, in sadhana one has to become conscious of these suppressed impulses and eliminate them – this may be called rising up, but that does not mean that they have to be raised up into action but only raised up before the consciousness so as to be cleared out of the being.

As for some men being able to control themselves and others being swept away, that is due to difference of temperament. Some men are sattwic and control comes easy to them, up to a certain point at least; others are more rajasic and find control difficult and often impossible. Some have a strong mind and mental will and others are vital men in whom the vital passions are stronger and more on the surface. Some do not think control necessary and let themselves go. In sadhana the mental or moral control has to be replaced by the spiritual mastery – for that mental control is only partial and it controls but does not liberate; it is only the psychic and spiritual that can do that. That is the main difference in this respect between the ordinary and the spiritual life.

*

The exacerbation of certain vital movements is a perfectly well-known phenomenon in yoga and does not mean that one has degenerated, but only that one has come to close grips instead of to a pleasant nodding acquaintance with the basic instincts of the earthly vital nature. I have had myself the experience of this rising to a height, during a certain stage of the spiritual development, of things that before hardly existed and seemed quite absent in the pure yogic life. These things rise up like that because they are fighting for their existence – they are not really personal to you and the vehemence of their attack is not due to any "badness" in the personal nature. I dare say seven sadhaks out of ten have a similar experience. Afterwards when they cannot effect their object which is to drive the sadhak out of his sadhana, the whole thing sinks and there is no longer any vehement trouble. I repeat that the only serious thing about it is the depression created in you and the idea of inability in the yoga that they take care to impress on the brain when they are at their work. If you can get rid of that, the violence of the vital attacks is only the phenomenon of a stage and does not in the end matter.

*

In fact all these ignorant vital movements originate from outside in the ignorant universal Nature; the human being forms in his superficial parts of being, mental, vital, physical, a habit of certain responses to these waves from outside. It is these responses that he takes as his own character (anger, desire, sex etc.) and thinks he cannot be otherwise. But that is not so; he can change. There is another consciousness deeper within him, his true inner being, which is his real self, but is covered over by the superficial nature. This the ordinary man does not know, but the yogi becomes aware of it as he progresses in his sadhana. As the consciousness of this inner being increases by sadhana, the surface nature and its responses are pushed out and can be got rid of altogether. But the ignorant universal Nature does not want to let go and throws the old movements on the sadhak and tries to get them inside again; owing to a habit the superficial nature gives the old responses. If one can get the firm knowledge that these things are from outside and not a real part of oneself, then it is easier for the sadhak to repel such returns, or if they lay hold, he can get rid of them sooner. That is why I say repeatedly that these things rise not in yourself, but from outside.

*

The one thing necessary is to arrive at a fixed and definite choice in the mind which one can always oppose to the vital disturbance. Disturbance in the vital will always come so long as the full peace has not descended there, but with a fixed resolution in the mind kept always to the front the acuteness of the disturbance can disappear and the road become shorter.

*

If you get peace, then to clean the vital becomes easy. If you simply clean and clean and do nothing else, you go very slowly — for the vital gets dirty again and has to be cleaned a hundred times. The peace is something that is clean in itself, so to get it is a positive way of securing your object. To look for dirt only and clean is the negative way.

THE LOWER VITAL

The cardinal defect, that which has been always standing in the way and is now isolated in an extreme prominence, is seated or at least is at present concentrated in the lower vital being. I mean that part of the vital-physical nature with its petty and obstinate egoism which actuates the external human personality, — that which supports its surface thoughts and dominates its habitual ways of feeling, character and action. I am not concerned here with the other parts of the being and I do not speak of anything in the higher mind, the psychic self or the higher and larger vital nature; for, when the lower vital rises, these are pushed into the background, if not covered over for the time, by this lower vital being and this external personality. Whatever there may be in these higher parts, aspiration to the Truth, devotion, or will to conquer the obstacles and the hostile forces, it cannot become integral, it cannot remain unmixed or unspoilt or continue to be effective so long as the lower vital and the external personality have not accepted the Light and consented to change.

It was inevitable that in the course of the sadhana these inferior parts of the nature should be brought forward in order that like the rest of the being they may make the crucial choice and either accept or refuse transformation. My whole work depends upon this movement; it is the decisive ordeal of this yoga. For the physical consciousness and the material life cannot change if this does not change. Nothing that may have been done before, no inner illumination, experience, power or Ananda is of any eventual value, if this is not done. If the little external personality is to persist in retaining its obscure and limited, its petty and ignoble, its selfish and false and stupid human consciousness, this amounts to a flat negation of the work and the sadhana. I have no intention of giving my sanction to a new edition of the old fiasco, a partial and transient spiritual opening within with no true and radical change in the law of the external nature. If, then, any sadhak refuses in practice to admit this change or if he refuses even to admit the necessity for any change of his lower vital being and his habitual external personality, I am entitled to conclude that, whatever his professions, he has not accepted either myself or my yoga. . . .

In the nature the resistance [of the lower vital being] takes certain characteristic forms which add to the confusion and to the difficulty of transformation. It is necessary to outline some of these forms because they are sufficiently common, in some in a less, in others in a greater degree, to demand a strong and clear exposure.

1. A certain vanity and arrogance and self-assertive rajasic vehemence which in this smaller vital being are, for those who have a pronounced strength in these parts, the deformation of the vital force and habit of leading and domination that certain qualities in the higher vital gave them. This is accompanied by an excessive *amour-propre* which creates the necessity of making a figure, maintaining by any means

position and prestige, even of posturing before others, influencing, controlling or "helping" them, claiming the part of a superior sadhak, one with greater knowledge and with occult powers. . . .

2. Disobedience and indiscipline. This lower part of the being is always random, wayward, self-assertive and unwilling to accept the imposition on it of any order and discipline other than its own idea or impulse. Its defects even from the beginning stand in the way of the efforts of the higher vital to impose on the nature a truly regenerating tapasya. . . .

3. Dissimulation and falsity of speech. This is an exceedingly injurious habit of the lower nature. . . .

4. A dangerous habit of constant self-justification. When this becomes strong in the sadhak, it is impossible to turn him in this part of his being to the right consciousness and action because at each step his whole preoccupation is to justify himself. His mind rushes at once to maintain his own idea, his own position or his own course of action. This he is ready to do by any kind of argument, sometimes the most clumsy and foolish or inconsistent with what he has been protesting the moment before, by any kind of mis-statement or any kind of device. This is a common misuse, but none the less a misuse of the thinking mind; but it takes in him exaggerated proportions and so long as he keeps to it, it will be impossible for him to see or live the Truth.

Whatever the difficulties of the nature, however long and painful the process of dealing with them, they cannot stand to the end against the Truth, if there is or if there comes in these parts the true spirit, attitude and endeavour. But if a sadhak continues out of self-esteem and self-will or out of tamasic inertia to shut his eyes or harden his heart against the Light, so long as he does that, no one can help him. The consent of all the being is necessary for the divine change, and it is the completeness and fulness of the consent that constitutes the integral surrender. But the consent of the lower vital must not be only a mental profession or a passing emotional adhesion; it must translate itself into an abiding attitude and a persistent and consistent action.

This yoga can only be done to the end by those who are in total earnest about it and ready to abolish their little human ego and its demands in order to find themselves in the Divine. It cannot be done in a spirit of levity or laxity; the work is too high and difficult, the adverse powers in the lower Nature too ready to take advantage of the least sanction or the smallest opening, the aspiration and tapasya needed too constant and intense. It cannot be done if there is a petulant self-assertion of the ideas of the human mind or wilful indulgence of the demands and instincts and pretensions of the lowest part of the being, commonly justified under the name of human nature. It cannot be done if you insist on identifying these lowest things of the Ignorance with the divine Truth or even the lesser truth permissible on the way. It cannot be done if you cling to your past self and its old mental, vital and physical formations and habits; one has continually to leave behind his past selves and to see, act and live from an always higher and higher conscious level. It cannot be done if you insist on "freedom" for your human mind and vital ego. All the parts of the human being are entitled to express and satisfy themselves in their own way at their own risk and peril, if he so chooses, as long as he leads the ordinary life. But to enter into a path of yoga whose whole object is to substitute for these human things the law and power of a greater Truth and the whole heart of whose method is surrender to the Divine Shakti, and yet to go on claiming this so-called freedom, which is no more than a subjection to certain ignorant cosmic Forces, is to indulge in a blind contradiction and to claim the right to lead a double life.

Least of all can this yoga be done if those who profess to be its sadhaks continue always to make themselves centres, instruments or spokesmen of the forces of the Ignorance which oppose, deny and ridicule its very principle and object. On one side there is the supramental realisation, the overshadowing and descending power of the supramental

Divine, the light and force of a far greater Truth than any yet realised on the earth, something therefore beyond what the little human mind and its logic regard as the only permanent realities, something whose nature and way and process of development here it cannot conceive or perceive by its own inadequate instruments or judge by its puerile standards; in spite of all opposition this is pressing down for manifestation in the physical consciousness and the material life. On the other side is this lower vital nature with all its pretentious arrogance, ignorance, obscurity, dullness or incompetent turbulence, standing for its own prolongation, standing against the descent, refusing to believe in any real reality or real possibility of a supramental or superhuman consciousness and creation, or, still more absurd, demanding, if it exists at all, that it should conform to its own little standards, seizing greedily upon everything that seems to disprove it, denying the presence of the Divine, – for it knows that without that presence the work is impossible, – affirming loudly its own thoughts, judgments, desires, instincts, and, if these are contradicted, avenging itself by casting abroad doubt, denial, disparaging criticism, revolt and disorder. These are the two things now in presence between which everyone will have to choose.

For this opposition, this sterile obstruction and blockade against the descent of the divine Truth cannot last for ever. Every one must come down finally on one side or the other, on the side of the Truth or against it. The supramental realisation cannot coexist with the persistence of the lower Ignorance; it is incompatible with continued satisfaction in a double nature.

*

There is only one way of escape from this siege of the lower vital nature. It is the entire rejection of all egoistic vital demand, claim and desire and the replacement of the dissatisfied vital urge by the purity of psychic aspiration. Not the satisfaction of these vital clamours nor, either, an ascetic retirement is the true solution, but the surrender of the vital being to the Divine and a single-minded consecration to the supreme Truth into which desire and demand cannot enter. For the nature of the supreme Truth is Light and Ananda, and where desire and demand are there can be no Ananda.

It is not the vital demand but the psychic urge that alone can bring the nature towards the supramental transformation; for it alone can change the mental and vital and show them their own true movement.

*

Sometimes the aspiration is felt at the navel, but that is part of the larger vital. The lower vital is below. The lower vital aspires by offering all its small movements in the fire of purification, by calling for the light and power to descend into it and rid it of its little greeds, jealousies, resistances and revolts over small matters, angers, vanities, sexualities etc. to be replaced by the right movements governed by selflessness, purity, obedience to the urge of the Divine Force in all things.

TRANSFORMATION OF THE PHYSICAL

A time comes when after a long preparation of the mind and vital being, it becomes necessary to open also the physical nature. But when that happens very often the vital exaltation which can be very great when the experience is on its own plane, falls away and the obscure obstructive physical and gross material consciousness appears in its unrelieved inertia. Inertia, tamas, stupidity, narrowness and limitation, an inability to progress, doubt, dullness, dryness, a constant forgetfulness of the spiritual experiences received are the characteristics of the unregenerated physical nature, when that is not pushed by the vital and is not supported either by the higher mental will and intelligence. This seems to be in part what has temporarily happened to you; but the way out is not to excite the physical by any vital revolt and outcry, or to blame for your condition either circumstances or the Mother, — for that will only make things worse and increase the tamas, dryness, dullness, inertia, — but to recognise that there is here an element of the universal Nature reflected in yours, which you must eliminate. And this can only be done by more and more surrender and aspiration and by so bringing in from beyond the vital and the mind the divine peace, light, power and presence. This is the only way towards the transformation and fulfilment of the physical nature.

*

It is always the effect of the physical consciousness being uppermost (so long as it is not entirely changed) that one feels like this — like an ordinary man or worse, altogether in the outer consciousness, the inner consciousness veiled, the action of yoga power apparently suspended. This happens in the earlier stages also, but it is not quite complete usually then because something of the mind and vital is active in the physical still, or even if the interruption of sadhana is complete, it does not last long and so one does not so much notice it. But when from the mental and vital stage of the yoga one comes down into the physical, this condition which is native to the physical consciousness fully manifests and is persistent for long periods. It happens because one has to come down and deal with this part directly by entering into it, — for if that is not done, there can be no complete change of the nature. What has to be done is to understand that it is a stage and to persist in the faith that it will be overcome. If this is done, then it will be easier for the Force, working behind the veil at first, then in front to bring out the yoga consciousness into this outer physical shell and make it luminous and responsive. If one keeps steadily the faith and quietude, then this can be more quickly done — if the faith gets eclipsed or the quietude disturbed by the long difficulty, then it takes longer but even then it will be done; for, though not felt, the Force is there at work. It can only be prevented if one breaks away or throws up the sadhana, because one becomes too impatient of the difficulty to go through with it. That is the one thing that should never be done.

*

This negation is the very nature of the physical resistance and the physical resistance is the whole base of the denial of the Divine in the world. All in the physical is persistent, obstinate, with a massive force of negation and inertia — if it were not so, sadhana would be extremely cursory. You have to face this character of the physical resistance and conquer it however often it may rise. It is the price of the transformation of the earth-consciousness.

*

It [the use of violence for the change of the physical] was done by some people, but I don't believe in its usefulness. No doubt the physical is an obstinate obstacle, but it must be enlightened, persuaded, pressed even to change, but not oppressed or violently driven. People use violence with the mind, vital, body because they are in a hurry, but my own observation has always been that it leads to more reactions and hindrances and not to a genuinely sound advance.

*

It is only by a more constant dynamic force descending into an unalterable equality and peace that the physical nature's normal tendency can be eradicated.

The normal tendency of the physical nature is to be inert and in its inertia to respond only to the ordinary vital forces, not to the higher forces. If one has a perfect equality and peace then one can be unaffected by the spreading of the inertia and bring down into it gradually or quickly the same peace with a force of the higher consciousness which can alter it. When that is there there can be no longer the difficulty and fluctuations with a preponderance of inertia such as now you are having.

*

The first means is not to get upset when it [inertia] comes or when it stays. The second is to detach yourself, not only yourself above but yourself below and not identify. The third is to reject everything that is raised by the inertia and not regard it as your own or accept it at all.

If you can do these things then there will be something in you that remains perfectly quiet even in the greatest inertia. Through that quiet part you can bring down peace, force, even light and knowledge into the inertia itself.

*

The physical sadhana is to bring down the higher light and power and peace and Ananda into the body consciousness, to get rid of the inertia of the physical, the doubts, limitations, external tendency of the physical mind, the defective energies of the vital physical (nerves) and bring in instead the true consciousness there so that the physical may be a perfect instrument for the Divine Will. The food and care for the body is only to get it into good condition, afterwards it would not be necessary to attend to such things.

TRANSFORMATION OF THE SUBCONSCIENT

So long as there is not the supramental change down to the subconscient, complete and full, the lower nature has always a hold on some part of the being.

*

As there is a superconscient (something above our present consciousness) above the head from which the higher consciousness comes down into the body, so there is also a subconscient (something below our consciousness) below the feet. Matter is under the control of this power, because it is that out of which it has been created – that is why matter seems to us to be quite unconscious. The material body is very much under the influence of this power for the same reason; it is why we are not conscious of what is going on in the body, for the most part. The outer consciousness goes down into this subconscient when we are asleep, and so it becomes unaware of what is going on in us when we are asleep except for a few dreams. Many of these dreams rise up from the subconscient and are made up of old memories, impressions etc. put together in an incoherent way. For the subconscient receives impressions of all we do or experience in our lives and keeps these impressions in it, sending up often fragments of them in sleep. It is a very important part of the being, but we can do nothing much with it by the conscious will. It is the higher Force working in us that in its natural course will open the subconscient to itself and bring down into it its control and light.

*

The subconscient is a dark and ignorant region, so that it is natural that the obscurer movements of the Nature should have more power there. It is so indeed with all the lower parts of the nature from the lower vital downwards. But it does send up good things also though more rarely. It has in the course of the sadhana to be illumined and made a support of the higher consciousness in the physical nature instead of a basis of the instinctive lower movements.

*

The subconscient is to be penetrated by the light and made a sort of bed-rock of truth, a store of right impressions, right physical responses to the Truth. Strictly speaking, it will not be subconscient at all, but a sort of bank of true values held ready for use.

THE SUBCONSCIENT AND PSYCHOANALYSIS

I find it difficult to take these psycho-analysts at all seriously when they try to scrutinise spiritual experience by the flicker of their torch-lights, — yet perhaps one ought to, for half-knowledge is a powerful thing and can be a great obstacle to the coming in front of the true Truth. This new psychology looks to me very much like children learning some summary and not very adequate alphabet, exulting in putting their a-b-c-d of the subconscient and the mysterious underground super-ego together and imagining that their first book of obscure beginnings (c-a-t cat, t-r-e-e tree) is the very heart of the real knowledge. They look from down up and explain the higher lights by the lower obscurities; but the foundation of these things is above and not below, *upari budhna esām.* The superconscient, not the subconscient, is the true foundation of things. The significance of the lotus is not to be found by analysing the secrets of the mud from which it grows here; its secret is to be found in the heavenly archetype of the lotus that blooms for ever in the Light above. The self-chosen field of these psychologists is besides poor, dark and limited; you must know the whole before you can know the part and the highest before you can truly understand the lowest. That is the promise of the greater psychology awaiting its hour before which these poor gropings will disappear and come to nothing.

*

Your practice of psycho-analysis was a mistake. It has, for the time at least, made the work of purification more complicated, not easier. The psycho-analysis of Freud is the last thing that one should associate with yoga. It takes up a certain part, the darkest, the most perilous, the unhealthiest part of the nature, the lower vital subconscious layer, isolates some of its most morbid phenomena and attributes to it and them an action out of all proportion to its true role in the nature. Modern psychology is an infant science, at once rash, fumbling and crude. As in all infant sciences, the universal habit of the human mind – to take a partial or local truth, generalise it unduly and try to explain a whole field of Nature in its narrow terms – runs riot here. Moreover, the exaggeration of the importance of suppressed sexual complexes is a dangerous falsehood and it can have a nasty influence and tend to make the mind and vital more and not less fundamentally impure than before.

It is true that the subliminal in man is the largest part of his nature and has in it the secret of the unseen dynamisms which explain his surface activities. But the lower vital subconscious which is all that this psycho-analysis of Freud seems to know, – and even of that it knows only a few ill-lit corners, – is no more than a restricted and very inferior portion of the subliminal whole. The subliminal self stands behind and supports the whole superficial man; it has in it a larger and more efficient mind behind the surface mind, a larger and more powerful vital behind the surface vital, a subtler and freer physical consciousness behind the surface bodily existence. And above them it opens to higher super-conscient as well as below them to lower subconscient ranges. If one wishes to purify and transform the nature, it is the power of these higher ranges to which one must open and raise to them and change by them both the subliminal and the surface being. Even this should be done with care, not prematurely or rashly, following a higher guidance, keeping always the right attitude; for otherwise the force that is drawn down may be too strong for an obscure and weak frame of nature. But to begin by opening up the lower subconscious, risking to raise up all that is foul or obscure in it, is to go out of one's way to invite trouble. First, one should make the higher mind and vital strong and firm and full of light and peace from above; afterwards one can open up or even dive into the subconscious with more safety and some chance of a rapid and successful change.

The system of getting rid of things by *anubhava* can also

be a dangerous one; for on this way one can easily become more entangled instead of arriving at freedom. This method has behind it two well-known psychological motives. One, the motive of purposeful exhaustion, is valid only in some cases, especially when some natural tendency has too strong a hold or too strong a drive in it to be got rid of by *vicāra* or by the process of rejection and the substitution of the true movement in its place; when that happens in excess, the sadhak has sometimes even to go back to the ordinary action of the ordinary life, get the true experience of it with a new mind and will behind and then return to the spiritual life with the obstacle eliminated or else ready for elimination. But this method of purposive indulgence is always dangerous, though sometimes inevitable. It succeeds only when there is a very strong will in the being towards realisation; for then indulgence brings a strong dissatisfaction and reaction, *vairāgya*, and the will towards perfection can be carried down into the recalcitrant part of the nature.

The other motive for *anubhava* is of a more general applicability; for in order to reject anything from the being one has first to become conscious of it, to have the clear inner experience of its action and to discover its actual place in the workings of the nature. One can then work upon it to eliminate it, if it is an entirely wrong movement, or to transform it if it is only the degradation of a higher and true movement. It is this or something like it that is attempted crudely and improperly with a rudimentary and insufficient knowledge in the system of psycho-analysis. The process of raising up the lower movements into the full light of consciousness in order to know and deal with them is inevitable; for there can be no complete change without it. But it can truly succeed only when a higher light and force are sufficiently at work to overcome, sooner or later, the force of the tendency that is held up for change. Many, under the pretext of *anubhava*, not only raise up the adverse movement, but support it with their consent instead of rejecting it, find justifications for continuing or repeating it and so go on playing with it, indulging its return, eternising it; afterwards when they want to get rid of it, it has got such a hold that they find themselves helpless in its clutch and only a terrible struggle or an intervention of divine grace can liberate them. Some do this out of a vital twist or perversity, others out of sheer ignorance; but in yoga, as in life, ignorance is not accepted by Nature as a justifying excuse. This danger is there in all improper dealings with the ignorant parts of the nature; but none is more ignorant, more perilous, more unreasoning and obstinate in recurrence than the lower vital subconscious and its movements. To raise it up prematurely or improperly for *anubhava* is to risk suffusing the conscious parts also with its dark and dirty stuff and thus poisoning the whole vital and even the mental nature. Always therefore one should begin by a positive, not a negative experience, by bringing down something of the divine nature, calm, light, equanimity, purity, divine strength into the parts of the conscious being that have to be changed; only when that has been sufficiently done and there is a firm positive basis, is it safe to raise up the concealed subconscious adverse elements in order to destroy and eliminate them by the strength of the divine calm, light, force and knowledge.

*

If you go down into your lower parts or ranges of nature, you must be always careful to keep a vigilant connection with the higher already regenerated levels of the consciousness and to bring down the Light and Purity through them into these nether still unregenerated regions. If there is not this vigilance, one gets absorbed in the unregenerated movement of the inferior layers and there is obscuration and trouble.

The safest way is to remain in the higher part of the consciousness and put a pressure from it on the lower to change. It can be done in this way, only you must get the knack and the habit of it. If you achieve the power to do that, it makes the progress much easier, smoother and less painful.

THE INCONSCIENT

There is another cause of the general inability to change which at present afflicts the sadhak. It is because the sadhana, as a general fact, has now and for a long time past come down to the Inconscient; the pressure, the call is to change in that part of the nature which depends directly on the Inconscient, the fixed habits, the automatic movements, the mechanical repetitions of the nature, the involuntary reactions to life, all that seems to belong to the fixed character of a man. This has to be done if there is to be any chance of a total spiritual change. The Force (generally and not individually) is working to make that possible, its pressure is for that,— for, on the other levels, the change has already been made possible (not, mind you, assured to everybody). But to open the Inconscient to light is a herculean task; change on the other levels is much easier. As yet this work has only begun and it is not surprising that there seems to be no change in things or people. It will come in time, but not in a hurry.

*

The extreme acuteness of your difficulties is due to the yoga having come down against the bed-rock of Inconscience which is the fundamental basis of all resistance in the individual and in the world to the victory of the Spirit and the Divine Work that is leading toward that victory. The difficulties themselves are general in the Ashram as well as in the outside world. Doubt, discouragement, diminution or loss of faith, waning of the vital enthusiasm for the ideal, perplexity and a baffling of the hope for the future are the common features of the difficulty. In the world outside there are much worse symptoms such as the general increase of cynicism, a refusal to believe in anything at all, a decrease of honesty, an immense corruption, a preoccupation with food, money, comfort, pleasure, to the exclusion of higher things,

and a general expectation of worse and worse things awaiting the world. All that, however acute, is a temporary
phenomenon for which those who know anything about the
workings of the world-energy and the workings of the Spirit
were prepared. I myself foresaw that this worst would come,
the darkness of night before the dawn; therefore I am not
discouraged. I know what is preparing behind the darkness
and can see and feel the first signs of its coming. Those who
seek for the Divine have to stand firm and persist in their
seeking; after a time, the darkness will fade and begin to
disappear and the Light will come.

10

Difficulties in Transforming the Nature

THE RESISTANCE OF THE NATURE

It is a mistake to think that any path of yoga is facile, that any is a royal road or short cut to the Divine, or that there can be, like a system of "French made easy" or "French without tears", also a system of "yoga made easy" or "yoga without tears". A few great souls prepared by past lives or otherwise lifted beyond the ordinary spiritual capacity may attain realisation more swiftly; some may have uplifting experiences at an early stage, but for most the *siddhi* of the path, whatever it is, must be the end of a long, difficult and persevering endeavour. One cannot have the crown of spiritual victory without the struggle or reach the heights without the ascent and its labour. Of all it can be said, "Difficult is that road, hard to tread like the edge of a razor."

*

When the soul draws towards the Divine, there may be a resistance in the mind and the common form of that is denial and doubt – which may create mental and vital suffering. There may again be a resistance in the vital nature whose principal character is desire and the attachment to the objects of desire, and if in this field there is conflict between the soul and the vital nature, between the Divine Attraction and the pull of the Ignorance, then obviously there may be much suffering of the mind and vital parts. The physical consciousness also may offer a resistance which is usually that of a fundamental inertia, an obscurity in the very stuff of the physical, an incomprehension, an inability to respond to the higher consciousness, a habit of helplessly responding to the lower mechanically, even when it does not want to do so; both vital and physical suffering may be the consequence. There is, moreover, the resistance of the Universal Nature which does not want the being to escape from the Ignorance into the Light. This may take the form of a vehement insistence in the continuation of the old movements, waves of them thrown on the mind and vital and body so that old ideas, impulses, desires, feelings, responses continue even after they are thrown out and rejected, and can return like an invading army from outside, until the whole nature, given to the Divine, refuses to admit them. This is the subjective form of the universal resistance, but it may also take an objective form, — opposition, calumny, attacks, persecution, misfortunes of many kinds, adverse conditions and circumstances, pain, illness, assaults from men or forces. There too the possibility of suffering is evident. There are two ways to meet all that — first that of the Self, calm, equality, a spirit, a will, a mind, a vital, a physical consciousness that remain resolutely turned towards the Divine and unshaken by all suggestion of doubt, desire, attachment, depression, sorrow, pain, inertia. This is possible when the inner being awakens, when one becomes conscious of the Self, of the inner Mind, the inner Vital, the inner Physical, for that can more easily attune itself to the divine Will, and then there is a division in the being as if there were two beings, one within, calm, strong, equal, unperturbed, a channel of the Divine Consciousness and Force, one without still encroached on by the lower Nature; but then the disturbances of the latter become something superficial which are no more than an outer ripple, — until these under the inner pressure fade and sink away and the outer being too remains calm, concentrated, unattackable. There is also the way of the psychic, — when the psychic being comes out in its inherent power, its consecration, adoration, love of the Divine, self-giving, surrender and imposes these on the mind, vital and physical consciousness and compels them to turn all their movements Godward. If the psychic is strong and master throughout, then there is no or little subjective suffering and the objective cannot affect either the soul or the other parts of the consciousness – the way is sunlit and a great joy and sweetness are the note of the whole sadhana. As for the outer attacks and adverse circumstances, that depends on the action of the Force transforming the relations of the being with the outer Nature; as the victory of the Force proceeds, they will be eliminated; but however long they last, they cannot impede the sadhana, for then even adverse things and happenings become a means for its advance and for the growth of the spirit.

DIFFICULTIES AND DEPRESSION

All who enter the spiritual path have to face the difficulties and ordeals of the path, those which rise from their own nature and those which come in from outside. The difficulties in the nature always rise again and again till you overcome them; they must be faced with both strength and patience. But the vital part is prone to depression when ordeals and difficulties rise. This is not peculiar to you, but comes to all sadhaks – it does not imply an unfitness for the sadhana or justify a sense of helplessness. But you must train yourself to overcome this reaction of depression, calling in the Mother's Force to aid you.

All who cleave to the path steadfastly can be sure of their spiritual destiny. If anyone fails to reach it, it can only be for one of the two reasons, either because they leave the path or because for some lure of ambition, vanity, desire, etc. they go astray from the sincere dependence on the Divine.

*

Thirst for the Divine is one thing and depression is quite another, nor is depression a necessary consequence of the thirst being unsatisfied, that may lead to a more ardent thirst or to a fixed resolution and persistent effort or to a more yearning call or to a psychic sorrow which is not at all identical with depression and despair. Depression is a clouded grey state in its nature and it is more difficult for light to come through clouds and greyness than through a clear atmosphere. That depression obstructs the inner light is a matter of general experience. The Gita says expressly, "Yoga should be practised persistently with a heart free from depression" – *anirvinnacetasā*. Bunyan in *The Pilgrim's Progress* symbolises it as the Slough of Despond, one of the perils of the way that has to be overcome. It is, no doubt, impossible to escape from attacks of depression, almost all sadhaks go through these attacks, but the principle is that one should react against them and not allow them by any kind of mental encouragement or acceptance of their suggestions to persist or grow chronic.

*

The rule in yoga is not to let the depression depress you, to stand back from it, observe its cause and remove the cause; for the cause is always in oneself, perhaps a vital defect somewhere, a wrong movement indulged or a petty desire causing a recoil, sometimes by its satisfaction, sometimes by its disappointment. In yoga a desire satisfied, a false movement given its head produces very often a worse recoil than disappointed desire.

What is needed for you is to live more deeply within, less in the outer vital and mental part which is exposed to these touches. The inmost psychic being is not oppressed by them; it stands in its own closeness to the Divine and sees the small surface movements as surface things foreign to the true Being.

*

All depression is bad as it lowers the consciousness, spends the energy, opens to adverse forces.

*

Never allow this idea "I am not able", "I am not doing enough" to come and vex you; it is a tamasic suggestion and brings depression and depression opens the way to the attacks of the wrong forces. Your position should be, "Let me do what I can; the Mother's force is there, the Divine is there to see that in due time all will be done."

*

When I spoke of being faithful to the light of the soul and the divine Call, I was not referring to anything in the past or to any lapse on your part. I was simply affirming the great need in all crises and attacks, — to refuse to listen to any suggestions, impulses, lures and to oppose to them all the call of the Truth, the imperative beckoning of the Light. In all doubt and depression, to say, "I belong to the Divine, I cannot fail"; to all suggestions of impurity and unfitness, to reply, "I am a child of Immortality chosen by the Divine; I have but to be true to myself and to Him — the victory is sure; even if I fell, I would rise again"; to all impulses to depart and serve some smaller ideal, to reply, "This is the greatest, this is the Truth that alone can satisfy the soul within me; I will endure through all tests and tribulations to the very end of the divine journey". This is what I mean by faithfulness to the Light and the Call.

THE SUNLIT PATH

Fits of depression and darkness and despair are a tradition in the path of Sadhana — in all Yogas, oriental or occidental, they seem to have been the rule. I know all about them myself — but my experience has led me to the perception that they are an unnecessary tradition and could be dispensed with if one chose. That is why whenever they come in you or others I try to lift up before them the gospel of faith. If still they come, one has to get through them as soon as possible and get back into the sun.

*

The change noted by X evidently indicates a great progress in the vital and physical being. There is nothing spiritually wrong in being glad and cheerful, on the contrary it is the right thing. As for struggles and aspiration, struggles are really not indispensable to progress and there are many people who get so habituated to the struggling attitude that they have all the time struggles and very little else. That is not desirable. There is a sunlit path as well as a gloomy one and it is the better of the two – a path in which one goes forward in absolute reliance on the Mother, fearing nothing, sorrowing over nothing. Aspiration is needed but there can be a sunlit aspiration full of light and faith and confidence and joy. If difficulty comes, even that can be faced with a smile.

*

The sunlit path can only be followed if the psychic is constantly or usually in front or if one has a natural spirit of faith and surrender or a face turned habitually towards the sun or psychic predisposition (e.g. a faith in one's spiritual destiny) or, if one has acquired the psychic turn. That does not mean that the sunlit man has no difficulties; he may have many, but he regards them cheerfully as "all in the day's work". If he gets a bad beating, he is capable of saying, "Well, that was a queer go but the Divine is evidently in a queer mood and if that is his way of doing things, it must be the right one; I am surely a still queerer fellow myself and that, I suppose, was the only means of putting me right." But everybody can't be of that turn, and surrender which would put everything right is, as you say, difficult. At least it is difficult to do completely. That is why we do not insist on total surrender at once, but are satisfied with a little to begin with, the rest to grow as it can.

DETACHMENT FROM DIFFICULTIES

It is inevitable that doubts and difficulties should arise in so arduous an undertaking as the transformation of the normal nature of man into the spiritual nature, the replacement of his system of externalised values and surface experience into profounder inner values and experience. But the doubts and difficulties cannot be overcome by giving them their full force; it can be rather done by learning to stand back from them and to refuse to be carried away; then there is a chance of the still small voice from within getting itself heard and pushing out these louder clamorous voices and movements from outside. It is the light from within that you have to make room for; the light of the outer mind is quite insufficient for the discovery of the inner values or to judge the truth of spiritual experience.

*

The thing is that it is unavoidable in the course of the sadhana that some parts of the being should be less open, less advanced, as yet less aware of the Peace and Force, less intimate to them than others. These parts have to be worked upon, and changed, but this can be done smoothly only if you are detached from them, able to regard them as not your very self, even though a part of the nature you have to change. Then when they appear with their defects, you will not be upset, not carried away by their movements, lost to the sense of the Peace and Force; you will be able to work on them (or rather let the Force work) as one would on a machine that has to be repaired or a work that has defects and has to be done better this time. If you identify yourself with these parts, then it is very troublesome. The work will still be done, the change made, but with delay, with bad upsettings, in a painful and not in a smooth way. That is why we always tell people to be calm and detached and look upon these things not as their true selves but as an outer part that has to be worked upon quietly until it is what it should be.

*

Suggestions come to all, even to the greatest sadhaks or to the Avatars – as they came to Buddha or Christ. Obstacles are there – they are part of Nature and they have to be overcome. What has to be attained is not to accept the suggestions, not to admit them as the truth or as one's own thoughts, to see them for what they are and keep oneself separate. Obstacles have to be looked at as something wrong in the machinery of human nature which has to be changed – they should not be regarded as sins or wrong-doings which make one despair of oneself and of the sadhana.

THE POSITIVE SIDE OF THE SADHANA

It is a mistake to dwell too much on the lower nature and its obstacles, which is the negative side of the sadhana. They have to be seen and purified, but preoccupation with them as the one important thing is not helpful. The positive side of experience of the descent is the more important thing. If one waits for the lower nature to be purified entirely and for all time before calling down the positive experience, one might have to wait for ever. It is true that the more the lower nature is purified, the easier is the descent of the higher Nature, but it is also and more true that the more the higher Nature descends, the more the lower is purified. Neither the complete purification nor the permanent and perfect manifestation can come all at once, it is a matter of time and patient progress. The two (purification and manifestation) go on progressing side by side and become more and more strong to play into each other's hands — that is the usual course of the sadhana.

*

The negative means [of purification] are not evil; they are useful for their object which is to get away from life. But from the positive point of view, they are disadvantageous, because they get rid of the powers of the being instead of divinising them for the transformation of life.

*

By negative I mean merely repressing the desires and wrong movements and egoism, by positive I mean the bringing down of light and peace and purity in those parts from above. I do not mean that these movements are not to be rejected — but all the energy should not be used solely for rejection. It must also be directed to the positive replacement of them by the higher consciousness. The more this consciousness comes, the easier also will the rejection be.

*

It is necessary to observe and know the wrong movements in you; for they are the source of your trouble and have to be persistently rejected if you are to be free.

But do not be always thinking of your defects and wrong movements. Concentrate more upon what you are to be, on the ideal, with the faith that, since it is the goal before you, it must and will come.

To be always observing faults and wrong movements brings depression and discourages the faith. Turn your eyes more to the coming light and less to any immediate darkness. Faith, cheerfulness, confidence in the ultimate victory are the things that help, — they make the progress easier and swifter.

Make more of the good experiences that come to you; one experience of the kind is more important than the lapses and failures. When it ceases, do not repine or allow yourself to be discouraged, but be quiet within and aspire for its renewal in a stronger form leading to a still deeper and fuller experience.

Aspire always, but with more quietude, opening yourself to the Divine simply and wholly.

DIFFICULTIES DUE TO THE HOSTILE FORCES

It is a fact always known to all yogis and occultists since the beginning of time, in Europe and Africa as in India, that wherever yoga or Yajna is done, there the hostile Forces gather together to stop it by any means. It is known that there is a lower nature and a higher spiritual nature – it is known that they pull different ways and the lower is strongest at first and the higher afterwards. It is known that the hostile Forces take advantage of the movements of the lower nature and try to spoil through them, smash or retard the siddhi. It has been said as long ago as the Upanishads (hard is the path to tread, sharp like a razor's edge); it was said later by Christ 'hard is the way and narrow the gate by which one enters into the kingdom of heaven' and also 'many are called, few chosen' – because of these difficulties. But it has also always been known that those who are sincere and faithful in heart and remain so and those who rely on the Divine will arrive in spite of all difficulties, stumbles or falls.

*

The mere intensity of the force does not show that it is a bad power; the Divine Force often works with a great intensity. Everything depends on the nature of the force and its working: what does it do, what seems to be its purpose? If it works to purify or open the system, or brings with it light or peace, or prepares the change of the thought, ideas, feelings, character in the sense of a turning towards a higher consciousness, then it is the right force. If it is dark or obscure or perturbs the being with rajasic or egoistic suggestions or excites the lower nature, then it is an adverse force.

*

The lower nature is ignorant and undivine, not in itself hostile but shut to the Light and Truth. The hostile forces are anti-divine, not merely undivine; they make use of the lower nature, pervert it, fill it with distorted movements and by that means influence man and even try to enter and possess or at least entirely control him.

*

The normal resistance of the lower Nature in human beings and the action of the Hostiles are two quite different things. The former is natural and occurs in everybody; the latter is an intervention from the non-human world. But this intervention can come in two forms. (1) They use and press on the lower Nature forces making them resist where they would otherwise be quiescent, making the resistance strong or violent where it would be otherwise slight or moderate, exaggerating its violence when it is violent. There is besides a malignant cleverness, a conscious plan and combination when the Hostiles act on these forces which is not evident in the normal resistance of the forces. (2) They sometimes invade with their own forces. When this happens there is often a temporary possession or at least an irresistible influence which makes the thoughts, feelings, actions of the person abnormal – a black clouding of the brain, a whirl in the vital, all acts as if the person could not help himself and were drawn by an overmastering force. On the other hand instead of a possession there may be only a strong Influence; then the symptoms are less marked, but it is easy for anyone acquainted with the ways of these forces to see what has happened. Finally it may be only an attack, not possession or influence; the person then is separate, is not overcome, resists.

There are some who are never touched by the hostile forces.

ATTACK BY THE HOSTILE FORCES

The hostile forces have a certain self-chosen function: it is to test the condition of the individual, of the work, of the earth itself and their readiness for the spiritual descent and fulfilment. At every step of the journey, they are there attacking furiously, criticising, suggesting, imposing despondency or inciting to revolt, raising unbelief, amassing difficulties. No doubt, they put a very exaggerated interpretation on the rights given them by their function, making mountains even out of what seems to us a mole-hill. A little trifling false step or mistake and they appear on the road and clap a whole Himalaya as a barrier across it. But this opposition has been permitted from of old not merely as a test or ordeal, but as a compulsion on us to seek a greater strength, a more perfect self-knowledge, an intenser purity and force of aspiration, a faith that nothing can crush, a more powerful descent of the Divine Grace.

*

This yoga is a spiritual battle; its very attempt raises all sorts of adverse forces and one must be ready to face difficulties, sufferings, reverses of all sorts in a calm unflinching spirit.

The difficulties that come are ordeals and tests and if one meets them in the right spirit, one comes out stronger and spiritually purer and greater.

No misfortune can come, the adverse forces cannot touch or be victorious unless there is some defect in oneself, some impurity, weakness or, at the very least, ignorance. One should then seek out this weakness in oneself and correct it.

When there is an attack from the human instruments of adverse forces, one should try to overcome it not in a spirit of personal hatred or anger or wounded egoism, but with a calm spirit of strength and equanimity and a call to the Divine Force to act. Success or failure lies with the Divine.

*

About the attacks and the action of the cosmic forces — these attacks very ordinarily become violent when the progress is becoming rapid and on the way to be definite — especially if they find they cannot carry out an effective aggression into the inner being, they try to shake by outside assaults. One must take it as a trial of strength, a call for gathering all one's capacities of calm and openness to the Light and Power, so as to make oneself an instrument for the victory of the Divine over the undivine, of the Light over the darkness in the world-tangle. It is in this spirit that you must face these difficulties till the higher things are so confirmed in you that these forces can attack no longer.

*

The hostiles when they cannot break the yoga by positive means, by positive temptations or vital outbreaks, are quite willing to do it negatively; first by depression, then by refusal at once of ordinary life and of sadhana.

*

One must not get into the habit of a state in which one is always in a struggle with suggestions and forces. People very easily fall into this and make it a habit — the vital part takes a sort of glowing satisfaction in crying out "I am attacked, overborne, suffering, miserable! How tragic is my fate! Why do you not help, O Divine? There is no help, nor Divine Grace? I am left to my misery and downfall etc. etc. etc." I do not want one more sadhak to fall into this condition – that is why I am calling Halt! before you get entangled into this kind of habit of constant struggle. It is what these forces want – to make you feel helpless, defeated, overcome. You must not allow it.

*

How can you have peace and quiet when you are always thinking of "lower forces" and "attacks" and "possessions" etc.? If you can look at things naturally and quietly, then only you can have quiet and peace.

*

There are two things that make it impossible for them [the hostile forces] to succeed even temporarily in any attack on the mind or the vital – first, an entire love, devotion and confidence that nothing can shake, secondly, a calm and equality in the vital as well as in the mind which has become the fundamental character of the inner nature. Suggestions then may still come, things go wrong outside, but the being remains invulnerable. Either of these two things is sufficient in itself – and in proportion as they grow, even the existence of the hostile forces becomes less and less of a phenomenon of the inner life – though they may still be there in the outer atmosphere.

POSSESSION BY THE HOSTILE FORCES

The Asuras and Rakshasas etc. do not belong to the earth, but to supraphysical worlds; but they act upon the earth-life and dispute the control of human life and character and action with the Gods. They are the Powers of Darkness combating the Powers of Light.

Sometimes they possess men in order to act through them, sometimes they take birth in a human body. When their use in the play is over, they will either change or disappear or no longer seek to intervene in the earth-play.

*

Epilepsy is not possession – it is an attack or at most a temporary seizure. Insanity always indicates possession. The hereditary conditions create a predisposition. It is not possible for a vital Force or Being to invade or take possession unless there are doors open for it to enter. The door may be a vital consent or affinity or a physical defect in the being.

*

Those who fall into insanity have lost the true touch and got into the wrong contact. It is due either to some impurity and unspiritual desire with which the seeker enters into the way or some insincerity, egoism and false attitude or to some weakness in the brain or nervous system which cannot bear the Power it has called down into it.

*

I must say however that it is not the push for union with the Divine nor is it the Divine Force that leads to madness – it is the way in which people themselves act with regard to their claim for these things. To be more precise, I have never known a case of collapse in yoga as opposed to mere difficulty or negative failure, – a case of dramatic disaster in which there was not one of three causes – or more than one of the three at work. First, some sexual aberration – I am not speaking of mere sexuality which can be very strong in the nature without leading to collapse – or an attempt to sexualise spiritual experience on an animal or gross material basis; second, an exaggerated ambition, pride or vanity trying to seize on spiritual force or experience and turn it to one's own glorification ending in megalomania; third, an unbalanced vital and a weak nervous system apt to follow its own imaginations and unruly impulses without any true mental will or strong mental will to steady or restrain it, and so at the mercy of the imaginations and suggestions of the adverse vital world when carried over the border into the intermediate zone of which I spoke in a recent message.

*

. . . to feel sympathy or any emotion of the weak philanthropic kind with those possessed by vital forces is most dangerous as it may bring an attack upon oneself which may take any form. One must do what is to be done but abstain from all such weakness.

THE EGO

Egoism is part of the machinery – a chief part – of universal Nature, first to develop individuality out of indiscriminate force and substance of Nature and, secondly, to make the individual (through the machinery of egoistic thought, feeling, will and desire) a tool of the universal forces. It is only when one gets into touch with a higher Nature that it is possible to get free of this rule of ego and subjection to these forces.

*

I suppose the ego came there first as a means of the outer consciousness individualising itself in the flux of Nature and, secondly, as an incentive for tamasic animal man to act and get something done. Otherwise he might merely have contented himself with food and sleep and done nothing else. With that incentive of ego (possession, vanity, ambition, eagerness for power etc. etc.) he began doing all sorts of things he might never otherwise have done. But now that he has to go higher, this ego comes badly in the way.

*

Your nature like that of almost everybody has been largely ego-centric and the first stages of the sadhana are with almost everybody ego-centric. The main idea in it is always one's own sadhana, one's own endeavour, one's own development, perfection, siddhi. It is inevitable for most, for without that personal endeavour there would not be sufficient will or push to bring about the first necessary changes. But none of these things – development, perfection or siddhi – can really come in any degree of completeness or unmixed finality until this ego-centric attitude changes into the God-centric; until it becomes the development, perfection, siddhi of the Divine Consciousness, its will and its instrumentation in this body – and that can only be when these things become secondary, and bhakti for the Divine, love for the Divine, oneness with the Divine in consciousness, will, heart and body, become the sole aim – the rest is then only the fulfilment of the Divine Will by the Divine Power.

*

I think you still give an exaggerated importance and attention to the ego and other elements that are interwoven in the nature of humanity and cannot be entirely got rid of except by the coming of a new consciousness which replaces them by higher movements. If one rejects centrally and with all sincerity the ego and rajas, their roots get loosened and sattwa can prevail in the nature, but the expulsion of all ego and rajas cannot be done by the will and its effort. After a certain stage of preparation, therefore, one must stress more on the positive side of the sadhana than on the negative side of rejection, – though this of course must remain to help the other. Still what is important is to develop the psychic within and bring down the higher consciousness from above. The psychic, as it grows and manifests, detects immediately all wrong movements or elements and at the same time supplies almost automatically the true element or movement which will replace them – this process is much easier and more effective than that of a severe tapasya of purification. The higher consciousness in descending brings peace and purity into all the inner parts; the inner being separates itself from the imperfect outer consciousness and at the same time the peace that comes carries in it a power which can throw out what contradicts the peace and purity. Ego can then slowly or swiftly but surely disappear – rajas and tamas change into their divine substitutes.

*

By tamasic ego is meant the ego of weakness, self-depreciation, despondency, unbelief. The rajasic ego is puffed up with pride and self-esteem or stubbornly asserts itself at every step or else wherever it can; the tamasic ego, on the contrary, is always feeling "I am weak, I am miserable, I have no capacity, I am not loved or chosen by the Divine, I am so bad and incapable – what can the Divine do for me?" Or else "I am especially chosen out for misfortune and suffering, all are preferred to me, all are progressing, I only am left behind, all abandons me, I have nothing before me but flight, death or disaster," etc., etc., or something or all of these things mixed together. Sometimes the rajasic and tamasic Ahankar mix together and subtly support each other. In both cases it is the "I" that is making a row about itself and clouding the true vision. The true spiritual or psychic vision is this: "Whatever I may be, my soul is a child of the Divine and must reach the Divine sooner or later. I am imperfect, but seek after the perfection of the Divine in me and that not I but the Divine Grace will bring about; if I keep to that, the Divine Grace itself will do all." The "I" has to take its proper place here as a small portion and instrument of the Divine, something that is nothing without the Divine but with the Grace can be everything that the Divine wishes it to be.

*

The right attitude is to see that as a separate being, as an ego, one has no importance whatever and the insistence on one's own desires, pride, position etc. is an ignorance, but one matters only as a spirit, as a portion of the Divine, not more than others but as all souls matter to the Soul of all.

*

It is so with everybody. Human nature is shot through in all its stuff with the thread of the ego; even when one tries to get away from it, it is in front or could be behind all the thoughts and actions like a shadow. To see that is the first step, to discern the falsity and absurdity of the ego-movements is the second, to discourage and refuse it at each step is the third, — but it goes entirely only when one sees, experiences and lives the One in everything and equally everywhere.

*

Why is it [to be concentrated on the Divine] selfishness? Selfishness is to live for oneself and not for something greater than the self. To be concentrated on the Divine at all times is to get out of the personal self and its aims into something greater and serve the aims of that greater Existence. It is no more selfishness than to live for others always would be selfishness.

HUMILITY

Humility before the Divine is also a *sine qua non* of the spiritual life, and spiritual pride, arrogance, or vanity and self-assurance press always downward. But confidence in the Divine and a faith in one's spiritual destiny (i.e. since my heart and soul seek for the Divine, I cannot fail one day to reach Him) are much needed in view of the difficulties of the Path.

*

It is only this habit of the nature — self-worrying and harping on the sense of deficiency that prevents you from being quiet. If you threw that out, it would be easy to be quiet. Humility is needful, but constant self-depreciation does not help; excessive self-esteem and self-depreciation are both wrong attitudes. To recognise any defects without exaggerating them is useful but, once recognised, it is no good dwelling on them always; you must have the confidence that the Divine Force can change everything and you must let the Force work.

*

A spiritual humility within is very necessary, but I do not think an outward one is very advisable (absence of pride or arrogance or vanity is indispensable of course in one's outer dealings with others) — it often creates pride, becomes formal or becomes ineffective after a time. I have seen people doing it to cure their pride, but I have not found it producing a lasting result.

*

As for the sense of superiority, that is a little difficult to avoid when greater horizons open before the consciousness, unless one is already of a saintly and humble disposition. There are men like Nag Mahashaya (among Sri Ramakrishna's disciples) in whom spiritual experience creates more and more humility; there are others like Vivekananda in whom it creates a great sense of strength and superiority — European critics have taxed him with it rather severely; there are others in whom it fixes a sense of superiority to men and humility to the Divine. Each position has its value. Take Vivekananda's famous answer to the Madras Pundit who objected to one of his assertions saying: "But Shankara does not say so", to whom Vivekananda replied: "No, but I, Vivekananda, say so", and the Pundit was speechless. That "I, Vivekananda," stands up to the ordinary eye like a Himalaya of self-confident egoism. But there was nothing false or unsound in Vivekananda's spiritual experience. For this was not mere egoism, but the sense of what he stood for and the attitude of the fighter who, as the representative of something very great, could not allow himself to be put down or belittled. This is not to deny the necessity of non-egoism and of spiritual humility, but to show that the question is not so easy as it appears at first sight.

*

Perhaps one could say that it [spiritual humility] is to be aware of the relativity of what has been done compared with what is still to be done – and also to be conscious of one's being nothing without the Divine Grace.

DESIRE

It is not yoga to give free play to the natural instincts and desires. Yoga demands mastery over the nature, not subjection to the nature.

*

Most men are, like animals, driven by the forces of Nature: whatever desires come, they fulfil them, whatever emotions come they allow them to play, whatever physical wants they have, they try to satisfy. We say then that the activities and feelings of men are controlled by their Prakriti, and mostly by the vital and physical nature. The body is the instrument of the Prakriti or Nature – it obeys its own nature or it obeys the vital forces of desire, passion, etc.

But man has also a mind and, as he develops, he learns to control his vital and physical nature by his reason and by his will. This control is very partial: for the reason is often deluded by vital desires and the ignorance of the physical and it puts itself on their side and tries to justify by its ideas, reasonings or arguments their mistakes and wrong movements. Even if the reason keeps free and tells the vital or the body, "Do not do this", yet the vital and the body often follow their own movement in spite of the prohibition – man's mental will is not strong enough to compel them.

When people do sadhana, there is a higher Nature that works within, the psychic and spiritual, and they have to put their nature under the influence of the psychic being and the higher spiritual self or of the Divine. Not only the vital and the body but the mind also has to learn the Divine Truth and obey the divine rule. But because of the lower nature and its continued hold on them, they are unable at first and for a long time to prevent their nature from following the old ways – even when they know or are told from within what to do or what not to do. It is only by persistent sadhana, by getting into the higher spiritual consciousness and spiritual nature that this difficulty can be overcome; but even for the strongest and best sadhaks it takes a long time.

*

No one can easily get rid of desires. What has first to be done is to exteriorize them, to push them out, on the surface and get the inner parts quiet and clear. Afterwards they can be thrown out and replaced by the true thing, a happy and luminous will one with the Divine's.

*

... if you want to do yoga, you must take more and more in all matters, small or great, the yogic attitude. In our path that attitude is not one of forceful suppression, but of detachment and equality with regard to the objects of desire. Forceful suppression stands on the same level as free indulgence; in both cases, the desire remains; in the one it is fed by indulgence, in the other it lies latent and exasperated by suppression. It is only when one stands back, separates oneself from the lower vital, refusing to regard its desires and clamours as one's own, and cultivates an entire equality and equanimity in the consciousness with respect to them that the lower vital itself becomes gradually purified and itself also calm and equal. Each wave of desire as it comes must be observed, as quietly and with as much unmoved detachment as you would observe something going on outside you, and allowed to pass, rejected from the consciousness, and the true movement, the true consciousness steadily put in its place.

*

All the ordinary vital movements are foreign to the true being and come from outside; they do not belong to the soul nor do they originate in it but are waves from the general Nature, Prakriti.

The desires come from outside, enter the subconscious vital and rise to the surface. It is only when they rise to the surface and the mind becomes aware of them, that we become conscious of the desire. It seems to us to be our own because we feel it thus rising from the vital into the mind and do not know that it came from outside. What belongs to the vital, to the being, what makes it responsible is not the desire itself, but the habit of responding to the waves or the currents of suggestion that come into it from the universal Prakriti.

*

The rejection of desire is essentially the rejection of the element of craving, putting that out from the consciousness itself as a foreign element not belonging to the true self and the inner nature. But refusal to indulge the suggestions of desire is also a part of the rejection; to abstain from the action suggested, if it is not the right action, must be included in the yogic discipline. It is only when this is done in the wrong way, by a mental ascetic principle or a hard moral rule, that it can be called suppression. The difference between suppression and an inward essential rejection is the difference between mental or moral control and a spiritual purification.

When one lives in the true consciousness one feels the desires outside oneself, entering from outside, from the universal lower Prakriti, into the mind and the vital parts. In the ordinary human condition this is not felt; men become aware of the desire only when it is there, when it has come inside and found a lodging or a habitual harbourage and so they think it is their own and a part of themselves. The first condition for getting rid of desire is, therefore, to become conscious with the true consciousness; for then it becomes much easier to dismiss it than when one has to struggle with it as if it were a constituent part of oneself to be thrown out from the being. It is easier to cast off an accretion than to excise what is felt as a parcel of our substance.

When the psychic being is in front, then also to get rid of desire becomes easy; for the psychic being has in itself no desires, it has only aspirations and a seeking and love for the Divine and all things that are or tend towards the Divine. The constant prominence of the psychic being tends of itself to bring out the true consciousness and set right almost automatically the movements of the nature.

*

Your theory is a mistaken one. The free expression of a passion may relieve the vital for a time, but at the same time it gives it a right to return always. It is not reduced at all. Suppression with inner indulgence in subtle forms is not a cure, but expression in outer indulgence is still less a cure. It is perfectly possible to go on without manifestation if one is resolute to arrive at a complete control, the control being not a mere suppression but an inner and outer rejection.

*

The difference between suppression (*nigraha*) and self-control (*samyama*) is that one says "I cannot help desiring but I will not satisfy my desire", while the other says "I refuse the desire as well as the satisfaction of the desire".

*

The desire for the Divine or for bhakti for the Divine is the one desire which can free one from all the others – at the core it is not a desire but an aspiration, a soul need, the breath of existence of the inmost being, and as such it cannot be counted among desires.

TRUE NEED AND DESIRE

Desire is a psychological movement, and it can attach itself to a "true need" as well as to things that are not true needs. One must approach even true needs without desire. If one does not get them, one must feel nothing.

*

The *necessities* of a sadhak should be as few as possible; for there are only a very few things that are real necessities in life. The rest are either utilities or things decorative to life or luxuries. These a yogin has a right to possess or enjoy only on one of two conditions –

(1) If he uses them during his sadhana solely to train himself in possessing things without attachment or desire and learn to use them rightly, in harmony with the Divine Will, with a proper handling, a just organisation, arrangement and measure – or,

(2) if he has already attained a true freedom from desire and attachment and is not in the least moved or affected in any way by loss or withholding or deprival. If he has any greed, desire, demand, claim for possession or enjoyment, any anxiety, grief, anger or vexation when denied or deprived, he is not free in spirit and his use of the things he possesses is contrary to the spirit of sadhana. Even if he is free in spirit, he will not be fit for possession if he has not learned to use things not for himself, but for the Divine Will, as an instrument, with the right knowledge and action in the

use, for the proper equipment of a life lived not for oneself but for and in the Divine.

*

As for the inconveniences, you should take them as a training in *samatā*. To be able to bear inconveniences is one of the most elementary necessities if one wants to enter into the true spirit of yoga.

ANGER AND VIOLENCE

I think you have always had an idea that to give expression to an impulse or a movement is the best way or even the only way to get rid of it. But that is a mistaken idea. If you give expression to anger, you prolong or confirm the habit of the recurrence of anger; you do not diminish or get rid of the habit. The very first step towards weakening the power of anger in the nature and afterwards getting rid of it altogether is to refuse all expression to it in act or speech. Afterwards one can go on with more likelihood of success to throw it out from the thought and feeling also. And so with all other wrong movements.

All these movements come from outside, from the universal lower Nature, or are suggested or thrown upon you by adverse forces – adverse to your spiritual progress. Your method of taking them as your own is again a wrong method; for by doing that you increase their power to recur and take hold of you. If you take them as your own, that gives them a kind of right to be there. If you feel them as *not* your own, then they have no right, and the will can develop more power to send them away. What you must always have and feel as yours is this will, the power to refuse assent, to refuse admission to a wrong movement. Or if it comes in, the power to send it away, without expressing it.

Of course the best way will be if you can keep the contact

more with the Mother and her Light and Force and receive and accept and follow only what comes from that higher force.

*

The fact that the anger comes with such force is itself enough to show that it is not in you that it is but that it comes from outside. It is a rush of force from the universal Nature that tries to take possession of the individual being and make that being act according to the will of this outside force and not according to the will of the soul within. These things come in the course of the sadhana because the sadhak is liberating himself from the lower nature and trying to turn towards the Mother and live in her divine consciousness and the higher nature. The forces of the lower nature do not want that and so they make these rushes in order to recover their rule. It is necessary when that comes, to remain quiet within remembering the Mother or calling her and reject the anger or whatever else comes, whenever it comes or however often it comes. If that is done, then these forces begin to lose their power to invade. It is easier if one clearly feels them to be outside forces and foreign to oneself; but even if you cannot feel that yet when they enter, still the mind must keep that idea and refuse to accept them as any longer a part of the nature.

*

It is true that anger and strife are in the nature of the human vital and do not go easily; but what is important is to have the will to change, and the clear perception that these things must go. If that will and perception are there, then in the end they will go. The most important help to it is, here also, for the psychic being to grow within – for that brings a certain kindliness, patience, charity towards all and one no longer regards everything from the point of view of one's own ego and its pain or pleasure, likings and dislikings. The second help is the growth of the inner peace which outward things cannot trouble. With the peace comes a calm wideness in which one perceives all as one self, all beings as the children of the Mother and the Mother dwelling in oneself and in all. It is that towards which your sadhana will move, for these are the things which come with the growth of the psychic and spiritual consciousness. Then these troubled reactions to outward things will no longer come.

*

An inner psychic or spiritual change is not brought about by violence. It is not a change of conduct that has to be done in the sadhaks, but a change of soul and spirit governing the mind and vital and body instead of the mind and vital governing. Violence is the drastic contradiction of that; it makes mental egoism and vital passion and fury or else cruelty the rulers. Violence in ordinary Nature does not justify violence in spiritual work.

*

The *Essays on the Gita** explain the ordinary Karmayoga as developed in the Gita, in which the work done is the ordinary work of human life with only an inward change. There too the violence to be used is not a personal violence done from egoistic motives, but part of the ordered system of social life. Nothing can spiritually justify individual violence done in anger or passion or from any vital motive. In our yoga our object is to rise higher than the ordinary life of men and in it violence has to be left aside altogether.

*

There is a truth in Ahimsa, there is a truth in destruction also. I do not teach that you should go on killing everybody every day as a spiritual dharma. I say that destruction can be done when it is part of the divine work commanded by the Divine. Non-violence is better than violence as a rule, and

* Sri Aurobindo's exposition of the Bhagavad Gita.

still sometimes violence may be the right thing. I consider dharma as relative; unity with the Divine and action from the Divine Will, the highest way.

SEX

What has this yoga got to do with sex and sex-contact? I have told you repeatedly that sex has to be got rid of and overcome before there can be siddhi in this yoga.

*

The whole principle of this yoga is to give oneself entirely to the Divine alone and to nobody and nothing else, and to bring down into ourselves by union with the Divine Mother-Power all the transcendent light, force, wideness, peace, purity, truth-consciousness and Ananda of the supramental Divine. In this yoga, therefore, there can be no place for vital relations or interchanges with others; any such relation or interchange immediately ties down the soul to the lower consciousness and its lower nature, prevents the true and full union with the Divine and hampers both the ascent to the supramental Truth-consciousness and the descent of the supramental Ishwari Shakti. Still worse would it be if this interchange took the form of a sexual relation or a sexual enjoyment, even if kept free from any outward act; therefore these things are absolutely forbidden in the sadhana. It goes without saying that any physical act of the kind is not allowed; but also any subtler form is ruled out. It is only after becoming one with the supramental Divine that we can find our true spiritual relations with others in the Divine; in that higher unity this kind of gross lower vital movement can have no place.

To master the sex-impulse, – to become so much master of the sex-centre that the sexual energy would be drawn upwards, not thrown outwards and wasted — it is so indeed that the force in the seed can be turned into a primal physical energy supporting all the others, *retas* into *ojas*. But no error can be more perilous than to accept the immixture of the sexual desire and some kind of subtle satisfaction of it and look on this as a part of the sadhana. It would be the most effective way to head straight towards spiritual downfall and throw into the atmosphere forces that would block the supramental descent, bringing instead the descent of adverse vital powers to disseminate disturbance and disaster. This deviation must be absolutely thrown away, should it try to occur and expunged from the consciousness, if the Truth is to be brought down and the work is to be done.

It is an error too to imagine that, although the physical sexual action is to be abandoned, yet some inward reproduction of it is part of the transformation of the sex-centre. The action of the animal sex-energy in Nature is a device for a particular purpose in the economy of the material creation in the Ignorance. But the vital excitement that accompanies it makes the most favourable opportunity and vibration in the atmosphere for the inrush of those very vital forces and beings whose whole business is to prevent the descent of the supramental Light. The pleasure attached to it is a degradation and not a true form of the divine Ananda. The true divine Ananda in the physical has a different quality and movement and substance; self-existent in its essence, its manifestation is dependent only on an inner union with the Divine. You have spoken of Divine Love; but Divine Love, when it touches the physical, does not awaken the gross lower vital propensities; indulgence of them would only repel it and make it withdraw again to the heights from which it is already difficult enough to draw it down into the coarseness of the material creation which it alone can transform. Seek the Divine Love through the only gate through which it will consent to enter, the gate of the psychic being, and cast away the lower vital error.

The transformation of the sex-centre and its energy is

needed for the physical siddhi; for this is the support in the body of all the mental, vital and physical forces of the nature. It has to be changed into a mass and a movement of intimate Light, creative Power, pure divine Ananda. It is only the bringing down of the supramental Light, Power and Bliss into the centre that can change it. As to the working afterwards, it is the supramental Truth and the creative vision and will of the Divine Mother that will determine it. But it will be a working of the conscious Truth, not of the Darkness and Ignorance to which sexual desire and enjoyment belong; it will be a power of preservation and free desireless radiation of the life-forces and not of their throwing out and waste. Avoid the imagination that the supramental life will be only a heightened satisfaction of the desires of the vital and the body; nothing can be a greater obstacle to the Truth in its descent than this hope of glorification of the animal in the human nature. Mind wants the supramental state to be a confirmation of its own cherished ideas and preconceptions; the vital wants it to be a glorification of its own desires; the physical wants it to be a rich prolongation of its own comforts and pleasures and habits. If it were to be that, it would be only an exaggerated and highly magnified consummation of the animal and the human nature, not a transition from the human into the Divine.

SEX: A MOVEMENT OF GENERAL NATURE

All movements are in the mass movements of Nature's cosmic forces, they are movements of universal Nature. The individual receives something of them, a wave or pressure of some cosmic force, and is driven by it; he thinks it is his own, generated in himself separately, but it is not so, it is part of a general movement which works just in the same way in others. Sex, for instance, is a movement of general Nature seeking for its play and it uses this or that one – a man vitally or physically "in love" as it is called with a woman is simply repeating and satisfying the world-movement of sex; if it had not been that woman, it would have been another; he is simply an instrument in Nature's machinery, it is not an independent movement. So it is with anger and other Nature-motives.

*

The sex exists for its own satisfaction and this or that person is only an excuse or occasion for its action or a channel for awakening its activity. It is from within, by the peace and purity from above coming into that part and holding it that it must disappear.

*

It is of course the universal sex-force that acts, but certain people are more full of it than others, have the sex-appeal as they now say in Europe. This sex-appeal is exercised especially by women even without any conscious intention of putting it on a particular person. Consciously they may turn it on a particular person, but it may exercise itself on many others whom they do not wish particularly to capture. All women have not the sex-appeal, but some force of sex-pull there is in most. There is of course a similar pull in men for women.

*

In most men the sexual is the strongest of all the impulses of Nature.

*

The terrestrial sex-movement is a utilisation by Nature of the fundamental physical energy for purposes of procreation. The thrill of which the poets speak, which is accompanied by a very gross excitement, is the lure by which she makes the vital consent to this otherwise unpleasing process;

there are numbers who experience a recoil of disgust after the act and repulsion from the partner in it because of the disgust, though they return to it when the disgust has worn off for the sake of this lure.

*

There are a number of women who can love with the mind, the psychic, the vital (heart), but they shrink from a touch on the body and even when that goes, the physical act remains abhorrent to them. They may yield under pressure, but it does not reconcile them to the act which always seems to them animal and degrading. Women know this, but men seem to find it hard to believe; but it is perfectly true.

*

There is no "delight" in the sex-affair, it is necessarily and can only be a passing excitement and pleasure which finally wears itself out with the wearing out of the body.

SEXUAL CONTINENCE

Doctors advise marriage because they think satisfaction of the sexual instinct is necessary for the health and repression causes disturbances in the system. This is true only when there is no true giving up of the sexual indulgence, but only a change in the way of indulging it. Nowadays a new theory has come up which confirms the Indian theory of Brahma-charya, viz. that by continence *retas* can be changed into *ojas* and the vigour and the power of the being enormously increase.

*

The sex-energy utilised by Nature for the purpose of reproduction is in its real nature a fundamental energy of Life. It can be used not for the heightening but for a certain intensification of the vital-emotional life; it can be controlled and diverted from the sex-purpose and used for aesthetic and artistic or other creation and productiveness or preserved for heightening of the intellectual or other energies. Entirely controlled it can be turned into a force of spiritual energy also. This was well known in ancient India and was described as the conversion of *retas* into *ojas* by Brahmacharya. Sex-energy misused turns to disorder and disintegration of the life-energy and its powers.

REJECTION OF THE SEXUAL IMPULSE

As to sexual impulse. Regard it not as something sinful and horrible and attractive at the same time, but as a mistake and wrong movement of the lower nature. Reject it entirely, not by struggling with it, but by drawing back from it, detaching yourself and refusing your consent; look at it as something not your own, but imposed on you by a force of Nature outside you. Refuse all consent to the imposition. If anything in your vital consents, insist on that part of you withdrawing its consent. Call in the Divine Force to help you in your withdrawal and refusal. If you can do this quietly and resolutely and patiently, in the end your inner will will prevail against the habit of the outer Nature.

*

As to the sexual impulse, for this also you must have no moral horror or puritanic or ascetic repulsion. This also is a power of life and while you have to throw away the present form of this power (that is the physical act), the force itself has to be mastered and transformed. It is often strongest in people with a strong vital nature and this strong vital nature can be made a great instrument for the physical realisation of the Divine Life. If the sexual impulse comes, do not be sorry or troubled but look at it calmly, quiet it down, reject all wrong suggestions connected with it and wait for the Higher Consciousness to transform it into the true force and Ananda.

*

... the right attitude is neither to worry always about the sex-weakness and be obsessed by its importance so as to be in constant struggle and depression over it, nor to be too careless so as to allow it to grow. It is perhaps the most difficult of all to get rid of entirely; one has to recognise quietly its importance and its difficulty and go quietly and steadily about the control of it. If some reactions of a slight character remain, it is not a thing to get disturbed about – only it must not be permitted to increase so as to disturb the sadhana or get too strong for the restraining will of the mental and higher vital being.

*

To think too much of sex even for suppressing it makes it worse. You have to open more to positive experience. To spend all the time struggling with the lower vital is a very slow method.

*

The idea that by fully indulging the sex-hunger it will be finished and disappear for ever is a deceptive pretence held out by the vital to the mind in order to get a sanction for its desire; it has no other *raison d'être* or truth or justification. If an occasional indulgence keeps the sex-desire simmering, a full indulgence would only sink you in its mire. This hunger like other hungers does not cease by temporary satiation; it revives itself after a temporary abeyance and wants again indulgence. Neither sops nor gorgings are the right treatment for it. It can only go by a radical psychic rejection or a full spiritual opening with the increasing descent of a consciousness that does not want it and has the truer Ananda.

*

There is a force of purity, not the purity of the moralist, but an essential purity of spirit, in the very substance of the being. When that comes, then sex-waves either cannot approach or they pass without imparting any impulse, without touching anywhere.

*

Strength and purity in the lower vital and wideness in the heart are the best condition for meeting others, especially women, and if that could always be there sex could hardly have a look in.

*

All that happens because the vital is conscious of sex in the approach and immediately assumes the "man to woman" attitude. To get rid of that, one must be able to look on the woman and feel her as to a human being only. That is difficult and needs a certain training; for even if the mind is able to take the position, the vital is unreliable and one has to be on guard that it does not suddenly or surreptitiously get in into the relation with its partiality for the sex-interchange.

*

In ordinary society people touch each other more or less freely according to the manners of the society. That is quite a different matter because there the sex-impulse is allowed within certain more or less wide or narrow limits and even the secret indulgence is common, although people try to avoid discovery. In Bengal when there is purdah touching between men and women is confined to the family, in Europe there is not such restriction so long as there is no excessive familiarity or indecency; but in Europe sex is now practically free. Here all sex-indulgence inner or outer is considered undesirable as an obstacle to the sadhana – as it very evidently is. For that reason any excessive familiarity of touch between men and women has to be avoided, anything also in the nature of caressing, as it creates or tends to create sex-tendency or even the strong sex-impulse. Casual touching has to be avoided also if it actually creates the sex-impulse. These are commonsense rules if the premiss is granted that sex has not to have any indulgence.

MARRIAGE

As to the question of marriage in general, we do not consider it advisable for one who desires to come to the spiritual life. Marriage means usually any amount of trouble, heavy burdens, a bondage to the worldly life and great difficulties in the way of single-minded spiritual endeavour. Its only natural purpose would be, if the sexual trend was impossible to conquer, to give it a restricted and controlled satisfaction.

*

It is only a minority that is called to the strict yogic life and there will be always plenty of people who will continue the race. Certainly, the yogi has no contempt or aversion for human nature; he understands it and the place given to each of its activities with a clear and calm regard.

*

If she consents to marry, that would be the best. All these vital disturbances proceed from suppressed sex-instinct, suppressed but not rejected and overcome.

A mental acceptance or enthusiasm for the sadhana is not a sufficient guarantee nor sufficient ground for calling people, especially young people, to begin it. Afterwards these vital instincts rise up and there is nothing sufficient to balance or prevail against them, — only mental ideas which do not prevail against the instincts, but on the other hand, also stand in the way of the natural social means of satisfaction. If she marries now and gets experience of the human vital life, then thereafter there may be a chance of her mental aspiration for sadhana turning into the real thing.

*

Regarding your question about a complementary soul and marriage, the answer is easy to give; the way of the spiritual life lies for you in one direction and marriage lies in quite another and opposite. All talk about a complementary soul is a camouflage with which the mind tries to cover the sentimental, sensational and physical wants of the lower vital nature. It is that vital nature in you which puts the question and would like an answer reconciling its desires and demands with the call of the true soul in you. But it must not expect a sanction for any such incongruous reconciliation from here. The way of the supramental yoga is clear; it lies not through concession to these things, — not, in your case, through satisfaction, under a spiritual cover if possible, of its craving for the comforts and gratifications of a domestic and conjugal life and the enjoyment of the ordinary emotional desires and physical passions, — but through the purification and transformation of the forces which these movements pervert and misuse. Not these human and animal demands, but the divine Ananda which is above and beyond them and which the indulgence of these degraded forms would prevent from descending, is the great thing that the aspiration of the vital being must demand in the sadhak.

FEAR

If you want to do yoga, you must get rid of fear. Yoga and fear do not go together.

*

It is true that what one fears has the tendency to come until one is able to look it in the face and overcome one's shrinking. One must learn to take one's foundation on the Divine and overcome the fear, relying on the help to carry one through all things even unpleasant and adverse. There is a Force that works even through them for the seeker and carries him towards his goal.

*

Yes, fear creates imaginary terrors — even if there is real danger, fear does not help; it clouds the intelligence, takes away presence of mind and prevents one seeing the right thing to do.

Let the Force at work increase, till it clears out the mixed consciousness altogether.

*

[Ways to remove fear:] By bringing down strength and calm into the lower vital (region below the navel). Also by will and imposing calm on the system when the fear arises. It can be done in either way or both together.

WEAKNESS, FATIGUE, INERTIA

A strong mind and body and life-force are needed in the sadhana. Especially steps should be taken to throw out tamas and bring strength and force into the frame of the nature.

*

The weakness of the body has to be cured, not disregarded. It can only be cured by bringing in strength from above, not by merely forcing the body.

*

Overstraining only increases the inertia — the mental and vital will may force the body, but the body feels more and more strained and finally asserts itself. It is only if the body itself feels a will and force to work that one can do that.

*

Physical fatigue like this in the course of the sadhana may come from various reasons:

1. It may come from receiving more than the physical is ready to assimilate. The cure is then quiet rest in conscious immobility receiving the forces but not for any other purpose than the recuperation of the strength and energy.

2. It may be due to the passivity taking the form of inertia – inertia brings the consciousness down towards the ordinary physical level which is soon fatigued and prone to *tamas*. The cure here is to get back into the true consciousness and to rest there, not in inertia.

3. It may be due to mere overstrain of the body – not giving it enough sleep or repose. The body is the support of the yoga, but its energy is not inexhaustible and needs to be husbanded; it can be kept up by drawing on the universal vital Force but that reinforcement too has its limits. A certain moderation is needed even in the eagerness for progress – moderation, not indifference or indolence.

*

The first rule is – there must be sufficient sleep and rest, not in excess but not too little.

The body must be trained to work, but not strained beyond its utmost capacity.

The outer means without the inner is not effective. Up to a certain point by a *progressive* training the body may be made more capable of work. But the important thing is to bring down the force for work and the Rasa of work in the body. The body will then do what is asked of it without grudging or feeling fatigue.

Even so, even when the force and Rasa are there, one must keep one's sense of measure.

Work is a means of self-dedication to the Divine, but it

must be done with the necessary inner consciousness in which the outer vital and physical also share.

A lazy body is certainly not a proper instrument for yoga – it must stop being lazy. But a fatigued and unwilling body also cannot receive properly or be a good instrument. The proper thing is to avoid either extreme.

*

It is quite true that the physical exercise is very necessary to keep off tamas. I am glad you have begun it and I trust you will keep it up.

Physical tamas in its roots can be removed only by the descent and the transformation, but physical exercise and regular activity of the body can always prevent a tamasic condition from prevailing in the body.

*

Even if there is physical fatigue sometimes, it is not inevitable that it should interfere with the sadhana. The inner movement can always go on.

SLEEP

This is not a yoga in which physical austerities have to be done for their own sake. Sleep is necessary for the body just as food is. Sufficient sleep must be taken, but no excessive sleep. What sufficient sleep is depends on the need of the body.

*

It is not a right method to try to keep awake at night; the suppression of the needed sleep makes the body tamasic and unfit for the necessary concentration during the waking hours. The right way is to transform the sleep and not suppress it, and especially to learn how to become more and more conscious in sleep itself. If that is done, sleep changes into an inner mode of consciousness in which the sadhana can continue as much as in the waking state, and at the same time one is able to enter into other planes of consciousness than the physical and command an immense range of informative and utilisable experience.

*

Sadhana can go on in the dream or sleep state as well as in the waking.

*

There is no reason at all why intensity of sadhana should bring insufficient sleep.

*

If you do not sleep enough the body and the nervous envelope will be weakened and the body and the nervous envelope are the basis of the sadhana.

*

It must be the want of sleep that keeps your nervous system exposed to weakness – it is a great mistake not to take sufficient sleep. Seven hours is the minimum needed. When one has a very strong nervous system one can reduce it to six, sometimes even five – but it is rare and ought not to be attempted without necessity.

*

The normal allowance of sleep is said to be 7 to 8 hours except in advanced age when it is said to be less. If one takes less (5 to 6 for instance) the body accommodates itself somehow, but if the control is taken off it immediately wants to make up for its lost arrears of the normal 8 hours. So often when one has tried to live on too little food, if one relaxes, the body becomes enormously rapacious for food until it has set right the credit and loss account. At least it often happens like that.

*

In sleep one very commonly passes from consciousness to deeper consciousness in a long succession until one reaches the psychic and rests there or else from higher to higher consciousness until one reaches rest in some silence and peace. The few minutes one passes in this rest are the real sleep which restores, – if one does not get it, there is only a half rest. It is when you come near to either of these domains of rest that you begin to see these higher kinds of dreams.

*

A long unbroken sleep is necessary because there are just ten minutes of the whole into which one enters into a true rest – a sort of Sachchidananda immobility of consciousness – and that it is which really restores the system. The rest of the time is spent first in travelling through various states of consciousness towards that and then coming out of it back towards the waking state. This fact of the ten minutes true rest has been noted by medical men, but of course they know nothing about Sachchidananda!

*

The consciousness in the night almost always descends below the level of what one has gained by sadhana in the waking consciousness, unless there are special experiences of an uplifting character in the time of sleep or unless the yogic consciousness acquired is so strong in the physical itself as to counteract the pull of the subconscient inertia. In ordinary sleep the consciousness in the body is that of the subconscient physical, which is a diminished consciousness, not awake and alive like the rest of the being. The rest of the being stands back and part of its consciousness goes out into other planes and regions and has experiences which are recorded in dreams. . . .

*

At night when one sinks into the subconscient after being in a good state of consciousness we find that state gone and we have to labour to get it back again. On the other hand, if the sleep is of the better kind one may wake up in a good condition. Of course, it is better to be conscious in sleep, if one can.

*

You have to start by concentrating before you sleep always with a specific will or aspiration. The will or aspiration may take time to reach the subconscient, but if it is sincere, strong and steady, it does reach after a time — so that an automatic consciousness and will are established in the sleep itself which will do what is necessary.

*

At night, you have to pass into sleep in the concentration — you must be able to concentrate with the eyes closed, lying down and the concentration must deepen into sleep — that is to say, sleep must become a concentrated going inside away from the outer waking state. If you find it necessary to sit for a time you may do so, but afterwards lie down keeping the concentration till this happens.

FOOD

Greed for food has to be overcome, but it has not to be given too much thought. The proper attitude to food is a certain equality. Food is for the maintenance of the body and one should take enough for that — what the body needs; if one gives less the body feels the need and hankers; if you give more, then that is indulging the vital. As for particular foods the palate likes, the attitude of the mind and vital should be, "If I get, I take; if I don't get, I shall not mind." One should not think too much of food either to indulge or unduly to repress – that is the best.

*

It is the attachment to food, the greed and eagerness for it, making it an unduly important thing in the life, that is contrary to the spirit of yoga. To be aware that something is pleasant to the palate is not wrong; only one must have no desire nor hankering for it, no exultation in getting it, no displeasure or regret at not getting it. One must be calm and equal, not getting upset or dissatisfied when the food is not tasty or not in abundance – eating the fixed amount that is necessary, not less or more. There should be neither eagerness nor repugnance.

To be always thinking about food and troubling the mind is quite the wrong way of getting rid of the food-desire. Put the food element in the right place in the life, in a small corner, and don't concentrate on it but on other things.

*

What is necessary is to take enough food and think no more about it, taking it as a means for the maintenance of the physical instrument only. But just as one should not overeat, so one should not diminish unduly – it produces a reaction which defeats the object – for the object is not to allow either the greed for food or the heavy tamas of the physical which is the result of excessive eating to interfere with the concentration on the spiritual experience and progress. If the body is left insufficiently nourished, it will think of food more than otherwise.

*

Too much eating makes the body material and heavy, eating too little makes it weak and nervous – one has to find the true harmony and balance between the body's need and the food taken.

*

It is true that as one reaches an advanced age a diminished diet may become desirable.

*

It is a fact that by fasting, if the mind and the nerves are solid or the will-force dynamic, one can get for a time into a state of inner energy and receptivity which is alluring to the mind and the usual reactions of hunger, weakness, intestinal disturbance, etc., can be wholly avoided. But the body suffers by diminution and there can easily develop in the vital a morbid overstrained condition due to the inrush of more vital energy than the nervous system can assimilate or co-ordinate. Nervous people should avoid the temptation to fast, it is often accompanied or followed by delusions and a loss of balance. Especially if there is a motive of hunger-strike or that element comes in, fasting becomes perilous, for it is then an indulgence of a vital movement which may easily become a habit injurious and pernicious to the sadhana. Even if all these reactions are avoided, still there is no sufficient utility in fasting, since the higher energy and receptivity ought to come not by artificial or physical means but by intensity of the consciousness and strong will for the sadhana.

*

The first thing I tell people when they want not to eat or sleep is that no yoga can be done without sufficient food and sleep (see the Gita on this point). Fasting or sleeplessness make the nerves morbid and excited and weaken the brain and lead to delusions and fantasies. The Gita says, yoga is not for one who eats too much or sleeps too much, neither is it for one who does not eat or does not sleep, but if one eats and sleeps suitably — *yuktāhārī yuktanidraḥ* — then one can

do it best. It is the same with everything else. How often
have I said that excessive retirement was suspect to me and
that to do nothing but meditate was a lop-sided and therefore unsound sadhana?

*

Not to eat as the method of getting rid of the greed of food is
the ascetic way. Ours is equanimity and non-attachment.

*

I think the importance of sattwic food from the spiritual
point of view has been exaggerated. Food is rather a question of hygiene, and many of the sanctions and prohibitions
laid down in ancient religions had more a hygienic than a
spiritual motive. The Gita's definitions seem to point in the
same direction – tamasic food, it seems to say, is what is
stale or rotten with the virtue gone out of it, rajasic food is
that which is too acrid, pungent, etc., heats the blood and
spoils the health, sattwic food is what is pleasing, healthy,
etc. It may well be that different kinds of food nourish the
action of the different gunas and so indirectly are helpful or
harmful apart from their physical action. But that is as far as
one can go confidently. What particular eatables are or are
not sattwic is another question and more difficult to determine. Spiritually, I should say that the effect of food depends more on the occult atmosphere and influences that
come with it than on anything in the food itself. Vegetarian-
ism is another question altogether; it stands, as you say, on a
will not to do harm to the more conscious forms of life for
the satisfaction of the belly.

As for the question of practising to take all kinds of food
with equal *rasa*, it is not necessary to practise nor does it
really come by practice. One has to acquire equality within
in the consciousness and as this equality grows, one can
extend it or apply it to the various fields of the activity of the
consciousness.

ILLNESS

The human body has always been in the habit of answering to whatever forces chose to lay hands on it and illness is the price it pays for its inertia and ignorance. It has to learn to answer to the one Force alone, but that is not easy for it to learn.

*

Attacks of illness are attacks of the lower nature or of adverse forces taking advantage of some weakness, opening or response in the nature, — like all other things that come and have got to be thrown away, they come from outside. If one can feel them so coming and get the strength and the habit to throw them away before they can enter the body, then one can remain free from illness. Even when the attack seems to rise from within, that means only that it has not been detected before it entered the subconscient; once in the subconscient, the force that brought it rouses it from there sooner or later and it invades the system. When you feel it just after it has entered, it is because though it came direct and not through the subconscient, yet you could not detect it while it was still outside. Very often it arrives like that frontally or more often tangentially from the side direct, forcing its way through the subtle vital envelope which is our main armour of defence, but it can be stopped there in the envelope itself before it penetrates the material body. Then one may feel some effect, e.g., feverishness or a tendency to cold, but there is not the full invasion of the malady. If it can be stopped earlier or if the vital envelope of itself resists and remains strong, vigorous and intact, then there is no illness; the attack produces no physical effect and leaves no traces.

*

All illnesses pass through the nervous or vital-physical sheath of the subtle consciousness and subtle body before they enter the physical. If one is conscious of the subtle body or with the subtle consciousness, one can stop an illness on its way and prevent it from entering the physical body. But it may have come without one's noticing, or when one is asleep or through the subconscient, or in a sudden rush when one is off one's guard; then there is nothing to do but to fight it out from a hold already gained on the body. Self-defence by these inner means may become so strong that the body becomes practically immune as many yogis are. Still this "practically" does not mean "absolutely". The absolute immunity can only come with the supramental change. For below the supramental it is the result of an action of a Force among many forces and can be disturbed by a disruption of the equilibrium established – in the supramental it is a law of the nature; in a supramentalised body immunity from illness would be automatic, inherent in its new nature.

*

The complete immunity from all illness for which our yoga tries can only come by a total and permanent enlightenment of the below from above resulting in the removal of the psychological roots of ill health – it can't be done otherwise.

*

Illness marks some imperfection or weakness or else opening to adverse touches in the physical nature and is often connected also with some obscurity or disharmony in the lower vital or the physical mind or elsewhere.

It is very good if one can get rid of illness entirely by faith and yoga-power or the influx of the Divine Force. But very often this is not altogether possible, because the whole nature is not open or able to respond to the Force. The mind may have faith and respond, but the lower vital and the body may not follow. Or, if the mind and vital are ready, the body may not respond, or may respond only partially, because it has the habit of replying to the forces which produce a particular illness, and habit is a very obstinate force in the material part of the nature. In such cases the use of the physical means can be resorted to, – not as the main means, but as a help or material support to the action of the Force. Not strong and violent remedies, but those that are beneficial without disturbing the body.

*

As for medical treatment it is sometimes a necessity. If one can cure by the Force as you have often done it is the best – but if for some reason the body is not able to respond to the Force (e.g. owing to doubt, lassitude or discouragement or for inability to react against the disease), then the aid of medical treatment becomes necessary. It is not that the Force ceases to act and leaves all to the medicines, – it will continue to act through the consciousness but take the support of the treatment so as to act directly on the resistance in the body, which responds more readily to physical means in its ordinary consciousness.

*

Care should be taken of the body certainly, the care that is needed for its good condition, rest, sleep, proper food, sufficient exercise; what is not good is too much preoccupation with it, anxiety, despondency in the illness, etc., for these things only favour the prolongation of ill-health or weakness. For such things as the liver attacks treatment can always be taken when necessary.

But it is always the right inner poise, quietude inward and outward, faith, the opening of the body consciousness to the Mother and her Force that are the true means of recovery – other things can only be minor aids and devices.

*

Above all, do not harbour that idea of an unfit body – all suggestions of that kind are a subtle attack on the will to siddhi and especially dangerous in physical matters. It has been cropping up in several people who are doing the yoga and the first business is to expel it bag and baggage. Appearances and facts may be all in its favour, but the first

condition of success for the yogin and indeed for anybody
who wants to do anything great or unusual is to be superior
to facts and disbelieve in appearances. Will to be free from
disease, however formidable, many-faced or constant its
attacks, and repel all contrary suggestions.

*

The feeling of illness is at first only a suggestion; it becomes
a reality because your physical consciousness accepts it. It is
like a wrong suggestion in the mind, – if the mind accepts it,
it becomes clouded and confused and has to struggle back
into harmony and clearness. It is so with the body consciousness and illness. You must not accept but reject it with
your physical mind and so help the body consciousness to
throw off the suggestion. If necessary, make a counter-
suggestion "No, I shall be well; I am and shall be all right."
And in any case call in the Mother's Force to throw out the
suggestion and the illness it is bringing.

*

Your theory of illness is rather a perilous creed – for illness
is a thing to be eliminated, not accepted or enjoyed. There *is*
something in the being that enjoys illness, it is possible even
to turn the pains of illness like any other pain into a form of
pleasure; for pain and pleasure are both of them degrada-
tions of an original Ananda and can be reduced into the
terms of each other or else sublimated into their original
principle of Ananda. It is true also that one must be able to
bear illness with calm, equanimity, endurance, even recognition of it, since it has come, as something that has to be
passed through in the course of experience. But to accept
and enjoy it means to help it to last and that will not do; for
illness is a deformation of the physical nature just as lust,
anger, jealousy, etc., are deformations of the vital nature
and error and prejudice and indulgence of falsehood are
deformations of the mental nature. All these things have to
be eliminated and rejection is the first condition of their

disappearance while acceptance has a contrary effect altogether.

*

Whatever it may be — the power of illness to prevent the sadhana ought not to exist. The yogic consciousness and its activities must be there whether there is health or illness.

*

There is a sort of traditional belief in many minds that the practice of yoga is inimical to the health of the body and tends to have a bad effect of one kind or another and even finally leads to a premature or an early dropping of the body. Ramakrishna seems to have held the view, if we can judge from his remarks about the connection between Keshav Sen's progress in spirituality and the illness which undermined him, that one was the result and the desirable result of the other, a liberation and release from life in this world, *mukti*. That may or may not be; but I find it difficult to believe that illness and deterioration of the body is the natural and general result of the practice of yoga or that that practice is the cause of an inevitable breakdown of health or of the final illnesses which bring about departure from the body. On what ground are we to suppose or how can it be proved that while non-yogis suffer from ill-health and die because of the disorders of Nature, yogis die of their yoga? Unless a direct connection between their death and their practice of yoga can be proved — and this could be proved with certainty only in particular cases and even then not with an absolute certainty — there is no sufficient reason to believe in such a difference. It is more rational to conclude that both yogis and non-yogis fall ill and die from natural causes and by the same dispensation of Nature; one might even advance the view, since they have the Yoga-Shakti at their disposal if they choose to use it, that the yogi falls ill and dies not because of but in spite of his yoga.

11

Human Relationships in Yoga

FRIENDSHIP, AFFECTION AND LOVE

The idea that all sadhaks must be aloof from each other and at daggers drawn is itself a preconceived idea that must be abandoned. Harmony and not strife is the law of yogic living. This preconceived idea arises perhaps from the old notion of Nirvana as the aim; but Nirvana is not the aim here. The aim here is fulfilment of the Divine in life and for that, union and solidarity are indispensable.

The ideal of the yoga is that all should be centred in and around the Divine and the life of the sadhaks must be founded on that firm foundation, their personal relations also should have the Divine for their centre. Moreover, all relations should pass from the vital to the spiritual basis with the vital only as a form and instrument of the spiritual – this means that, from whatever relations they have with each other, all jealousy, strife, hatred, aversion, rancour and other evil vital feelings should be abandoned, for they can be no part of the spiritual life. So, also, all egoistic love and attachment will have to disappear – the love that loves only for the ego's sake and, as soon as the ego is hurt and dissatisfied, ceases to love or even cherishes rancour and hate. There must be a real living and lasting unity behind the love. It is understood of course that such things as sexual impurity must disappear also.

That is the ideal, but as for the way of attainment, it may

differ for different people. One way is that in which one leaves everything else to follow the Divine alone. This does not mean an aversion for anybody any more than it means aversion for the world and life. It only means an absorption in one's central aim, with the idea that once that is attained it will be easy to found all relations on the true basis, to become truly united with others in the heart and the spirit and the life, united in the spiritual truth and in the Divine. The other way is to go forward from where one is, seeking the Divine centrally and subordinating all else to that, but not putting everything else aside, rather seeking to transform gradually and progressively whatever is capable of such transformation. All the things that are not wanted in the relation – sex impurity, jealousy, anger, egoistic demand – drop away as the inner being grows purer and is replaced by the unity of soul with soul and the binding together of the social life in the hoop of the Divine.

It is not that one cannot have relations with people outside the circle of the sadhaks, but there too if the spiritual life grows within, it must necessarily affect the relation and spiritualise it on the sadhak's side. And there must be no such attachment as would make the relation an obstacle or a rival to the Divine. Attachment to family etc. often is like that and, if so, it falls away from the sadhak. That is an exigence which, I think, should not be considered excessive. All that, however, can be progressively done; a severing of existing relations is necessary for some, it is not so for all. A transformation, however gradual, is indispensable, – severance where severance is the right thing to do.

P.S. I must repeat also that each case differs – one rule for all is not practical or practicable. What is needed by each for his spiritual progress is the one desideratum to be held in view.

*

Friendship or affection is not excluded from the yoga. Friendship with the Divine is a recognised relation in the sadhana. Friendships between the sadhaks exist and are encouraged by the Mother. Only, we seek to found them on a surer basis than that on which the bulk of human friendships are insecurely founded. It is precisely because we hold friendship, brotherhood, love to be sacred things that we want this change – because we do not want to see them broken at every moment by the movements of the ego, soiled and spoiled and destroyed by the passions, jealousies, treacheries to which the vital is prone – it is to make them truly sacred and secure that we want them rooted in the soul, founded on the rock of the Divine. Our yoga is not an ascetic yoga: it aims at purity, but not at a cold austerity. Friendship and love are indispensable notes in the harmony to which we aspire. It is not a vain dream, for we have seen that even in imperfect conditions, when a little of the indispensable element is there at the very root, the thing is possible. It is difficult and the old obstacles still cling obstinately? But no victory can be won without a fixed fidelity to the aim and a long effort. There is no other way than to persevere.

*

In yoga friendship can remain but attachment has to fall away or any such engrossing affection as would keep one tied to the ordinary life and consciousness.

*

Human affection is obviously unreliable because it is so much based upon selfishness and desire; it is a flame of the ego sometimes turbid and misty, sometimes more clear and brightly coloured – sometimes tamasic based on instinct and habit, sometimes rajasic and fed by passion or the cry for vital interchange, sometimes more sattwic and trying to be or look to itself disinterested. But fundamentally it depends on a personal need or a return of some kind inward or outward and when the need is not satisfied or the return ceases or is not given, it most often diminishes or dies or exists only as a tepid or troubled remnant of habit from the past or else turns for satisfaction elsewhere. The more intense it is, the more it is apt to be troubled by tumults, clashes, quarrels, egoistic disturbances of all kinds, selfishness, exactions, lapses even to rage and hatred, ruptures. It is not that these affections cannot last — tamasic instinctive affections last because of habit in spite of everything dividing the persons, e.g. certain family affections; rajasic affections can last sometimes in spite of all disturbances and incompatibilities and furious ruptures because one has a vital need of the other and clings because of that or because both have that need and are constantly separating to return and returning to separate or proceeding from quarrel to reconciliation and from reconciliation to quarrel; sattwic affections last very often from duty to the ideal or with some other support though they may lose their keenness or intensity or brightness. But the true reliability is there only when the psychic element in human affections becomes strong enough to colour or dominate the rest. For that reason friendship is or rather can oftenest be the most durable of the human affections because there there is less interference of the vital and even though a flame of the ego it can be a quiet and pure fire giving always its warmth and light. Nevertheless reliable friendship is almost always with a very few; to have a horde of loving, unselfishly faithful friends is a phenomenon so rare that it can be safely taken as an illusion. . . . In any case human affection whatever its value has its place, because through it the psychic being gets the emotional experiences it needs until it is ready to prefer the true to the apparent, the perfect to the imperfect, the divine to the human. As the consciousness has to rise to the higher level so the activities of the heart also have to rise to that higher level and change their basis and character. Yoga is the founding of all life and consciousness in the Divine, so also love and affection must be rooted in the Divine and a spiritual and psychic oneness in the Divine must be their foundation — to reach the Divine first leaving other things

aside or to seek the Divine alone is the straight road towards
that change. That means no attachment – it need not mean
turning affection into disaffection or chill indifference.

*

Human love is mostly vital and physical with a mental
support – it can take an unselfish, noble and pure form and
expression only if it is touched by the psychic. It is true, as
you say, that it is more usually a mixture of ignorance,
attachment, passion and desire. But whatever it may be, one
who wishes to reach the Divine must not burden himself
with human loves and attachments, for they form so many
fetters and hamper his steps, turning him away besides from
the concentration of his emotions on the one supreme object
of love.

There is such a thing as psychic love, pure, without
demand, sincere in self-giving, but it is not usually left pure
in the attraction of human beings to one another. One must
also be on one's guard against the profession of psychic love
when one is doing sadhana, – for that is most often a cloak
and justification for yielding to a vital attraction or attachment.

*

One can have a psychic feeling of love for someone, a
universal love for all creatures, but one has to give oneself
only to the Divine.

*

The love of the sadhak should be for the Divine. It is only
when he has that fully that he can love others in the right
way.

*

There is a love in which the emotion is turned towards the
Divine in an increasing receptivity and growing union. What

it receives from the Divine it pours out on others, but freely without demanding a return — if you are capable of that, then that is the highest and most satisfying way to love.

RELATIONS BETWEEN MEN AND WOMEN

The only relation permissible between a sadhak and sadhika here is the same as between a sadhak and sadhak or between a sadhika and sadhika — a friendly relation as between followers of the same path of yoga and children of the Mother.

*

In a general way the only method for succeeding in having between a man and a woman the free and natural yogic relations that should exist between a sadhak and a sadhika in this yoga is to be able to meet each other without thinking at all that one is a man and another a woman — both are simply human beings, both sadhaks, both striving to serve the Divine and seeking the Divine alone and none else. Have that fully in yourself and no difficulty is likely to come.

*

Our experience is that it is only when both are in the true consciousness centred round the Divine that there is some chance of a true meeting in the Divine. Otherwise, with the personal relation that forms there comes in either disappointment and alienation or else reactions that are not pure.

*

As for turning all to the Divine, that is a counsel of perfection for those who don't care to carry any luggage. But otherwise friendship between man and man or man and woman or woman and woman is not forbidden, provided it is the true thing and sex does not come in and also provided it does not turn one away from the goal. If the central aim is strong, that is sufficient. . . . When I spoke of personal relation, I certainly did not mean pure indifference, for indifference does not create a relation: it tends to non-relation altogether. Emotional friendship need not be an obstacle.

*

It is certainly easier to have friendship between man and man or between woman and woman than between man and woman, because there the sexual intrusion is normally absent. In a friendship between man and woman the sexual turn can at any moment come in a subtle or in a direct way and produce perturbations. But there is no impossibility of friendship between man and woman pure of this element; such friendships can exist and have always existed. All that is needed is that the lower vital should not look in at the back door or be permitted to enter. There is often a harmony between a masculine and a feminine nature, an attraction or an affinity which rests on something other than any open or covert lower vital (sexual) basis — it depends sometimes predominantly on the mental or the psychic or on the higher vital, sometimes on a mixture of these for its substance. In such a case friendship is natural and there is little chance of other elements coming in to pull it downwards or break it.

It is also a mistake to think that the vital alone has warmth and the psychic is something frigid without any flame in it. A clear limpid goodwill is a very good and desirable thing. But that is not what is meant by psychic love. Love is love and not merely goodwill. Psychic love can have a warmth and a flame as intense and more intense than the vital, only it is a pure fire, not dependent on the satisfaction of ego-desire or on the eating up of the fuel it embraces. It is a white flame, not a red one; but white heat is not inferior to the red variety in its ardour. It is true that the psychic love does not usually get its full play in human relations and human nature; it finds the fullness of its fire and ecstasy more easily when it is lifted towards the Divine. In the human relation the psychic love gets mixed up with other elements which seek at once to use

it and overshadow it. It gets an outlet for its own full
intensities only at rare moments. Otherwise it comes in only
as an element, but even so it contributes all the higher things
in a love fundamentally vital − all the finer sweetness,
tenderness, fidelity, self-giving, self-sacrifice, reachings of
soul to soul, idealising sublimations that lift up human love
beyond itself, come from the psychic. If it could dominate
and govern and transmute the other elements, mental, vital,
physical, of human love, then love could be on the earth
some reflection or preparation of the real thing, an integral
union of the soul and its instruments in a dual life. But even
some imperfect appearance of that is rare.

Our view is that the normal thing is in yoga for the entire
flame of the nature to turn towards the Divine and the rest
must wait for the true basis: to build higher things on the
sand and mire of the ordinary consciousness is not safe. That
does not necessarily exclude friendships or comradeships,
but these must be subordinate altogether to the central fire.
If anyone makes meanwhile the relation with the Divine his
one absorbing aim, that is quite natural and gives the full
force to the sadhana. Psychic love finds itself wholly when it
is the radiation of the diviner consciousness for which we are
seeking; till then it is difficult for it to put out its undimmed
integral self and figure.

FAMILY TIES

When one enters the spiritual life, the family ties which
belong to the ordinary nature fall away − one becomes
indifferent to the old things. This indifference is a release.
There need be no harshness in it at all. To remain tied to the
old physical affections would mean to remain tied to the
ordinary nature and that would prevent the spiritual progress.

It [the child's indebtedness to his father for bringing him up] is a law of human society, not a law of Karma. The child did not ask the father to bring him into the world – and if the father has done it for his own pleasure, it is the least he can do to bring up the child. All these are social relations (and it is not at all a one-sided debt of the child to the father, either), but whatever they are, they cease once one takes to the spiritual life. For the spiritual life does not at all rest on the external physical relations; it is the Divine alone with whom one has then to do.

*

What you write about the family ties is perfectly correct. It creates an unnecessary interchange and comes in the way of a complete turning to the Divine. Relations after taking up yoga should be less based on a physical origin or the habits of the physical consciousness and more and more on the basis of sadhana – of sadhak with sadhaks, of others as souls travelling the same path or children of the Mother than in the ordinary way or with the old viewpoint.

*

It is necessary if you want to progress in your Sadhana that you should make the submission and surrender of which you speak sincere, real and complete. This cannot be as long as you mix up your desires with your spiritual aspiration. It cannot be as long as you cherish vital attachment to family, child or anything or anybody else. If you are to do this Yoga, you must have only one desire and aspiration, to receive the spiritual Truth and manifest it in all your thoughts, feelings, actions and nature. You must not hunger after any relations with anyone. The relations of the Sadhak with others must be created for him from within, when he has the true consciousness and lives in the Light. They will be determined within him by the power and will of the Divine Mother according to the supramental Truth for the divine life and divine work; they must not be determined by his mind and his vital desires.

MIXING WITH OTHERS

When one is with another for some time talking etc., there is always some vital interchange, unless one rejects what comes from the others instinctively or deliberately. If one is impressionable, there may be a strong impression or influence from the other. Then when one goes to another person it is possible to pass it on to the other. That is a thing which is constantly happening. But this thing happens without the knowledge of the transmitter. When one is conscious, one can prevent it happening.

*

... the ordinary movements of interchange are harmless provided they are kept within moderate limits. What creates a difficulty in the sadhana is that one may easily draw in undesirable influences or pass them on to others. It is the reason why at certain stages a limitation of talk, intercourse etc. is often advisable. But the true remedy is to become inwardly conscious, to know and be able to repel any undesirable incursion or influence, to be able when speaking, mixing etc. to keep a defence round one and allow to pass in only what one can accept and nothing else. Also to measure what one can give out safely and what one cannot. When one has the consciousness and the practice, this working becomes almost automatic.

*

That [mixing with people, laughing, joking, etc.] is a kind of vital expansiveness, it is not vital strength — this expansiveness is also expensive. For when there is this mixing, the vitally strong get strength from it but the vitally weak expend what strength they have and become weaker.

*

I think no rule can be laid down applicable to all. There are some who have the expansive tendency of the vital, others who have the concentrative. The latter are absorbed in their own intensity of endeavour and certainly they gather from that a great force for progress and are saved the expense and loss of energy which frequently comes to the more communicative and also make themselves less open to reactions from others (though this cannot be altogether avoided). The others need to communicate what is in them and cannot wait for the full fullness before they use what they have. Even they may need to give out as well as to take in in order to progress. The only thing is that they must balance the two tendencies, concentrating to receive from above as much or more than they open sideways to distribute.

*

It is a matter of temperament. Some are psychically and vitally sensitive and responsive to all that comes from anywhere; others are solid of nerve and walled against invasion. It is not at all a question of strength or weakness. The first have a greater sense of life and answer to life; they suffer more from life and get more from it. It is the difference between the Greek and the Roman. Even without egoism the difference remains because it is of the temperament. In yoga the first type are more able to feel everything directly and know everything in detail by close experience; it is their great advantage. The others have to use the mind to know and their grasp is less intimate.

*

It is true that one has to try to keep the inner condition under all circumstances, even the most adverse; but that does not mean that one has to accept, unnecessarily, unfavourable conditions when there is no good reason for their being allowed to go on. Especially, the nervous system and the physical cannot bear an excessive strain as well as the mind and higher vital; your fatigue came from the strain of living in one consciousness and at the same time exposing yourself too much to prolonged contacts from the ordinary consciousness. A certain amount of self-defence is necessary – so that the consciousness may not be pulled down or out constantly into the ordinary atmosphere or the physical strained by being forced into activities that have become foreign to you. Those who practise yoga often seek refuge in solitude from these difficulties; that is unnecessary here, but all the same you need not submit to being put under this kind of useless strain always.

*

How are you going to find the right external relations by withdrawing altogether from external relations? And how do you propose to be thoroughly transformed and unified by living only in the internal life, without any test of the transformation and unity by external contact and the ordeals of the external work and life? Thoroughness includes external work and relations and not a retired inner life only.

*

It is true that mixing with others too closely tends to lower the condition, if they are not themselves in the right attitude and live very much in the vital. In all contacts what you have to do is to remain within, keep a detached attitude and not allow yourself to be troubled by the difficulties that arise in work or the movements of people, but keep yourself the true movement. Do not be caught by the desire to "help" others – do and speak yourself the right thing from the inner poise and leave the help to come to them from the Divine. Nobody can really help – only the Divine Grace.

*

The idea of helping others is a subtle form of the ego. It is only the Divine Force that can help. One can be its instrument, but you should first learn to be a fit and egoless instrument.

*

To concentrate most on one's own spiritual growth and experience is the first necessity of the sadhak – to be eager to help others draws away from the inner work. To grow in the spirit is the greatest help one can give to others, for then something flows out naturally to those around that helps them.

TALKING WITH OTHERS

In talking one has the tendency to come down into a lower and more external consciousness because talking comes from the external mind. But it is impossible to avoid it altogether. What you must do is to learn to get back at once to the inner consciousness – this so long as you are not able to speak always from the inner being or at least with the inner being supporting the action.

*

Talking of an unnecessary character tires the inner being because the talk comes from the outer nature while the inner has to supply the energy which it feels squandered away.

Even those who have a strong inner life, take a long time before they can connect it with the outer speech and action. Outer speech belongs to the externalising mind – that is why it is so difficult to connect it with the inner life.

*

Chat of that kind has indeed a very tiring effect when one is at all in the stream of true experience, because it dissipates the energy uselessly and makes the mind movement a thing of valueless shreds and patches instead of gathered and poised in itself so as to receive.

*

The condition which you feel is one which is very well known in sadhana. It is a sort of passage or transition, a state of inwardness which is growing but not yet completed – at that time to speak or throw oneself outward is painful. What is necessary is to be very quiet and remain within oneself all the time until the movement is completed, – one should not speak or only a little and in a low quiet way nor concentrate the mind on outward things. You should also not mind what people say or question, – although they are practising sadhana, they know nothing about these conditions and if one becomes quiet or withdrawn they think one must be sad or ill. . . .

The condition lasts often for a number of days, sometimes many, until something definite begins. Remain confident and quiet.

*

Yes, of course, complete truth of speech is very important for the sadhak and a great help for bringing Truth into the consciousness. It is at the same time difficult to bring the speech under control; for people are accustomed to speak what comes to them and not to supervise and control what they say. There is something mechanical about speech and to bring it to the level of the highest part of the consciousness is never easy. That is one reason why to be sparing in speech is helpful. It helps to a more deliberate control and prevents the tongue from running away with one and doing whatever it likes.

To stand back means to become a witness of one's own mind and speech, to see them as something separate from oneself and not identify oneself with them. Watching them as a witness, separate from them, one gets to know what they are, how they act and then put a control over them, reject what one does not approve and think and speak only what one feels to be true. This cannot, of course, be done all at once. It takes time to establish this attitude of separateness, still more time to establish the control. But it can be done by practice and persistence.

*

The psychic self-control that is desirable in these surroundings and in the midst of discussion would mean among other things:

1. Not to allow the impulse of speech to assert itself too much or say anything without reflection, but to speak always with a conscious control and only what is necessary and helpful.

2. To avoid all debate, dispute or too animated discussion and simply say what has to be said and leave it there. There should also be no insistence that you are right and the others wrong, but what is said should only be thrown in as a contribution to the consideration of the truth of the matter.

3. To keep the tone of speech and the wording very quiet and calm and uninsistent.

4. Not to mind at all if others are heated and dispute, but remain quiet and undisturbed and yourself speak only what can help things to be smooth again.

5. If there is gossip about others and harsh criticism (especially about sadhaks), not to join — for these things are helpful in no way and only lower the consciousness from its higher level.

6. To avoid all that would hurt or wound others.

*

On the whole you are right. Useless conversation which lowers the consciousness or brings back something of a past consciousness is better avoided. Talking about sadhana also comes under the category when it is merely mental discussion of a superficial kind.

*

The Light left you because you spoke of it to someone who was not an *adhikārī*. It is safest not to speak of these experiences except to a Guru or to one who can help you. The passing away of an experience as soon as it is spoken of is a frequent happening and for that reason many yogis make it a rule never to speak of what happens within them, unless it is a thing of the past or a settled realisation that nothing can take away. A settled permanent realisation abides, but these were rather things that come to make possible an opening in the consciousness to something more complete – to prepare it for realisation.

*

It is not very advisable to discuss either myself or the Ashram or spiritual things with hostile minds or unbelievers. These discussions usually bring on the Sadhak a stress of the opposing atmosphere and cannot be helpful to his progress. Reserve is the best attitude; one need not be concerned to dispel their bad will or their ignorance.

*

If you want to be an instrument of the Truth, you must always speak the truth and not falsehood. But this does not mean that you must tell everything to everybody. To conceal the truth by silence or refusal to speak is permissible, because the truth may be misunderstood or misused by those who are not prepared for it or who are opposed to it – it may even be made a starting-point for distortion or sheer falsehood. But to speak falsehood is another matter. Even in jest it should be avoided, because it tends to lower the consciousness.

HARMONY WITH OTHERS

There are two attitudes that a sadhak can have: either a quiet equality to all regardless of their friendliness or hostility or a general goodwill.

*

The inequality of feelings towards others, liking and disliking, is ingrained in the nature of the human vital. This is because some harmonise with one's own vital temperament, others do not; also there is the vital ego which gets displeased when it is hurt or when things do not go or people do not act according to its preferences or its idea of what they should do. In the self above there is a spiritual calm and equality, a goodwill to all or at a certain stage a quiet indifference to all except the Divine; in the psychic there is an equal kindness or love to all fundamentally, but there may be special relations with one − but the vital is always unequal and full of likes and dislikes. By the sadhana the vital must be quieted down; it must receive from the self above its quiet goodwill and equality to all things and from the psychic its general kindness or love. This will come, but it may take time to come.

*

Those one lives with have always some ways and manners that do not agree with one's own and may grate on the mind. To observe quietly and not resent is part of the discipline in life. Not to be moved or affected at all but to see with equanimity the play of one Nature in all is the discipline of sadhana.

*

I would suggest that in your relations with others, − which seem always to have been full of disharmony, − when incidents occur, it would be much better for you not to take the standpoint that you are all in the right and they are all in the wrong. It would be wiser to be fair and just in reflection, seeing where you have gone astray, and even laying stress on your own fault and not on theirs. This would probably lead to more harmony in your relations with others; at any rate, it would be more conducive to your inner progress, which is more important than to be the top-dog in a quarrel.

*

It is the petty ego in each that likes to discover and talk about the "real or unreal" defects of others – and it does not matter whether they are real or unreal; the ego has no right to judge them, because it has not the right view or the right spirit. It is only the calm, disinterested, dispassionate, all-compassionate and all-loving Spirit that can judge and see rightly the strength and weakness in each being.

*

Do not dwell much on the defects of others. It is not helpful. Keep always quiet and peace in the attitude.

*

There is no harm in seeing and observing if it is done with sympathy and impartiality – it is the tendency unnecessarily to criticise, find fault, condemn others (often quite wrongly) which creates a bad atmosphere both for oneself and others. And why this harshness and cocksure condemnation? Has not each man his own faults – why should he be so eager to find fault with others and condemn them? Sometimes one has to judge but it should not be done hastily or in a censorious spirit.

*

Yes, one's bad thoughts and good thoughts can have a bad or a good effect on others, though they have not always because they are not strong enough – but still that is the tendency. It is therefore always said by those who have this knowledge that we should abstain from bad thoughts of others for this reason. It is true that both kinds of thought come equally to the mind in its ordinary state; but if the mind and mental will are well developed, one can establish a control over one's thoughts as well as over one's acts and prevent the bad ones from having their play. But this mental control is not enough for the sadhak. He must attain to a quiet mind and in the silence of the mind receive only the Divine thought-forces or other divine Forces and be their field and instrument.

*

Do not think whether people agree with you or do not agree with you or whether you are good or bad, but think that "the Mother loves me and I am the Mother's". If you base your life on that thought, everything will soon become easy.

*

If you want to have knowledge or see all as brothers or have peace, you must think less of yourself, your desires, feelings, people's treatment of you, and think more of the Divine — living for the Divine, not for yourself.

*

The inner loneliness can only be cured by the inner experience of union with the Divine; no human association can fill the void. In the same way, for the spiritual life the harmony with others must be founded not on mental and vital affinities, but on the divine consciousness and the union with the Divine. When one feels the Divine and feels others in the Divine, then the real harmony comes. Meanwhile what there can be is the goodwill and unity founded on the feeling of a common divine goal and the sense of being all children of the Mother. . . . Real harmony can come only from a psychic or a spiritual basis.

*

To be alone with the Divine is the highest of all privileged
states for the sadhak, for it is that in which inwardly he
comes nearest to the Divine and can make all existence a
communion in the chamber of the heart as well as in the
temple of the universe. Moreover that is the beginning and
base of the real oneness with all, for it establishes that
oneness in its true base, on the Divine, for it is in the Divine
that he meets and unites with all and no longer in a precarious interchange of the mental and vital ego. So do not fear
loneliness but put your trust in the Mother and go forward
on the Path in her strength and Grace.

12

Other Aspects of Sri Aurobindo's Teaching and Method of Practice

REBIRTH, KARMA AND DESTINY

If evolution is a truth and is not only a physical evolution of species, but an evolution of consciousness, it must be a spiritual and not only a physical fact. In that case, it is the individual who evolves and grows into a more and more developed and perfect consciousness and obviously that cannot be done in the course of a brief single human life. If there is the evolution of a conscious individual, then there must be rebirth. Rebirth is a logical necessity and a spiritual fact of which we can have the experience. Proofs of rebirth, sometimes of an overwhelmingly convincing nature, are not lacking, but as yet they have not been carefully registered and brought together.

*

... a life is only one brief episode in a long history of spiritual evolution in which the soul follows the curve of the line set for the earth, passing through many lives to complete it. It is an evolution out of material inconscience to consciousness and towards the Divine Consciousness, from ignorance to Divine Knowledge, from darkness through half-light to Light, from death to Immortality, from suffering to the Divine Bliss. Suffering is due first to the Ignorance, secondly to the separation of the individual consciousness from the Divine Consciousness and Being, a separation created by the Ignorance — when that ceases, when one lives in the Divine and no more in one's separated smaller self, then only suffering can altogether cease.

*

Note that the idea of rebirth and the circumstances of the new life as a reward or punishment of *puṇya* or *pāpa* is a crude human idea of "justice" which is quite unphilosophical and unspiritual and distorts the true intention of life. Life here is an evolution and the soul grows by experience, working out by it this or that in the nature, and if there is suffering, it is for the purpose of that working out, not as a judgment inflicted by God or Cosmic Law on the errors or stumblings which are inevitable in the Ignorance.

*

Suffering is not inflicted as a punishment for sin or for hostility – that is a wrong idea. Suffering comes like pleasure and good fortune as an inevitable part of life in the ignorance. The dualities of pleasure and pain, joy and grief, good fortune and ill-fortune are the inevitable results of the ignorance which separates us from our true consciousness and from the Divine. Only by coming back to it can we get rid of suffering. Karma from the past lives exists, much of what happens is due to it, but not all. For we can mend our karma by our own consciousness and efforts. But the suffering is simply a natural consequence of past errors, not a punishment, just as a burn is the natural consequence of playing with fire. It is part of the experience by which the soul through its instruments learns and grows until it is ready to turn to the Divine.

*

Each person follows in the world his own line of destiny which is determined by his own nature and actions – the meaning and necessity of what happens in a particular life cannot be understood except in the light of the whole course of many lives. But this can be seen by those who can get beyond the ordinary mind and feelings and see things as a whole, that even errors, misfortunes, calamities are steps in the journey, – the soul gathering experience as it passes through and beyond them until it is ripe for the transition which will carry it beyond these things to a higher consciousness and higher life. When one comes to that line of crossing, one has to leave behind one the old mind and feelings. One looks then on those who are still fixed in the pleasures and sorrows of the ordinary world with sympathy and wherever it is possible with spiritual helpfulness, but no longer with attachment. One learns that they are being led through all their stumblings and trusts to the Universal Power that is watching and supporting their existence to do for them whatever for them is the best. But the one thing that is really important for us is to get into the greater Light and the Divine Union – to turn to the Divine alone, to put our trust there alone whether for ourselves or for others.

*

The soul takes birth each time, and each time a mind, life and body are formed out of the materials of universal nature according to the soul's past evolution and its need for the future.

When the body is dissolved, the vital goes into the vital plane and remains there for a time, but after a time the vital sheath disappears. The last to dissolve is the mental sheath. Finally the soul or psychic being retires into the psychic world to rest there till a new birth is close.

This is the general course for ordinarily developed human beings. There are variations according to the nature of the individual and his development. For example, if the mental is strongly developed, then the mental being can remain; so also can the vital, provided they are organized by and centred around the true psychic being; they share the immortality of the psychic.

The soul gathers the essential elements of its experiences in life and makes that its basis of growth in the evolution;

when it returns to birth it takes up with its mental, vital, physical sheaths so much of its Karma as is useful to it in the new life for further experience.

*

You must avoid a common popular blunder about reincarnation. The popular idea is that Titus Balbus is reborn again as John Smith, a man with the same personality, character, attainments as he had in his former life with the sole difference that he wears coat and trousers instead of a toga and speaks in cockney English instead of popular Latin. That is not the case. What would be the earthly use of repeating the same personality or character a million times from the beginning of time till its end? The soul comes into birth for experience, for growth, for evolution till it can bring the Divine into Matter. It is the central being that incarnates, not the outer personality – the personality is simply a mould that it creates for its figures of experience in that one life. In another birth it will create for itself a different personality, different capacities, a different life and career. . . .

As the evolving being develops still more and becomes more rich and complex, it accumulates its personalities, as it were. Sometimes they stand behind the active elements, throwing in some colour, some trait, some capacity here and there, – or they stand in front and there is a multiple personality, a many-sided character or a many-sided, sometimes what looks like a universal capacity. But if a former personality, a former capacity is brought fully forward, it will not be to repeat what was already done, but to cast the same capacity into new forms and new shapes and fuse it into a new harmony of the being which will not be a reproduction of what was before. . . .

Another thing. It is not the personality, the character that is of the first importance in rebirth – it is the psychic being who stands behind the evolution of the nature and evolves with it. The psychic when it departs from the body, shedding even the mental and vital on its way to its resting place, carries with it the heart of its experiences, – not the physical events, not the vital movements, not the mental buildings, not the capacities or characters, but something essential that it gathered from them, what might be called the divine element for the sake of which the rest existed. That is the permanent addition, it is that that helps in the growth towards the Divine. That is why there is usually no memory of the outward events and circumstances of past lives – for this memory there must be a strong development towards unbroken continuance of the mind, the vital, even the subtle physical; for though it all remains in a kind of seed memory, it does not ordinarily emerge.

*

But too much importance must not be given to past lives. For the purpose of this yoga one is what one is and, still more, what one will be. What one was has a minor importance.

THE AVATAR AND THE VIBHUTI

Surely for the earth-consciousness the very fact that the Divine manifests himself is the greatest of all splendours. Consider the obscurity here and what it would be if the Divine did not directly intervene and the Light of Lights did not break out of the obscurity – for that is the meaning of the manifestation.

*

The Avatar is necessary when a special work is to be done and in crises of the evolution. The Avatar is a special manifestation while for the rest of the time it is the Divine working within the ordinary human limits as a Vibhuti.

*

An Avatar, roughly speaking, is one who is conscious of the presence and power of the Divine born in him or descended into him and governing from within his will and life and action; he feels identified inwardly with this divine power and presence.

A Vibhuti is supposed to embody some power of the Divine and is enabled by it to act with great force in the world, but that is all that is necessary to make him a Vibhuti: the power may be very great, but the consciousness is not that of an inborn or indwelling Divinity. This is the distinction we can gather from the Gita which is the main authority on this subject.

*

An Avatar or Vibhuti have the knowledge that is necessary for their work, they need not have more. There was absolutely no reason why Buddha should know what was going on in Rome. An Avatar even does not manifest all the Divine omniscience and omnipotence; he has not come for any such unnecessary display; all that is behind him but not in the front of his consciousness. As for the Vibhuti, the Vibhuti need not even know that he is a power of the Divine. Some Vibhutis like Julius Caesar for instance have been atheists. Buddha himself did not believe in a personal God, only in some impersonal and indescribable Permanent.

*

There are two sides of the phenomenon of Avatarhood, the Divine Consciousness and the instrumental personality. The Divine Consciousness is omnipotent but it has put forth the instrumental personality in Nature under the conditions of Nature and it uses it according to the rules of the game — though also sometimes to change the rules of the game. If Avatarhood is only a flashing miracle, then I have no use for it. If it is a coherent part of the arrangement of the omnipotent Divine in Nature, then I can understand and accept it.

*

I put forward two propositions which appear to me indispensable unless we are to reverse all spiritual knowledge in favour of modern European ideas about things: first, the Divine Manifestation, even when it manifests in mental and human ways, has behind it a consciousness greater than the mind and not bound by the petty mental and moral conventions of this very ignorant human race – so that to impose these standards on the Divine is to try to do what is irrational and impossible. Secondly, this Divine Consciousness behind the apparent personality is concerned with only two things in a fundamental way – the truth above and here below the Lila and the purpose of the incarnation or manifestation, and it does what is necessary for that in the way its greater than human consciousness sees to be the necessary and intended way.

*

Men's way of doing things well is through a clear mental connection; they see things and do things with the mind and what they want is a mental and human perfection. When they think of a manifestation of Divinity, they think it must be an extraordinary perfection in doing ordinary human things – an extraordinary business faculty, political, poetic or artistic faculty, an accurate memory, not making mistakes, not undergoing any defeat or failure. Or else they think of things which they call superhuman like not eating food or telling cotton-futures or sleeping on nails or eating them. All that has nothing to do with manifesting the Divine. . . . These human ideas are false.

The Divinity acts according to another consciousness, the consciousness of the Truth above and the Lila below and It acts according to the need of the Lila, not according to man's ideas of what It should or should not do. This is the first thing one must grasp, otherwise one can understand nothing about the manifestation of the Divine.

THE GURU

Up to now no liberated man has objected to the Guruvada; it is usually only people who live in the mind or vital and have the pride of the mind and the arrogance of the vital that find it below their dignity to recognise a Guru.

*

No, surrender to the Divine and surrender to the Guru are not the same thing. In surrendering to the Guru, it is to the Divine in him that one surrenders — if it were only to a human entity, it would be ineffective. But it is the consciousness of the Divine Presence that makes the Guru a real Guru, so that even if the disciple surrenders to him thinking of the human being to whom he surrenders, that Presence will still make it effective.

*

One can have a Guru inferior in spiritual capacity (to oneself or to other Gurus) carrying in him many human imperfections and yet, if you have the faith, the bhakti, the right spiritual stuff, you can contact the Divine through him, attain to spiritual experiences, to spiritual realisation, even before the Guru himself. Mark the "If", for that proviso is necessary; it is not every disciple who can do that with every Guru. From a humbug you can acquire nothing but his humbuggery. The Guru must have something in him which makes the contact with the Divine possible, something which works even if he is not in his outer mind quite conscious of its action. If there is nothing at all spiritual in him, he is not a Guru, only a pseudo. Undoubtedly, there can be considerable differences of spiritual realisation between one Guru and another; but much depends on the inner relation between Guru and *śiṣya*. One can go to a very great spiritual man and get nothing or only a little from him; one can go to a man of less spiritual capacity and get all he has to give – and more. The causes of this disparity are various and subtle; I need not expand on them here. It differs with each man. I believe the Guru is always ready to give what can be given, if the disciple can receive, or it may be, when he is ready to receive. If he refuses to receive or behaves inwardly or outwardly in such a way as to make reception impossible or if he is not sincere or takes up the wrong attitude, then things become difficult. But if one is sincere and faithful and has the right attitude and if the Guru is a true Guru, then, after whatever time, *it* will come.

*

Ramakrishna had the siddhi himself before he began giving to others – so had Buddha. I don't know about the others. By perfection of course is meant siddhi in one's own path – realisation. Ramakrishna always put that as a rule that one should not become a teacher to others until one has the full authority.

*

The Guru is the Guide in the yoga. When the Divine is accepted as the Guide, He is accepted as the Guru.

*

It is not usual to use the word Guru in the supramental yoga, here everything comes from the Divine himself. But if anybody wants it he can use it for the time being.

*

The relation of Guru and disciple is only one of many relations which one can have with the Divine, and in this yoga which aims at a supramental realisation, it is not usual to give it this name; rather, the Divine is regarded as the Source, the living Sun of Light and Knowledge and Consciousness and spiritual realisation, and all that one receives is felt as coming from there and the whole being remoulded by the Divine Hand. This is a greater and more intimate relation than that of the human Guru and disciple, which is more of a limited mental ideal. Nevertheless, if the mind still needs the more familiar mental conception, it can be kept so long as it is needed; only do not let the soul be bound by it and do not let it limit the inflow of other relations with the Divine and larger forms of experience.

RELIGION

The Divine Truth is greater than any religion or creed or scripture or idea or philosophy – so you must not tie yourself to any of these things.

*

... you say that you ask only for the Truth and yet you speak like a narrow and ignorant fanatic who refuses to believe in anything but the religion in which he was born. All fanaticism is false, because it is a contradiction of the very nature of God and of Truth. Truth cannot be shut up in a single book, Bible or Veda or Koran, or in a single religion. The Divine Being is eternal and universal and infinite and cannot be the sole property of the Mussulmans or of the Semitic religions only, – those that happened to be in a line from the Bible and to have Jewish or Arabian prophets for their founders. Hindus and Confucians and Taoists and all others have as much right to enter into relation with God and find the Truth in their own way. All religions have some truth in them, but none has the whole truth; all are created in time and finally decline and perish. Mahomed himself never pretended that the Koran was the last message of God and there would be no other. God and Truth outlast these religions and manifest themselves anew in whatever way or form the Divine Wisdom chooses. You cannot shut up God in the limitations of your own narrow brain or dictate to the Divine Power and Consciousness how or where or through whom it shall manifest; you cannot put up your puny barriers against the divine Omnipotence. These again are simple truths which are now being recognised all over the world; only the childish in mind or those who vegetate in some formula of the past deny them.

*

There is nothing noble besides in fanaticism — there is no nobility of motive, though there may be a fierce enthusiasm of motive. Religious fanaticism is something psychologically low-born and ignorant — and usually in its action fierce, cruel and base. Religious ardour like that of the martyr who sacrifices himself only is a different thing.

*

I do not take the same view of the Hindu religion as J. Religion is always imperfect because it is a mixture of man's spirituality with his endeavours that come in in trying to sublimate ignorantly his lower nature. Hindu religion appears to me as a cathedral-temple, half in ruins, noble in the mass, often fantastic in detail but always fantastic with a significance — crumbling or badly outworn in places, but a cathedral-temple in which service is still done to the Unseen and its real presence can be felt by those who enter with the right spirit. The outer social structure which it built for its approach is another matter.

*

The Ashram has nothing to do with Hindu religion or culture or any religion or nationality. The Truth of the Divine which is the spiritual reality behind all religions and the descent of the supramental which is not known to any religion are the sole things which will be the foundation of the work of the future.

*

Nothing depends on the numbers. The numbers of Buddhism or Christianity were so great because the majority professed it as a creed without its making the least difference to their external life. If the new consciousness were satisfied with that, it could also and much more easily command homage and acceptance by the whole earth. It is because it is a greater consciousness, the Truth-Consciousness, that it will insist on a real change.

*

Well-known or unknown has absolutely no importance from the spiritual point of view. It is simply the propagandist spirit. We are not a party or a church or religion seeking adherents or proselytes. One man who earnestly pursues the yoga is of more value than a thousand well-known men.

*

As for propaganda I have seen that it is perfectly useless for us – if there is any effect, it is a very trifling and paltry effect not worth the trouble. If the Truth has to spread itself, it will do it of its own motion; these things are unnecessary.

*

Then, again, I don't believe in advertisement except for books etc., and in propaganda except for politics and patent medicines. But for serious work it is a poison. It means either a stunt or a boom – and stunts and booms exhaust the thing they carry on their crest and leave it lifeless and broken high and dry on the shores of nowhere – or it means a movement. A movement in the case of a work like mine means the founding of a school or a sect or some other damned nonsense. It means that hundreds or thousands of useless people join in and corrupt the work or reduce it to a pompous farce from which the Truth that was coming down recedes into secrecy and silence. It is what has happened to the "religions" and is the reason of their failure. If I tolerate a little writing about myself, it is only to have a sufficient counter-weight in that amorphous chaos, the public mind, to balance the hostility that is always aroused by the presence of a new dynamic Truth in this world of ignorance. But the utility ends there and too much advertisement would defeat that object. I am perfectly "rational", I assure you, in my methods and I do not proceed merely on any personal dislike of fame. If and so far as publicity serves the Truth, I am quite ready to tolerate it; but I do not find publicity for its own sake desirable.

BEAUTY

Beauty is as much an expression of the Divine as Knowledge, Power or Ananda.

*

Beauty is the special divine Manifestation in the physical as Truth is in the mind, Love in the heart, Power in the vital. Supramental beauty is the highest divine beauty manifesting in Matter.

*

Beauty is the way in which the physical expresses the Divine – but the principle and law of Beauty is something inward and spiritual and expresses itself through the form.

*

Beauty is Ananda taking form – but the form need not be a physical shape. One speaks of a beautiful thought, a beautiful act, a beautiful soul. What we speak of as beauty is Ananda in manifestation; beyond manifestation beauty loses itself in Ananda or, you may say, beauty and Ananda become indistinguishably one.

*

There is a certain state of Yogic consciousness in which all things become beautiful to the eye of the seer, simply because they spiritually are — because they are a rendering in line and form of the quality and force of existence, of the consciousness, of the Ananda that rules the worlds, — of the hidden Divine. What a thing is to the exterior sense may not be, often is not beautiful for the ordinary aesthetic vision, but the Yogin sees in it the something More which the external eye does not see, he sees the soul behind, the self and spirit, he sees too lines, hues, harmonies and expressive dispositions which are not to the first surface sight visible or seizable. It may be said that he brings into the object something that is in himself, transmutes it by adding out of his own being to it — as the artist too does something of the same kind but in another way. It is not quite that, however; what the Yogin sees, what the artist sees, is there, his is a transmuting vision because it is a revealing vision; he discovers behind what the object appears to be, the something More that it is. . . .

But there is one thing more that can be said, and that makes a big difference. In the Yogin's vision of universal beauty, all becomes beautiful, but all is not reduced to a single level. There are gradations, there is a hierarchy in this All-Beauty and we see that it depends on the ascending power (Vibhuti) of Consciousness and Ananda that expresses itself in the object. All is the Divine, but some things are more divine than others. In the artist's vision too there are or can be gradations, a hierarchy of values.

ART, POETRY, MUSIC, LITERATURE

Music, painting, poetry and many other activities which are of the mind and vital can be used as part of spiritual development or of the work and for a spiritual purpose: it depends on the spirit in which they are done.

*

Art, poetry, music are not yoga, not in themselves things spiritual any more than philosophy is a thing spiritual or Science. There lurks here another curious incapacity of the modern intellect – its inability to distinguish between mind and spirit, its readiness to mistake mental, moral and aesthetic idealisms for spirituality and their inferior degrees for spiritual values. It is mere truth that the mental intuitions of the metaphysician or the poet for the most part fall far short of a concrete spiritual experience; they are distant flashes, shadowy reflections, not rays from the centre of Light. It is not less true that, looked at from the peaks, there is not much difference between the high mental eminences and the lower climbings of this external existence. All the energies of the Lila are equal in the sight from above, all are disguises of the Divine. But one has to add that all can be turned into a first means towards the realisation of the Divine. . . . All things in the Lila can turn into windows that open on the hidden Reality. Still so long as one is satisfied with looking through windows, the gain is only initial; one day one will have to take up the pilgrim's staff and start out to journey there where the Reality is for ever manifest and present. Still less can it be spiritually satisfying to remain with shadowy reflections, a search imposes itself for the Light which they strive to figure. But since this Reality and this Light are in ourselves no less than in some high region above the mortal plane, we can in the seeking for it use many of the figures and activities of life; as one offers a flower, a prayer, an act to the Divine, one can offer too a created form of beauty, a song, a poem, an image, a strain of music, and gain through it a contact, a response or an experience. And when that divine consciousness has been entered or when it grows within, then too its expression in life through these things is not excluded from yoga; these creative activities can still have their place, though not intrinsically a greater place than any other that can be put to divine use and service. Art, poetry, music, as they are in their ordinary functioning, create mental and vital, not spiritual values; but they can be turned to a higher end, and then, like all things that are capable of linking our consciousness to the Divine, they are transmuted and become spiritual and can be admitted as part of a life of yoga. All takes new values not from itself, but from the consciousness that uses it; for there is only one thing essential, needful, indispensable, to grow conscious of the Divine Reality and live in it and live it always.

*

It is obvious that poetry cannot be a substitute for Sadhana; it can be an accompaniment only. If there is a feeling (of devotion, surrender etc.), it can express and confirm it; if there is an experience, it can express and strengthen the force of experience. As reading of books like the Upanishads or Gita or singing of devotional songs can help, especially at one stage or another, so this can help also. Also it opens a passage between the external consciousness and the inner mind or vital. But if one stops at that, then nothing much is gained. Sadhana must be the main thing and Sadhana means the purification of the nature, the consecration of the being, the opening of the psychic and the inner mind and vital, the contact and presence of the Divine, the realisation of the Divine in all things, surrender, devotion, the widening of the consciousness into the cosmic Consciousness, the Self one in all, the psychic and the spiritual transformation of the nature. If these things are neglected and only poetry and mental development and social contact occupy all the time, then that is not Sadhana. Also the poetry must be written in the true spirit, not for fame or self-satisfaction, but as a means of contact with the Divine through inspiration or of the expression of one's own inner being as it was written formerly by those who left behind them so much devotional and spiritual poetry in India; it does not help if it is written only in the spirit of the western artist or *litterateur*. Even works or meditation cannot succeed unless they are done in the right spirit of consecration and spiritual aspiration gathering up the whole being and dominating all else.

*

To be a literary man is not a spiritual aim, but to use literature as a means of spiritual expression is another matter. Even to make expression a vehicle of a superior power helps to open the consciousness. The harmonising rests on that principle.

*

The use of your writing is to keep you in touch with the inner source of inspiration and intuition so as to wear thin the crude *external* crust in the consciousness and encourage the growth of the inner being.

*

Literature and art are or can be a first introduction to the inner being – the inner mind, vital; for it is from there that they come. And if one writes poems of Bhakti, poems of divine seeking, etc., or creates music of that kind, it means that there is a Bhakta or seeker inside who is supporting himself by that self-expression. There is also the point of view behind Lele's answer to me when I told him that I wanted to do Yoga but for work, for action, not for San-nyasa and Nirvana, – but after years of spiritual effort I had failed to find the way and it was for that I had asked to meet him. His first answer was, "It would be easy for you as you are a poet."

*

I have always told you that you ought not to stop your poetry and similar activities. It is a mistake to do so out of asceticism or with the idea of tapasya. One can stop these things when they drop of themselves, because one is full of experience and so interested in one's inner life that one has no energy to spare for the rest. Even then, there is no rule for giving up; for there is no reason why poetry etc. should not be part of sadhana. The love of applause, the desire for fame, the ego-reaction have to be given up, but that can be done without giving up the activity itself. Your vital needs some activity — most vitals do — and to deprive it of its outlet, an outlet that can be helpful and not harmful, makes it sulking, indifferent and desponding or else inclined to revolt at any moment and throw up the sponge. Without the assent of the vital it is difficult to do sadhana — it non-co-operates, or it watches with a grim, even if silent dissatisfaction ready to express at any moment doubt and denial; or it makes a furious effort and then falls back saying: "I have got nothing." The mind by itself cannot do much, it must have support from the vital and for that the vital must be in a cheerful and acquiescent state. It has the joy of creation and there is nothing spiritually wrong in creative action. Why deny your vital this joy of outflow?

*

When you can sing out of your inner consciousness in which you feel the Mother moving all your actions, there is no reason why you should not do it. The development of capacities is not only permissible but right, when it can be made part of the yoga; one can give not only one's soul, but all one's powers to the Divine.

*

What you write is perfectly true, that all human greatness and fame and achievement are nothing before the greatness of the Infinite and the Eternal. There are two possible deductions from that: first that all human action has to be renounced and one should go into a cave; the other is that one should grow out of ego so that the activities of the nature may become one day consciously an action of the Infinite and Eternal. I myself never gave up poetry or other creative human activities out of *tapasya*; they fell into a subordinate position because the inner life became stronger and stronger slowly: nor did I really drop them, only I had so heavy a work laid upon me that I could not find time to go on. But it took me years and years to get the ego out of them or the vital absorption, but I never heard anybody say nor did it ever occur to me that that was a proof that I was not born for Yoga.

*

Every artist almost (there can be rare exceptions) has got something of the public man in him in his vital-physical parts, which makes him crave for the stimulus of an audience, social applause, satisfied vanity, appreciation, fame. That must go absolutely if you want to be a yogi, – your art must be a service not of your own ego, not of anyone or anything else but solely of the Divine.

*

It is your aim to write from the Divine and for the Divine – you should then try to make all equally a pure transcription from the inner source and where the inspiration fails return upon your work so as to make the whole worthy of its origin and its object. All work done for the Divine, from poetry and art and music to carpentry or baking or sweeping a room, should be made perfect even in its smallest external detail as well as in the spirit in which it is done; for only then is it an altogether fit offering.

MENTAL DEVELOPMENT, READING AND STUDY

It does not help for spiritual knowledge to be ignorant of things of this world.

*

Knowledge is always better than ignorance. It makes things possible hereafter if not at the moment, while ignorance actively obstructs and misleads.

*

The development of the mind is a useful preliminary for the Sadhak; it can also be pursued along with the Sadhana on condition that it is not given too big a place and does not interfere with the one important thing, the Sadhana itself.

*

Mental development may or may not help sadhana – if the mind is too intellectually developed on certain rationalistic lines, it may hinder.

*

Sadhana is the aim of a sadhak, not mental development. But if he has spare time, those who have the mental turn will naturally spend it in reading or study of some kind.

*

Reading and study are only useful to acquire information and widen one's field of data. But that comes to nothing if one does not know how to discern and discriminate, judge, see what is within and behind things.

*

Intelligence does not depend on the amount one has read, it is a quality of the mind. Study only gives it material for its work as life also does. There are people who do not know how to read and write who are more intelligent than many highly educated people and understand life and things better. On the other hand, a good intelligence can improve itself by reading because it gets more material to work on and grows by exercise and by having a wider range to move in. But book-knowledge by itself is not the real thing, it has to be used as a help to the intelligence but it is often only a help to stùpidity or ignorance – ignorance because knowledge of facts is a poor thing if one cannot see their true significance.

*

... there are two kinds of understanding – understanding by the intellect and understanding in the consciousness. It is good to have the former if it is accurate, but it is not indispensable. Understanding by the consciousness comes if there is faith and openness, though it may come only gradually and through steps of experience. But I have seen people without education or intellectuality understand in this way perfectly well the course of the yoga in themselves, while intellectual men make big mistakes, e.g. take a neutral mental quietude for the spiritual peace and refuse to come out of it in order to go farther.

*

Reading good books can be of help in the early mental stage – they prepare the mind, put it in the right atmosphere, can even, if one is very sensitive, bring some glimpses of realisation on the mental plane. Afterwards the utility diminishes – you have to find every knowledge and experience in yourself.

*

Yes, the real knowledge comes of itself from within by the touch of the Divine. Reading can be only a momentary help to prepare the mind. But the real knowledge does not come by reading. Some preparation for the inner knowledge may be helpful – but the mind should not be too superficially active or seek to know only for curiosity's sake.

*

To read what will help the yoga or what will be useful for the work or what will develop the capacities for the divine purpose. Not to read worthless stuff or for mere entertain-

ment or for a dilettante intellectual curiosity which is of the
nature of a mental dram-drinking. When one is established
in the highest consciousness, one can read nothing or everything; it makes no difference – but that is still far off.

*

One can say generally that newspaper reading or novel
reading is not helpful to the sadhana and is at least a
concession to the vital which is not yet ready to be absorbed
in the sadhana – unless and until one is able to read in the
right way with a higher consciousness which is not only not
"disturbed" by the reading or distracted by it from the
concentrated yoga-consciousness but is able to make the
right use of what is read from the point of view of the inner
consciousness and the inner life.

*

If one is always in the inner consciousness then one can be
not dispersed even when doing outward things – or if one is
conscious of the Divine at all times and in all one does, then
also can one read newspapers or do much correspondence
without dispersion. But even then though there is not
dispersion, yet there is less intensity of consciousness when
reading a newspaper or writing a letter than when one is not
putting part of oneself into quite external things. It is only
when the consciousness is quite *siddha* that there is not even
this difference. That does not mean one should not do
external things at all, for then one gets no training in joining
the two consciousnesses. But one must recognise that certain things do disperse the consciousness or lower it or
externalise it more than others. Especially one should not
deceive or pretend to oneself that one is not dispersed by
them when one is.

*

You are mistaken in thinking that the sadhana of X, Y, and
Z does not suffer by the dispersion of their minds in all

directions. They would have been far farther on the path if they did a concentrated yoga – even, Y who has an enormous receptivity and is eager for progress might have gone thrice as far as he has done. Moreover, your nature is intense in all it does and it was therefore quite its natural path to take the straight way. Naturally, when once the higher consciousness is settled and both the vital and physical sufficiently ready for the sadhana to go on of itself, strict tapasya will no longer be necessary. But till then we consider it very useful and helpful and in many cases indispensable. But we do not insist on it when the nature is not willing. I see too that those who get into the direct line, (there are not yet very many), get of themselves the tendency to give up these mind-dispersing interests and occupations and throw themselves fully into the sadhana.

WESTERNERS AND INDIAN YOGA

The best way to answer your letter will be, I think, to take separately the questions implied in it. I will begin with the conclusion you have drawn of the impossibility of the yoga for a non-oriental nature.

I cannot see any ground for such a conclusion; it is contrary to all experience. Europeans throughout the centuries have practised with success spiritual disciplines which were akin to oriental yoga and have followed, too, ways of the inner life which came to them from the East. Their non-oriental nature did not stand in their way. The approach and experiences of Plotinus and the European mystics who derived from him were identical, as has been shown recently, with the approach and experiences of one type of Indian yoga. Especially, since the introduction of Christianity, Europeans have followed its mystic disciplines which were one in essence with those of Asia, however much they may have differed in forms, names and symbols. If the question be of Indian yoga itself in its own characteristic forms, here too the supposed inability is contradicted by experience. In early times Greeks and Scythians from the West as well as Chinese and Japanese and Cambodians from the East followed without difficulty Buddhist or Hindu disciplines; at the present day an increasing number of occidentals have taken to Vedantic or Vaishnava or other Indian spiritual practices and this objection of incapacity or unsuitableness has never been made either from the side of the disciples or from the side of the Masters. I do not see, either, *why* there should be any such unbridgeable gulf; for there is no essential difference between the spiritual life in the East and the spiritual life in the West; what difference there is has always been of names, forms and symbols or else of the emphasis laid on one special aim or another or on one side or another of psychological experience. Even here differences are often alleged which do not exist or else are not so great as they appear. I have seen it alleged by a Christian writer (who does not seem to have shared your friend Angus' objection to these scholastic small distinctions) that Hindu spiritual thought and life acknowledged or followed after only the Transcendent and neglected the Immanent Divinity, while Christianity gave due place to both Aspects; but in point of fact, Indian spirituality, even if it laid the final stress on the Highest beyond form and name, yet gave ample recognition and place to the Divine immanent in the world and the Divine immanent in the human being. Indian spirituality has, it is true, a wider and more minute knowledge behind it; it has followed hundreds of different paths, admitted every kind of approach to the Divine and has thus been able to enter into fields which are outside the less ample scope of occidental practice; but that makes no difference to the essentials, and it is the essentials alone that matter.

Your explanation of the ability of many Westerners to practise Indian yoga seems to be that they have a Hindu temperament in a European or American body. As Gandhi is inwardly a moralistic Westerner and Christian, you say, so the other non-oriental members of the Ashram are essentially Hindus in outlook. But what exactly is this Hindu outlook? I have not myself seen anything in them that can be so described nor has the Mother. My own experience contradicts entirely your explanation. I knew very well Sister Nivedita (she was for many years a friend and a comrade in the political field) and met Sister Christine, – the two closest European disciples of Vivekananda. Both were Westerners to the core and had nothing at all of the Hindu outlook; although Sister Nivedita, an Irish woman, had the power of penetrating by an intense sympathy into the ways of life of the people around her, her own nature remained non-oriental to the end. Yet she found no difficulty in arriving at realisation on the lines of Vedanta. Here in this Ashram I have found the members of it who came from the West (I include especially those who have been here longest) typically occidental with all the quality and also all the difficulties of the Western mind and temperament and they have had to cope with their difficulties, just as the Indian members have been obliged to struggle with the limitations and obstacles created by their temperament and training. No doubt, they have accepted in principle the conditions of the yoga, but they had no Hindu outlook when they came and I do not think they have tried to acquire one. Why should they do so? It is not the Hindu outlook or the Western that fundamentally matters in yoga, but the psychic turn and the spiritual urge, and these are the same everywhere.

What are the differences after all from the viewpoint of yoga between the sadhak of Indian and the sadhak of occidental birth? You say the Indian has his yoga half done for him, – first, because he has his psychic much more directly open to the Transcendent Divine. Leaving out the adjective, (for it is not many who are by nature drawn to the Transcendent, most seek more readily the Personal, the Divine immanent here, especially if they can find it in a human body,) there is there no doubt an advantage. It arises simply from the strong survival in India of an atmosphere of spiritual seeking and a long tradition of practice and experience, while in Europe the atmosphere has been lost, the tradition interrupted, and both have to be rebuilt. There is an absence too of the *essential* doubt which so much afflicts the minds of Europeans or, it may be added, Europeanised Indians, although that does not prevent a great activity of a practical and very operative kind of doubt in the Indian sadhak. But when you speak of indifference to fellow human beings in any deeper aspect, I am unable to follow your meaning. My own experience is that the attachment to persons — to mother, father, wife, children, friends — not out of sense of duty or social relationship, but through close heart-ties is quite as strong as in Europe and often more intense; it is one of the great disturbing forces in the way, some succumbing to the pull and many, even advanced sadhaks, being still unable to get it out of their blood and their vital fibre. The impulse to set up a "spiritual" or a "psychic" relationship with others — very usually covering a vital mixture which distracts them from the one aim — is a persistently common feature. There is no difference here between the Western and Eastern human nature. Only the teaching in India is of long standing that all must be turned towards the Divine and everything else either sacrificed or changed into a subordinate and ancillary movement or made by sublimation a first step only towards the seeking for the Divine. This no doubt helps the Indian sadhak if not to become single-hearted at once, yet to orientate himself more completely towards the goal. It is not always for him the Divine alone, though that is considered the highest state; but the Divine, chief and first, is easily grasped by him as the ideal.

The Indian sadhak has his own difficulties in his approach to the yoga — at least to this yoga — which a Westerner has in less measure. Those of the occidental nature are born of the dominant trend of the European mind in the immediate past. A greater readiness of essential doubt and sceptical reserve; a habit of mental activity as a necessity of the nature which makes it more difficult to achieve a complete mental silence; a stronger turn towards outside things born of the plentitude of active life (while the Indian commonly suffers from defects born rather of a depressed or suppressed vital force); a habit of mental and vital self-assertion and sometimes an aggressively vigilant independence which renders difficult any completeness of internal surrender even to a greater Light and Knowledge, even to the divine Influence – these are frequent obstacles. But these things are not universal in Westerners, and they are, on the other hand, present in many Indian sadhaks; they are, like the difficulties of the typical Indian nature, superstructural formations, not the very grain of the being. They cannot permanently stand in the way of the soul, if the soul's aspiration is strong and firm, if the spiritual aim is the chief thing in the life. They are impediments which the fire within can easily burn away if the will to get rid of them is strong, and which it will surely burn away in the end, – though less easily,– even if the outer nature clings long to them and justifies them – provided that the fire, the central will, the deeper impulse is behind all, real and sincere.

This conclusion of yours about the incapacity of the non-oriental for Indian yoga is simply born of a too despondently acute sense of your own difficulties; you have not seen those equally great that have long troubled or are still troubling others. Neither to Indian nor to European can the path of yoga be smooth and easy; their common human nature is there to see to that. To each his own difficulties seem enormous and radical and even incurable by their continuity and persistence and induce long periods of despondency and crises of despair. To have faith enough or enough psychic sight to react at once or almost at once and prevent these attacks is given hardly to two or three in a hundred. But one ought not to settle down into a fixed idea of one's own incapacity or allow it to become an obsession; for such an attitude has no true justification and unnecessarily renders the way harder. Where there is a soul that has once become awake, there is surely a capacity within that can outweigh all surface defects and can in the end conquer.

If your conclusion were true, the whole aim of this yoga would be a vain thing; for we are not working for a race or a people or a continent or for a realisation of which only Indians or only orientals are capable. Our aim is not, either, to found a religion or a school of philosophy or a school of yoga, but to create a ground of spiritual growth and experience and a way which will bring down a greater Truth beyond the mind but not inaccessible to the human soul and consciousness. All can pass who are drawn to that Truth, whether they are from India or elsewhere, from the East or from the West. All may find great difficulties in their personal or common human nature; but it is not their physical origin or their racial temperament that can be an insuperable obstacle to their deliverance.

Notes on the Texts

The passages in this book (with a few exceptions) have been selected from the following volumes of the Sri Aurobindo Birth Centenary Library (SABCL), published between 1970 and 1973 by the Sri Aurobindo Ashram, Pondicherry:

Volume 9 – *The Future Poetry and Letters on Poetry, Literature and Art*

Volume 16 – *The Supramental Manifestation and Other Writings*

Volume 22 – *Letters on Yoga [I]*

Volume 23 – *Letters on Yoga [II]*

Volume 24 – *Letters on Yoga [III]*

Volume 25 – *The Mother*

Volume 26 – *On Himself*

Volume 27 – *Supplement*

References to the SABCL texts are listed below in an abbreviated form. The pages of this book are set in **bold type**; the volumes and page numbers of the SABCL are set in roman type. For example:

3: 26:95-97 = the passage on page 3 of this book is taken from SABCL Volume 26, pages 95-97.

Where more than one passage occurs on a page, the first reference is to the first passage *beginning* on that page, the second reference is to the second passage, and so on.

Facsimile of Sri Aurobindo's handwriting. 24:1639.

Epigraph. Not a letter: from the booklet *Thoughts and Glimpses*. 16:394.

Introduction. Not a letter: written in 1934 for the pamphlet *The Teaching of Sri Aurobindo and Sri Aurobindo's Ashram*. **3**: 26:95-97.

Part One. 7: 24:1639; 23:516-17. **8:** 26:509-10. **9:** 22:148-49; 24:
1271; 26:176. **10:** 23:503; 23:503. **11:** 24:1313-14; 23:519. **12:**
22:146; 23:849. **13:** 23:869; 27:415-16. **14:** 24:1656-57. **15:** 22:137;
22:144. **16:** 26:99-100; 23:676. **17:** 22:121-22. **18:** 23:512. **19:**
23:512-15.

Part Two. 23: 22:157-61. **26:** 22:39; 22:41-42. **27:** 22:44. **28:** 23:580;
22:69-70. **29:** 22:70. **30:** 22:72; 22:39. **31:** 22:73; 22:74. **32:** 22:74;
22:365. **33:** 22:369; 22:369; 22:85-86. **34:** 23:779-80. **35:** 23:794;
22:92; 22:88; 22:104. **36:** 22:105; 25:57-58; 26:115. **37:** 22:97;
22:97; 22:99-101. **40:** 22:101-02. **41:** 22:114-15.

Part Three. 43: 22:47; 26:415-16. **45:** 22:1-2; 22:236-37. **46:** 22:234;
22:235. **47:** 22:252-53. **48:** 24:1499-1500; 22:233. **49:** 23:1020-21;
22:307. **50:** 22:311; 22:313; 24:1602; 22:314. **51:** 22:252; 22:300;
24:1315; 24:1429-30. **52:** 26:208; 22:346. **53:** 22:334. **54:** 22:325;
22:345; 22:310; 22:320-21. **55:** 22:326-27. **56:** *At the Feet of the
Mother and Sri Aurobindo*, 1985 ed., p.191. **57:** 22:265; 22:270. **58:**
22:282-84. **59:** 22:277; 22:288-89. **61:** 26:110-11; 22:298-99; 22:297.
62: 22:251. **63:** 24:1154. **64:** 24:1154-55; 22:264; 22:259-60. **65:**
22:257; 22:239. **66:** 22:239-40; 22:242-43. **67:** 22:177-78. **68:** 22:90;
24:1126. **69:** 26:167; 22:20-21. **70:** 22:8-9. **71:** 22:13; 26:146. **72:**
22:10; *Mother India*, Oct. 1975, pp.795-97.

Part Four. 77: 23:1081; 23:1081; 23:509-10. **78:** 23:510-11. **80:**
22:27-28; 22:20; 22:259. **81:** 22:242; 22:173; 22:168. **82:** 23:586;
22:384-85; 22:385; 22:385. **83:** 22:383-84. **84:** 22:424; 22:389;
22:390; 22:391. **85:** 22:478; 24:1506. **86:** 26:38; 26:197-98. **87:**
22:107; 24:1203. **88:** 25:65; 25:65; 23:1081; 25:67-68; 25:69. **89:**
25:69; 26:455; 25:105. **90:** 25:105; 25:139; 25:139; 24:1207; 25:142.
91: 25:157; 25:139; 23:608-09. **92:** 23:609. **93:** 23:611; 24:1632;
23:611.

Part Five. 95: 23:545; 23:545; 23:545; 23:551. **96:** 23:551-52;
23:549; 22:12-13. **97:** 23:857; 24:1463; 23:505. **98:** 23:603-04;
25:123-24; 23:604-05. **99:** 23:605; *Mother India*, Nov. 1987, p.679.
100: 23:604; 25:121; 25:131-32. **101:** 23:603; 23:585; 23:601-02;
23:586-87. **103:** 23:588-89. **104:** 23:612; 25:135. **105:** 23:598; 23:
583. **106:** 24:1717; 24:1717; 24:1717; 24:1719; 24:1720; 24:1718.
107: 25:336; 24:1707; 23:566; 23:566; 23:566. **108:** 24:1670; 24:
1172; 23:569; 23:565; 23:566. **109:** 23:566; 23:566; 23:567; 23:567;
23:567. **110:** 23:576; 22:166; 23:572; 23:572-73. **112:** 23:584; 25:
347. **113:** 23:630; 23:623; 23:631; 23:625. **114:** 23:625; 23:879. **115:**

23:880-81; *Guidance from Sri Aurobindo*: Volume I, 1974 ed., p.110. **116**: 23:560; 25:205-06; 23:561. **117**: 23:562; 23:903-04; 24:1642. **118**: 23:641-42; 23:636. **119**: 23:642-43. 23:637-38; 23:643. **120**: 23:644; 23:649; 23:649; 23:657; 23:638. **121**: 23:648; 23:640. **122**: 23:656; 23:657-58. **123**: 23:1074; 23:658. **124**: 23:660; 22:143; 23:839; 23:661; 23:661-62. **126**: 23:662-63; 23:663-64; 24:1369; 23:597. **127**: 23:650-51. **Part Six. 129**: 23:669; 23:677. **130**: 22:145-46; 23:674; 22:151-52. **131**: 23:528-29. **133**: 25:200-01; 25:207; 23:533; 25:203. **134**: 23: 691; 23:689-90. **135**: 23:529-30. **136**: 23:687; 23:692; 23:691-92; 23:706; 23:713-14. **137**: 23:714; 23:704. **138**: 23:694; 23:694-95. **139**: 23:693; 24:1463-64; 23:701. **140**: 23:701; 23:700; 23:705. **141**: 23:714-15; 23:715; 23:861-62. **142**: 23:861; 23:862-63; 25: 211-12. **143**: 23:678; 23:716-17; 23:717; 23:716. **144**: 23:717; 25:199; 25: 199; 23:536. **145**: 25:200; 25:199. **146**: 23:721-23. **148**: 23:731; 23:839. **149**: 23:736; 23:723-25. **151**: 23:723; 23:723; 23:517-18. **153**: 23:740; 23:735-36; 23:743. **154**: 23:743; 23:743; 23:743; 23: 539. **155**: 23:727-28; 23:726-27; 23:727; 23:739. **156**: 23:739; 23: 730; 23:728; 23:735; 23:753. **157**: 23:754; 23:755. **158**: 23:764; 23:764; 23:765; 23:764; 23:766; 23:782-83. **159**: 23:776; 23:776; 23:880; 23:787-89. **162**: 23:763; 23:760. **163**: 23:784; 23:780; 23: 780; 23:786. **164**: 23:777; 23:777; 23:777. **165**: 9:507; 23:745-46. **166**: 23:746; 23:745. **167**: 23:533-34; 23:782. **168**: 23:525-26. **Part Seven. 171**: 22:188-89. **172**: 23:877; 23:884-85; 23:877. **173**: 23:877-78; 23:878. **174**: 23:1012; 23:996-97. **175**: 23:997-98; 23:991-94. **179**: 23:995; 23:1002; 23:1003. **180**: 23:1006; 23:1010-11. **181**: 23:1005; 23:1075; 23:1071. **182**: 23:1071; 23:1078; 23:1072; 23: 1075. **183**: 23:916-17; 22:105-06. **184**: 23:1073-74; 23:1070; 22:316-17. **185**: 23:1071. **186**: 23:1072-73; 23:1070; 24:1157; 23:1070-71. **187**: 23:1054; 23:1053. **188**: 23:1052-53; 23:886. **189**: 23:936-38. **191**: 26:90; 23:939-40. **192**: 23:932; 23:931; 23:1051; 22:76. **193**: 23:903; 23:948. **194**: 22:456-57; 23:955; 23:1055. **195**: 23:951-52; 23:952; 23:952. **196**: 24:1500; 24:1487; 23:1023-25. **199**: 23:1031-32; 23:1032; 23:1033. **Part Eight. 201**: 24:1143; 22:98-99. **203**: 24:1094; 24:1095; 23:902-03. **204**: 24:1609; 24:1095-96. **205**: 24:1092; 24:1098. **206**: 24:1115; 24:1097; 24:1107-08. **207**: 24:1109; 24:1108; 22:341-42. **208**: 24: 1098-99; 23:636-37; 24:1099. **209**: 24:1100; 24:1105; 24:1093. **210**: 24:1093; 24:1093-94; 24:1211; 22:115-16. **211**: 24:1163-70. **219**:

24:1126; 24:1128; 24:1136-37. **220:** 24:1151. **221:** 24:1150; 24:1147-48. **222:** 24:1148; 24:1170; 24:1197. **223:** 24:1192; 24:1174; 24:1175. **224:** 24:1220. **225:** 24:1163; 24:1677; 24:1189; 24:1189. **226:** 24:1185; 24:1185; 24:1184; 24:1186. **227:** 24:1187; 24:1188; 24:1211-12. **228:** 24:1665-66. **229:** 22:95; 22:106. **230:** 22:18-19. **231:** 24:1223; 24:1224. **232:** 24:1160; 24:1314; 23:554. **234:** 22:94; 24:1227. **235:** 24:1231; 24:1229. **236:** 24:1229; 24:1232-33; 24:1232. **Part Nine.** **239:** 23:892-93; 23:1004-05; 23:892. **240:** 24:1244; 24:1244; 24:1245. **241:** 24:1245; 24:1243. **242:** 24:1251; 24:1244; 24:1253. **243:** 22:327; 22:334-35. **244:** 24:1296; 22:347-48; 24:1266-67. **245:** 24:1268; 24:1266. **246:** 24:1624-26. **248:** 24:1357; 24:1356; 24:1356; 24:1304. **249:** 24:1301; 24:1304-05; 24:1303-04. **250:** 24:1326; 24:1292; 24:1292; 24:1293. **251:** 24:1297-98. **252:** 24:1337-38. **253:** 24:1409-10. **254:** 24:1327; 23:654; 24:1305-11. **258:** 24:1312. **259:** 24:1324; 24:1315. **260:** 24:1427. **261:** 24:1434; 24:1438; 24:1439. **262:** 24:1437-38; 24:1432; 24:1593; 24:1597. **263:** 24:1593-94. 24:1594. **264:** 24:1608-09; 24:1605-08. **267:** 24:1679. **268:** 24:1609; 24:1611. **Part Ten.** **271:** 24:1629-30; 24:1616-17. **273:** 24:1615. **274:** 24:1634; 24:1347-48. **275:** 24:1345; 25:328; 24:1425; 26:156. **276:** 24:1358-59; 24:1610. **277:** 24:1724-25; 24:1707-08. **278:** 24:1754; 23:906. **279:** 24:1690; 24:1690; 24:1687. **280:** 24:1731; 24:1737-38. **281:** 24:1733; 24:1731-32. **282:** 24:1734; 24:1639-40. **283:** 24:1741-42; 24:1748; 24:1716. **284:** 23:655; 24:1739; 22:394-95. **285:** 24:1770; 24:1769; 24:1766-67. **286:** 24:1765; 23:1087-88; 24:1376. **287:** 24:1372-73; 24:1377. **288:** 24:1753-54. **289:** 24:1389; 24:1370; 24:1375; 23:553. **290:** 24:1392; 24:1387; 24:1388. **291:** 24:1387-88; 24:1396; 24:1395. **292:** 24:1399; 24:1465-66. **293:** 24:1397-98; 24:1398-99. **294:** 24:1402; 24:1402-03. **295:** 24:1395-96; 24:1400; 24:1399-1400. **296:** 24:1400; 24:1410. **297:** 24:1408-09; 24:1412. **298:** 24:1415; 24:1415; 22:491. **299:** 24:1513; 24:1507-09. **301:** 24:1519-20. **302:** 24:1520; 24:1521; 24:1519; 24:1517. **303:** 24:1525; 24:1514; 24:1527; 24:1516. **304:** 24:1531; 23:1069-70. **305:** 24:1530; 24:1531; 24:1513-14. **306:** 24:1538; 24:1540; 24:1539; 24:1523. **307:** 24:1528; 24:1513; 24:1529-30. **308:** 23:811; 24:1416; 24:1416. **309:** 24:1416; 24:1417; 24:1463; 24:1463; 24:1463. **310:** 24:1186-87; 24:1463-64. **311:** 24:1462; 23:916; 24:1476; 24:1479. **312:** 24:1481; 24:1481; 24:1477; 24:1477; 24:1477. **313:** 24:1484; 24:1485; 24:1485-86. **314:** 24:1481-82; 24:1482; 24:1482; 24:1467. **315:** 24:1465; 24:1466;

24:1467. **316**: 24:1468; 24:1471; 24:1470. **317**: 24:1471; 24:1473-74.
318: 24:1563; 24:1564; 24:1564-65. **319**: 24:1571; 24:1568. **320**:
24:1573; 24:1576; 24:1563. **321**: 24:1572; 24:1566. **322**: 24:1581;
24:1561-62. **Part Eleven**. **323**: 23:803-05. **324**: 23:818-19. **325**: 23:819; 23:808-
09. **327**: 23:763-64; 23:815; 23:814; 23:815. **328**: 23:816; 23:816;
23:820; 23:816-17. **329**: 23:817-18. **330**: 23:812. **331**: 23:812-13;
23:812; 25:133. **332**: 23:835; 23:841; 23:833; 23:833-34. **333**: 23:
834; *At the Feet of the Mother and Sri Aurobindo*, 1985 ed., p.194.
334: 23:1064-65; 23:834-35; 23:828. **335**: 22:151; 24:1550; 24:1553;
24:1551. **336**: 23:925; 24:1553. **337**: 24:1555-56; 24:1549-50. **338**:
23:925-26; 26:380; 24:1559. **339**: 23:826; 23:822; *At the Feet of the
Mother and Sri Aurobindo*, 1985 ed., p.133; 25:240. **340**: 23:827;
23:826; 23:826; 23:838-39. **341**: 25:194; 23:825; 23:814. **342**: 23:
814. **Part Twelve**. **343**: 22:47; 22:461. **344**: 22:441; 24:1636; 22:460-61.
345: 22:433. **346**: 22:451-52. **347**: 22:455; 22:401; 22:401. **348**:
22:406-07; 22:410; 22:408. **349**: 22:421-22; 22:410-11. **350**: 23:620;
23:615; 23:618-19. **351**: 23:619; 23:614; 23:615; 23:614-15. **352**:
24:1281; 26:483. **353**: 22:490; 22:139; *Sri Aurobindo Circle*, 1976,
p.i. **354**: 26:138; 23:855; 23:855; 26:375-76. **355**: 25:361; 9:491;
9:491; 9:491. **356**: 9:332-33; 23:859. **357**: 22:198-200. **358**: 26:278-
79. **359**: 9:505; 9:512; 26:279; 24:1302. **360**: 23:857-58; 26:280. **361**:
23:679; 9:505-06; 24:1277. **362**: 24:1261-62; 9:513; 24:1270; 24:
1272; 24:1277; 24:1278-79. **363**: 24:1251; 24:1273; 9:513; 24:1279.
364: 24:1283; 23:837; 23:836-37. **365**: 23:555-60.

PHOTOGRAPHS

Cover photograph. Sri Aurobindo, c. 1918-20, about age fifty.
Photograph facing facsimile of Sri Aurobindo's handwriting. Sri
Aurobindo, c. 1918-20.
Photograph facing Epigraph. Sri Aurobindo, April 1950, age
seventy-seven, by Henri Cartier-Bresson.

Glossary of Names and Terms

The philosophical and psychological terms below are defined as far as possible in Sri Aurobindo's own words.

abhimāna — hurt pride and self-pity mixed with resentment because one feels mistreated by a loved one.

Absolute, the — the supreme reality of that transcendent Being which we call God. Indian thought calls it Brahman, European thought the Absolute because it is a self-existent which is absolved of all bondage to relativities.

acañcalatā — quiet; absence of restlessness.

Adesh — imperative command from the Divine.

Adhara — support, receptacle; the mental-vital-physical system as a vessel of the spiritual consciousness.

adhikārī — one who has capacity (for doing Yoga).

adverse forces — *see* **hostile forces**

Adya Shakti — the original power; the supreme divine Consciousness and Power above the universe; the transcendent Mother.

adhyātma-jīvana — the spiritual life.

Adwaita (*advaita*) — Non-duality, Monism, monistic Vedanta.

Ahankar — ego-sense; egoism.

Ahimsa — non-injuring and non-killing.

Ahriman — in the Zoroastrian religion, the god of darkness, evil and destruction.

Ahura Mazda — in the Zoroastrian religion, the supreme deity and creator of the world, the god of light and good and creative expansion.

ājñācakra — the centre of consciousness between the eyebrows, governing the dynamic mind, will, vision, mental formation.

anāhata — the centre of consciousness in the heart, governing the emotional being; also called *hṛtpadma*.

Ananda — bliss, delight; the essential principle of delight.

Anandamaya — full of Ananda.

anirviṇṇacetasā — with a heart free from depression.

annamaya puruṣa — the physical being.

anubhava — experience.

āsana — fixed posture, set position of the body.

ascent and descent — the two-sided practice of the Integral Yoga, an ascent of the consciousness to the higher planes, a descent of the power of the higher planes into the earth-consciousness so as to drive out the power of darkness and ignorance and control the nature.

Ashram — the house or houses of a Teacher or Master of spiritual philosophy in which he receives and lodges those who come to him for the teaching and practice.

aspiration — the call of the being for higher things, for the Divine, for all that belongs to the higher or divine consciousness.

Asura — Titan; adversary of the Gods; hostile being of the mentalised vital plane.

Asuro-Rakshaso-Pishachic prakriti — Nature under the influence of the hostile beings of the higher, middle and lower vital planes (the Asuras, Rakshasas and Pishachas).

Atman — the Self; the Spirit; the original and essential nature of our existence; the spiritual being above the mind. In its nature the Atman is transcendent or universal (Paramatma, Atma); when it individualises and becomes a central being, it is then the Jivatman.

Augustine, St. — (354-430), a great saint, bishop of Hippo and one of the four Latin fathers of the Christian Church. After a life of sensuality and religious scepticism Augustine suddenly embraced Christianity and became one of its foremost exponents.

avasthā — status.

Avatar — divine incarnation; one in whom the Divine Consciousness has descended into human birth for a great world-work; the word *avatara* means a descent: it is the coming down of the Divine below the line which divides the divine from the human world or status.

Avidya — the Ignorance; the Ignorance of oneness; the consciousness of Multiplicity; the relative and multiple consciousness. *See also* **Ignorance**

bāhyapūjā — external worship.

Bhakta — a lover and devotee of the Divine.

Bhakti — love for the Divine, devotion to the Divine; the delight of the heart in God.

Bhakti Yoga — the yoga of love and devotion.

Bilwamangal — Vaishnava saint who from a sensuous life turned entirely Godward after being rebuked by a courtesan with whom he was infatuated.

Brahma — the first member of the Hindu trinity (Brahma, Vishnu and Shiva); the Creator, he is the Eternal's Personality of Existence.

Brahmacharya — complete sex-purity.

Brahman — the Reality, the Eternal, the Infinite, the Absolute, the Supreme Being, the One beside whom there is nothing else existent.

brahmarandhra — the opening in the subtle body located at the top of the head; through this passage there is the communication between the higher consciousness and the lower in the body.

brahmavyaktikarāṇi yoge — signs accompanying (or helpful to) the opening to the higher consciousness in yoga.

buddheḥ parataḥ — supreme over the intellect.

Buddhi — the thinking mind proper; the mental power of understanding; the discerning intelligence and enlightened will; the discriminating principle of mind, at once intelligence and will.

caitya puruṣa — the psychic being.

cakra — see **centres**

calm — a still, unmoved condition which no disturbance can affect; a strong and positive quietude, firm and solid.

central being — the portion of the Divine in us which supports all the rest and survives through death and birth. It has two forms – above, it is the Jivatman, our true being, of which we become aware when the higher self-knowledge comes; below, it is the psychic being which stands behind mind, body and life.

centres (of consciousness) — centres (chakras) of the inner being; centres of consciousness which connect the inner being with the outer personality. These centres are supposed to be attached to the spinal cord, but in fact they are in the subtle body; by their opening through yoga, the yogic or inner consciousness develops and one escapes from the limitations of the surface consciousness. *See ājñācakra; anāhata; maṇipūra; mūlādhāra; sahasradala; svādhiṣṭhāna; viśuddha.*

Chaitanya — Sri Krishna Chaitanya (1486-1533), a Vaishnava saint whose mode of worshipping Krishna with ecstatic song and dance had a profound effect on Vaishnavism in Bengal.

chakras — *see* **centres**

Chandi — a name of Durga, the goddess who is the conquering and protecting aspect of the Universal Mother.

Chit (*cit*) — pure consciousness; the essential consciousness of the Spirit; the free and all-creative self-awareness of the Absolute.

Chit Shakti — Consciousness-Force.

chitta (*citta*) — the basic stuff of mental consciousness; the stuff of mixed mental-vital-physical consciousness out of which arise the movements of thought, emotion, sensation, impulse, etc.

Christine, Sister — Christine Greenstidel (1866-?), an American disciple of Swami Vivekananda.

cinmaya — consisting of pure consciousness; transcendental.

cit — *see* **Chit**

citta — *see* **Chitta**

consciousness — the self-aware force of existence. The essence of consciousness is the power to be aware of itself and its objects; but it is not only power of awareness of self and things, it is or has also a dynamic and creative energy. Consciousness is not synonymous with mentality, which is only a middle term; below mentality, it sinks into vital and material movements which are for us subconscient; above, it rises into the Supramental which is for us the superconscient.

Consciousness-Force — the Conscious Force that builds the worlds; a universal Energy that is the power of the Cosmic Spirit working out the cosmic and individual truth of things.

consecration — the devoting of all that comes to one, all one's experience and progress to the Divine.

conversion — a turning of the being away from lower things towards the Divine.

cosmic being — the manifold self-expression of the spirit.

cosmic consciousness — the consciousness of the universe, of the cosmic spirit and cosmic Nature, with all the beings and forces within it. In the cosmic consciousness the limits of the ego, personal mind and body disappear and one becomes aware of a cosmic vastness which is or is filled by a cosmic spirit and aware also of the direct play of cosmic forces.

Daityas — demons who warred against the gods and interfered with sacrifices.

Daivic nature — divine nature, godly nature.

descent — *see* **ascent and descent**

desire-soul — the surface soul in us, which works in our vital cravings, our emotions, aesthetic faculty and mental seeking for power, knowledge and happiness; the true soul is the subliminal psychic essence.

Deva — God, Godhead.

Devi — Goddess; the Divine Shakti.

Dharma — law; the deepest law of our nature; the right law of individual and social life; literally that which one lays hold of and which holds things together.

dharma-jīvana — the religious life.

dharmasādhana — the means of fulfilment of Dharma.

dhyāna — meditation; mental concentration, whether in thought, vision or knowledge.

Divine, the — the Supreme Being from which all comes and in which all lives. In its supreme Truth the Divine is absolute and infinite peace, consciousness, existence, power and delight. The Transcendent, the Cosmic (Universal) and the Individual are three powers of the Divine, overarching, underlying and penetrating the whole of manifestation.

Divine Force — *see* **Force, the**

Divine Grace — *see* **Grace, the**

Divine Mother — *see* **Mother, the**

Divine Presence — *see* **Presence, the**

Divine Shakti — *see* **Shakti**

Divine Will — *see* **Will, Divine**

Durga — the goddess who is the Energy of Shiva; she is the conquering and protecting aspect of the Universal Mother.

dynamic mind — that part of the mind proper which is concerned with the putting out of mental forces for the realisation of ideas; it thinks, plans and acts in order to achieve things.

earth-consciousness — the separate global consciousness of the earth which evolves with the evolution of life on the planet.

ego — the separative sense of individuality which makes each being conceive of itself as an independent personality. Ego implies the identification of one's existence with the outer mental, vital and physical self.

emotional being — the emotional vital.

emotional vital, the — that part of the higher vital being which is the seat of various feelings, such as love, joy, sorrow, hatred, and the rest.

environmental consciousness — something that each person carries around him, outside his body, by which he is in touch with others and with the universal forces.

equality — *samatā*, equality of soul and mind to all things and happenings, equanimity founded on the sense of the one Self, the one Divine everywhere; the capacity to remain unmoved within in all conditions.

Eternal, the — *see* **Brahman**

evolution — the progressive unfolding of Spirit out of the density of material consciousness; a heightening of the force of consciousness in the manifest being so that it may be raised into the greater intensity of what is still unmanifest, from matter into life, from life into mind, from mind into the spirit.

exteriorisation — the consciousness going out of the body.

externalising mind — that part of the mind proper which is concerned with the expression of ideas in life (not only by speech, but by any form it can give).

faith — a dynamic intuitive conviction in the inner being of the truth of supersensible things which cannot be proved by any physical evidence but which are a subject of experience; the soul's witness to something not yet manifested, achieved or realised, but which yet the Knower within us feels to be true or supremely worth following or achieving; the soul's belief in the Divine's existence, wisdom, power, love and grace.

Falsehood — not Ignorance (Avidya), but an extreme result of it. Falsehood is created by an Asuric power which intervenes in this creation and is not only separated from Truth and therefore limited in knowledge and open to error, but in revolt against the Truth or in the habit of seizing the Truth only to pervert it. This Power puts forth its own perverted consciousness as true knowledge and its willful distortions or reversals of the Truth as the verity of things. Whenever these perversions created out of the stuff of the Ignorance are put forward as the Truth of things, that is the Falsehood, in the yogic sense.

Force, the — the Divine Force, the one Energy that alone exists and alone makes universal or individual action possible, for this Force is the Divine itself in the body of its power; in the individual it is a Force for illumination, transformation, purification, for all that has to be done in the yoga.

Force, the Mother's — the higher Force of the Divine that descends from above to transform the nature; the Divine Force which works to remove the ignorance and change the nature into the divine nature.

Gandhi, Mahatma — Mohandas K. Gandhi (1869-1948), national leader who helped India win independence from British rule through his creed of non-violent civil disobedience.

Gita — short form of Bhagavad Gita, "the Song of the Blessed Lord", being the spiritual teachings of Sri Krishna spoken to Arjuna on the battlefield of Kurukshetra; it occurs as an episode in the Mahabharata.

Gnosis — a supreme totally self-aware and all-aware Intelligence. The Divine Gnosis is the Supermind.

God — the Absolute, the Spirit, the Self spaceless and timeless, the Self manifest in the Cosmos and Lord of Nature. God is the All and that which transcends the All.

Godhead — the one supreme divine Being.

Gods — Personalities and Powers of the dynamic Divine.

Grace, the (Divine Grace) — the help of a higher Divine Force other than the force of Karma, which can lift the sadhak beyond the present possibilities of his nature.

Guna — quality, character, property; the three Gunas of Nature, her qualities or modes, are sattwa, rajas and tamas.

Guru — the Guide in the yoga; one who has realised the Truth and himself possesses and is able to communicate the light, the experience.

Guruvada — the doctrine that stresses the indispensability of the Guru to the spiritual seeker.

higher consciousness — the higher spiritual or divine consciousness.

Higher Mind — *see* **spiritualised mind**

higher vital — *see* **vital, the**

hostile forces — anti-divine, not merely undivine forces that are in revolt against the Divine, against the Truth and Light, and opposed to the yoga.

hṛtpadma — the heart-centre of consciousness, governing the emotional being; also called *anāhata*.

Ignorance, the — Avidya, the Ignorance of oneness; the separative consciousness and the egoistic mind and life that flow from it and all that is natural to the separative consciousness and the egoistic mind and life; the consciousness of the divided Many divorced from the unifying knowledge of the One Reality.

Ilumined Mind — *see* **spiritualised mind**

Immanent, the — the one pure and absolute Existence present in all things and beings even as all things and beings exist in It and by It, and nothing can be or happen without this indwelling and all-supporting Presence.

Impersonal, the — not a He, but an It. The Impersonal Brahman is inactive, aloof, indifferent, not concerned with what happens in the universe; It is everywhere, all-pervading, without form or limit in any place or time.

Inconscience, the — the Supreme's state of self-involved, self-oblivious consciousness and force which is at the basis of the material world; this state is the apparent opposite of the Supreme and in it there can be darkness, inertia, insensibility, disharmony and disintegration. Not really inconscient at all, it is rather a complete "sub"-conscience, a supposed or involved consciousness.

inner being — the inner mind, inner vital, inner physical, with the psychic behind as the inmost.

inner mind — that which lies behind the surface mind (our ordinary mentality); this inner or subliminal mind senses directly all the things of the mind-plane, is open to the action of a world of mental forces, and can feel the ideative and other imponderable influences which act upon the material world and the life-plane but which at present we can only infer and cannot directly experience.

inner physical — the physical part of the inner being.

inner vital — the vital part of the inner being.

Insentience — absence of sense-perception.

Integral Yoga — a union (*yoga*) in all the parts of our being with the Divine and a consequent transmutation of all their now jarring elements into the harmony of a higher divine consciousness and existence; this yoga implies not only the realisation of God but the entire consecration and change of the inner and outer life till it is fit to manifest a divine consciousness and become part of a divine work.

intellect — that part of the mind proper which is concerned with ideas and knowledge in their own right; its function is to observe, inquire, understand and judge.

Intermediate Zone — a zone of formations, a borderland where all the worlds meet, mental, vital, subtle physical, pseudo-spiritual, but there is no order or firm foothold; this zone is a passage between the physical and the true spiritual realms.

Intuition — *see* **spiritualised mind**

Intuitive Mind — *see* **spiritualised mind**

Ishwara — Lord, Master; the Divine, the Supreme Being.

Ishwara-Shakti — the active Divine Being and Power; the dual principle of the Lord (Ishwara) and his executive Power (Shakti).

Ishwari — feminine of Ishwara, "she who has mastery".

Ishwari Shakti — the Divine Conscious Force and World Mother.

Jagai and Madhai — Jagannath and Madhava, two Brahmin brothers who were notorious ruffians, subjecting people to all sorts of harassment; they were converted into saints by contact with the Vaishnava saint, Chaitanya.

Japa — repetition of a mantra or a name of God.

Jiva — *see* **Jivatman**

Jivanmukta — a living liberated man.

Jivatman (Jiva) — the individual Self; the individualised self or spirit of the created being; the Spirit individualised and upholding the living being in its evolution from birth to birth. The full term is Jivatman — the Atman or eternal self of the living being (Jiva). The Jivatman in its essence does not change or evolve: it stands above the personal evolution; within the evolution itself it is represented by the evolving psychic being which supports all the rest of the nature.

Jnana — knowledge, wisdom; supreme self-knowledge.

Karma — action, work; the work or function of a man; action entailing its consequences, the chain of act and consequence.

Karmayoga — the yoga of (desireless) works.

kartavyam karma — the thing to be done, the work we have to do.

Keshav Sen — Keshab Chandra Sen (1838-84), a religious and social reformer of Bengal, leader of the Brahmo Samaj of India.

kevala — essential, indeterminate, absolute.

Knowledge, the — the knowledge of the One Reality, the consciousness of Unity.

Krishna — the Lord of Ananda, Love and bhakti; as an incarnation he manifests the union of wisdom (*jñāna*) and works and leads the world evolution through this towards union with the Divine by Ananda, Love and bhakti.

Kundalini — the Kundalini Shakti, the Yogic Power imaged as a serpent that is ordinarily coiled and asleep in the lowest centre of consciousness at the base of the spine.

Laya — extinction, dissolution; annullation of the individual soul in the Infinite.

Lele — Vishnu Bhaskar Lele (d. 1938), a Maharashtrian yogi under whose guidance Sri Aurobindo achieved complete silence of the mind and immobility of the whole consciousness.

Life — Being at labour in Matter to express itself in terms of Conscious Force; an energy of Spirit subordinated to action of mind and body, which fulfils itself through mentality and physicality and acts as a link between them.

life-force (Prana) — the life-energy itself, not material energy, but rather a different principle supporting Matter and involved in it. It supports and occupies all forms and without it no physical form could have come into being or could remain in being.

Light, the — primarily a spiritual manifestation of the Divine Reality illuminative and creative; spiritual Light is not knowledge, but the illumination that comes from above and liberates the being from obscurity and darkness.

Lila — play, game; the cosmic play, the divine play.

lower vital — *see* **vital, the**

Madhai — *see* **Jagai and Madhai**

Mahabharata — the epic poem dealing with the great war between the Pandavas and the Kauravas, said to have been composed by Krishna Dwaipayana Vyasa.

Mahakali — the Divine Mother's Power of force and strength.

Maheshwari — the Divine Mother's Power of wisdom, wideness, compassion, majesty and all-ruling greatness.

maṇipūra — the navel centre of consciousness, governing the higher vital; also called *nābhipadma*.

manomayaḥ puruṣaḥ — the mental being.

Mantra — set words or sounds having a spiritual significance or power; sacred syllable, name or mystic formula.

Many, the — *see* **One and the Many, the**

material vital — that part of the lower vital turned entirely to physical things, full of desires and greeds and seekings for pleasure on the physical plane.

Matter — Being manifest as substance; substance of the one Conscious Being. A self-formed mask and robe of the divine Spirit, Matter is not fundamentally real, but a form of the force of Conscious Being.

Maya — illusion, the power of self-illusion in Brahman; the formative self-conception of the Eternal.

Mayavada — Illusionism, the doctrine which holds that the world is Maya, i.e., an illusion.

mechanical mind — a part of the mind closely connected with the physical mind; its nature is to go on repeating without use whatever has happened — recent events, impressions, old habitual thoughts or ways of thinking and feeling.

mental physical — mechanical mind.

mental plane — a world of mental existence in which neither life, nor matter, but mind is the first determinant; mind there is not determined by material conditions or by the life-force, but itself determines and uses them for its own satisfaction.

mental vital — that part of the higher vital being which gives a mental expression by thought, speech or otherwise to the emotions, desires, passions, sensations and other movements of the vital being.

mind — the words "mind" and "mental" are used to connote specially the part of the nature which has to do with cognition and intelligence, with ideas, with mental or thought perceptions, the reactions of thought to things, with the truly mental movements and formations, mental vision and will etc. that are part of man's intelligence. The ordinary mind has three main parts: mind proper, vital mind, and physical mind.

The **mind proper** is divided into three parts: the thinking mind or intellect, concerned with ideas and knowledge in their own right; the dynamic mind, concerned with the putting out of mental forces for the realisation of the ideas; and the externalising mind, concerned with the expression of ideas in life.

The **vital mind** or desire mind is a mind of dynamic will, action, desire; it is occupied with force and achievement and satisfaction and possession, with enjoyment and suffering, giving and taking, growth and expansion, etc.

The **physical mind** is that part of the mind which is concerned with physical things only; limited by the physical view and experience of things, it mentalises the experience brought by the contact of outward life and things, but does not go beyond that. The mechanical mind, closely connected with the physical mind, goes on repeating without use whatever has happened.

Overtopping the ordinary mind, hidden in our own super-conscient parts, there are higher ranges of Mind, gradations of spiritualised mind leading to the Supermind. In ascending order they are: Higher Mind, Illumined Mind, Intuitive Mind, Intuition and Overmind. *See* **spiritualised mind**

mithyā — an illusion, a lie.

mind, inner — *see* **inner mind**

Moksha (*mokṣa*) — liberation, spiritual liberation.

Mother, the (Divine Mother) — the consciousness and force of the Divine; the Divine in its consciousness-force. The Mother is the divine Conscious Force that dominates all existence, upholding us and the universe.

Mukti — liberation, spiritual liberation, the release of the soul from the bondage of Ignorance.

Muladhar (*mūlādhāra*) — the lowest centre of consciousness at the base of the spine, governing the physical down to the subconscient.

nābhipadma — the navel centre of consciousness, governing the higher vital; also called *maṇipūra*.

Nag Mahashaya — Durga Charan Nag (1846-99), a prominent householder disciple of Sri Ramakrishna; he was an embodiment of humility and self-sacrifice.

Nature — Prakriti, the outer or executive side of the Conscious Force which forms and moves the worlds. The higher, divine Nature (Para Prakriti) is free from Ignorance and its consequences; the lower Nature (Prakriti) is a mechanism of active Force put forth for the working of the evolutionary Ignorance. The lower nature of an individual is his mind, life and body.

nigraha — forceful suppression; coercion of the nature.

Nirananda — joylessness.

Nirvana — extinction, not necessarily of all being, but of being as we know it, extinction of ego, desire and egoistic action and mentality.

niścala-nīravatā — silence; motionless soundlessness.

Nivedita, Sister — Margaret Noble (1867-1911), an Irishwoman who was one of the closest Western disciples of Swami Vivekananda.

Non-Being — Non-Existence, Nothingness.

occultism — the knowledge and right use of the hidden forces of nature; true occultism means a search into supraphysical realities and an unveiling of the hidden laws of being and Nature, of all that is not obvious on the surface.

ojas — physical (and vital physical) energy; a primal physical energy supporting all the other energies of the body, vital, mental, spiritual.

OM — the mantra or expressive sound symbol of the Brahman Consciousness.

One and the Many, the — the Being is one, but this oneness is infinite and contains in itself an infinite plurality or multiplicity of itself; the infinite multiplicity of the One and the eternal unity of the Many are the two realities or aspects of the one reality on which the Manifestation is founded.

opening — the release of the consciousness by which it begins to admit into itself the working of the Divine Life and Power; the ability of the consciousness on the various levels to receive the descent of the Higher Consciousness above.

Overhead planes — *see* **spiritualised mind**

outer being — the surface being, our ordinary exterior mind, life, body consciousness.

Overmind — *see* **spiritualised mind**

pāpa — sin, demerit, vice.

Para Prakriti —the supreme Nature; a supreme Consciousness-Force which manifests the multiple Divine as the Many. *See also* **Nature**

Parvati — consort of Shiva; a benevolent aspect of the Divine Mother.

Patanjali — author of the *Yogasutras*, a classic text of Yogic thought and practice often referred to as Rajayoga.

peace — a deep quietude bringing not merely a release but a certain happiness or Ananda of itself, a harmony that gives a feeling of liberation and full satisfaction.

Person, the — the human birth in this world is on its spiritual side a complex of two elements, a spiritual Person and a soul of personality; the former is man's eternal being, the latter is his cosmic and mutable being. *See also* **Purusha**

physical consciousness — the physical mind, the physical vital as well as the body consciousness proper.

physical, inner — *see* **inner physical**

physical mind — *see* **mind**

physical nature — not the body alone, but the whole physical mind, vital, material nature.

physical self — the physical conscious being; the material being; *annamaya purusa.*

physical, the — the physical consciousness and body.

physical vital — the part of the vital that is turned entirely upon physical things, full of desires and greeds and seekings for pleasure on the physical plane.

Plotinus — (c. 205-70), Greek philosopher, born in Egypt, who founded the anti-materialistic Neoplatonist school.

possession (by hostile forces) — an intervention from the non-human worlds in which the hostile forces act on humans.

Prakriti (*prakrti*) — Nature; Nature-Force; the Lord's executive force; the outer or executive side of the Conscious Force which forms and moves the worlds. *See also* **Nature**

Prana — *see* **life-force**

prānamaya purusa — the vital being.

prāna-śarira-netā — master of life and body.

prāyopaveśana — fasting for a long time.

prema — love, divine love.

Presence, the — the sense and perception of the Divine as a Being felt as present in one's existence and consciousness or in relation with it.

psychic — of or relating to the soul (as distinguished from the mind and vital). Used in the sense of the Greek word "psyche", meaning "soul", the term "psychic" refers to all the movements and experiences of the soul, those which rise from or directly touch the psychic being. It does not refer to all the more inward and all the abnormal experiences in which the mind and vital predominate; such experiences, in Sri Aurobindo's terminology, would be called psychological (surface or occult), not psychic.

psychic, the — psychic being; psychic essence; soul.

psychic being — the evolving soul of the individual, the divine portion in him which evolves from life to life, growing by its experiences until it becomes a fully conscious being. From its place behind the heart-centre, the psychic being supports the mind, life and body, aiding their growth and development. The term "soul" is often used as a synonym for "psychic being", but strictly speaking there is a distinction: the soul is the psychic essence, the psychic being is the soul-personality put forward and developed by the psychic essence to represent it in the evolution. *See also* **psychic**

psychic entity — psychic essence.

psychic essence — the soul in its essence; the divine essence in the individual, the divine spark which supports the evolution of the being in Nature. In the course of the evolution the psychic essence grows and takes form as the psychic being.

psychicisation — the psychic change in which the psychic being comes forward to dominate the mind, vital and physical and change the lower nature.

pulling — drawing down too eagerly the divine force or a spiritual experience, instead of letting it descend quietly.

puṇya — merit, virtue.

purity — freedom from soil or mixture. The divine purity is that in which there is no mixture of the turbid ignorant movements of the lower nature.

Purusha (*puruṣa*) — Conscious Being; essential Being supporting the play of Prakriti (Nature); a Consciousness behind that is the lord, witness, enjoyer, upholder and source of sanction for Nature's works; the true or spiritual Person.

Purushottama — the supreme divine Person; the Supreme Being who is superior both to the mutable Being and the Immutable.

quiet — absence of restlessness or disturbance.

rajas — the quality that energises and drives to action; the quality of action and passion and struggle impelled by desire and instinct; the force of kinesis. Rajas is one of the three Gunas or modes of Nature.

rajasic — of the nature of rajas.

Rajayoga — a system of yoga primarily using the process of mental concentration; its aim is to still the habitual mental movements so that the mind, cast into an absorbed trance, can lose itself in the divine consciousness.

rajoguna — the quality of rajas.

Rakshasi Maya — the illusions of the powers of darkness.

Ramakrishna — Sri Ramakrishna Paramahansa (1836-1886), a great saint and spiritual teacher of modern India.

Rasa — taste, liking, pure taste of enjoyment; the response of the mind, the vital feeling and the sense to a certain "taste" in things.

realisation — the reception in the consciousness and the establishment there of the fundamental truths of the Divine; the making real to ourselves and in ourselves of the Self, the transcendent and universal Divine.

Reality, the — a Truth of all existence which is greater and more abiding than all its formations and manifestations; behind the appearance of the universe is the Reality of an infinite existence, an infinite consciousness, an infinite force and will, an infinite delight of being.

receptivity — the power to receive the Divine Force and to feel its presence and allow it to work, guiding one's sight and will and action; the capacity of admitting and retaining the divine workings.

rejection — rejection of the falsehood of the mental, vital and physical Powers and Appearances that still rule the earth-Nature.

retas — semen.

Rig-veda — the Veda of the Riks (words of illumination), the most ancient of the sacred books of India.

Rishi — seer, sage.

Sachchidananda (Sat-Chit-Ananda) — the One Divine Being with a triple aspect of Existence (Sat), Consciousness (Chit) and Delight (Ananda). God is Sachchidananda; He manifests Himself as infinite Existence of which the essentiality is Consciousness, of which again the essentiality is bliss, is self-delight.

sadhak — one who practises a spiritual discipline; one who is getting or trying to get spiritual realisation.

sadhana — spiritual practice or discipline; the practice of yoga; the practice by which perfection (*siddhi*) is attained.

sadhika — female sadhak.

sahasradala — the thousand-petalled lotus, the centre of consciousness located just above the head, which commands the higher thinking mind, houses the still higher illumined mind, and opens to the intuition.

Samadhi — inner trance; yogic trance in which the mind acquires the capacity of withdrawing from its limited waking activities into freer and higher states of consciousness.

Samarpana — surrender.

samatā — equality, equanimity; equality of soul and mind to all things and happenings.

saṁyama — self-control; a spiritual control of the nature.

Sankhya — one of the six systems of orthodox Indian philosophy whose method is based on the analysis, enumeration and discriminative setting forth of the principles of our being.

sannyasa — renunciation, especially of life and action; in the Indian tradition, the final stage of the developing human life, that of the free, super-social man who has renounced the world.

sannyasi — one who practises sannyasa; an ascetic.

śānti — peace; spiritual peace.

sarvaṁ khalvidaṁ brahma — all this is the Brahman.

sat — Being, Existence; Pure Existence.

Sat-Chit-Ananda — *see* **Sachchidananda**

sattwa — the quality that illumines and clarifies; the quality of light, harmony, purity and peace; the force of equilibrium. Sattwa is one of the three Gunas or modes of Nature.

sattwic — of the nature of sattwa.

Satyagraha — "insistence on truth"; in the Indian national movement the name given to the non-violent resistance advocated by Mahatma Gandhi and others.

Saul of Tarsus — (afterwards St. Paul), a first century Jew who was a bitter enemy of Christianity until he was converted through a vision on the road to Damascus; he then became the leading missionary of the Christian Church and one of its greatest theologians.

Self, the — the Atman, the universal Spirit, the self-existent Being, the conscious essential Existence, one in all. The Self is being, not a being; it is the original and essential nature of our existence.

Self-knowledge — the knowledge of the Self.

Shakta — a worshipper of Shakti.

Shakti — Force, Power; the Divine Power; the Power of the Mother; the consciousness and power of the Divine; the Mother and Energy of the worlds.

Shankara — short for Shankaracharya, eighth century Indian philosopher and theologian, most famous exponent of the Adwaita Vedanta school of philosophy called Mayavada (Illusionism).

Shantimaya Shiva — Shiva full of peace.

sheaths — the oldest Vedantic knowledge tells us of five degrees of our being, the material, the vital, the mental, the ideal, the spiritual or beatific and to each of these grades of our soul there corresponds a grade of our substance, a sheath as it was called in the ancient figurative language.

Shiva — the third member of the Hindu Trinity; the Lord of spiritual austerity, Shiva is the Eternal's Personality of Force.

siddha — perfected by yoga; one perfect in the yoga; the perfected soul.

siddhi — perfection, success, accomplishment of the aims of yoga; an extraordinary or occult power.

silence — freedom from thoughts and vital movements, when the whole consciousness is quite still; not only cessation of thoughts but a stillness of the mental and vital substance.

sincerity — to mean what one says, feel what one professes, be earnest in one's will; sincerity in the sadhak means that he is really in earnest in his aspiration for the Divine and refuses all other will or impulse except the Divine's; it means to allow no part of the being to contradict the highest aspiration towards the Divine.

śiṣya — pupil, disciple.

soul — the psychic essence or entity, the divine essence in the individual; a spark of the Divine that comes down into the manifestation to support the evolution of the individual. In the course of the evolution, the soul grows and evolves in the form of a soul-personality, the psychic being. The term "soul" is often used as a synonym for "psychic being".

Spirit — the Consciousness above mind, the Atman or universal Self which is always in oneness with the Divine.

spiritual — of the spirit. All contacts with the Self, the Higher Consciousness, the Divine above are spiritual.

spiritualisation — the spiritual change in which there is the established descent of the divine peace, light, knowledge, power, bliss from above, the awareness of the Self and the Divine and of a higher cosmic consciousness and the change of the whole nature to that.

spiritualised mind, gradations of — higher ranges of Mind overtopping our normal Mind and leading to Supermind; these successive states, levels or graded powers of being are hidden in our own superconscious parts. In ascending order the gradations of spiritualised mind are:

Higher Mind — a luminous thought-mind whose instrumentation is through an elevated thought-power and comprehensive mental sight. In the Higher Mind one becomes constantly and closely aware of the Self, the One everywhere and knows and sees habitually with that awareness.

Illumined Mind — a mind no longer of higher thought, but of spiritual light; here the clarity of the intelligence, its tranquil daylight, gives place or subordinates itself to an intense lustre, a splendour and illumination of the Spirit.

Intuitive Mind — a mind of intuitive reason characterised by its intuitions, its inspirations, its swift revelatory vision, its luminous insight and discrimination; it is a kind of truth-vision, truth-hearing, truth-memory, direct truth-discernment.

Intuition — a power of consciousness nearer and more intimate than the lower ranges of spiritual mind to the original knowledge by identity; it gets the Truth in flashes and turns these flashes of Truth-perception into intuitions – intuitive ideas. Intuition is always an edge or ray or outleap of a superior light. What is thought-knowledge in the Higher Mind becomes illumination in the Illumined Mind and direct intimate vision in the Intuition.

Overmind — full of lights and powers, the Overmind sees calmly, steadily, in great masses and large extensions of space and time and relation, globally; it creates and acts in the same way. The Overmind is a delegate of the Supramental Consciousness, its delegate to the cosmic Ignorance. The Supramental is the total Truth-Consciousness; the Overmind draws down the truths separately and gives them a separate identity.

sthiratā — calm.

subconscient, the — the subconscient or subconscious of the individual is that submerged part of his being in which there is no waking conscious and coherent thought, will, feeling or organised reaction, but which yet receives obscurely the impressions of all things and stores them up; from it too all sorts of stimuli, of persistent habitual movements can surge up into dream or into the waking state. In the ordinary man the subconscient includes the larger part of the vital being and the physical mind and the secret body-consciousness. It is not to be confused with the subliminal: the subconscient is a nether diminished consciousness, the subliminal is an inner consciousness larger than our surface existence.

subconscious, the — *see* subconscient, the

subliminal — inner, not on the waking surface.

subliminal, the — the inner being, taken in its entirety of inner mind, inner life, inner physical, with the soul or psychic entity supporting them. The subliminal in man is the largest part of his nature; it is not subconscient, but conscient and greater than the waking consciousness. The subconscient is that which is below the ordinary physical consciousness, the subliminal that which is behind and supports it.

subliminal being — *see* subliminal, the

subtle body — a subtler material existence behind our outer body which provides the substance not only of our physical but of our vital and mental sheaths.

śuddhā bhakti — pure devotion and love for the Divine.

sūkṣma śarīra — the subtle body.

Superconscient, the (the Superconscience) — something above our present consciousness from which the higher consciousness comes down into the body; it includes the higher planes of mental being as well as the native heights of supramental and pure spiritual being.

Supermind — the Supramental, the Truth-Consciousness, the Divine Gnosis, the highest divine consciousness and force operative in the universe. A principle of consciousness superior to mentality, it exists, acts and proceeds in the fundamental truth and unity of things and not like the mind in their appearances and phenomenal divisions. Its fundamental character is knowledge by identity, by which the Self is known, the Divine Sachchidananda is known, but also the truth of manifestation is known because this too is that.

Supramental, the — *see* **Supermind**

surrender — to consecrate everything in oneself to the Divine, to offer all one is and has, not to insist on one's ideas, desires, habits, etc. but to allow the divine Truth to replace them by its knowledge, will and action everywhere.

svādhiṣṭhāna — the abdominal centre of consciousness, governing the lower vital.

symbol — the form of one plane that represents a truth of another.

Taittiriya Upanishad — a Vedantic treatise belonging to the Krishna Yajurveda.

tamas — the quality that hides or darkens; the quality of ignorance, inertia and obscurity, of incapacity and inaction; the force of inconscience. Tamas is one of the three Gunas or modes of Nature.

tamasic — of the nature of tamas.

Tantra — a yogic system based on the principle of Consciousness-Power (conceived of as the Divine Mother) as the Supreme Reality; its method of discipline is to raise Nature in man into manifest power of Spirit.

Tantric — relating to Tantra; a follower of the Tantra system of philosophy and yoga.

Tapas — force, spiritual power, will; concentration of energy to effect an end.

Tapasya — effort, energy, austerity of the personal will; concentration of the will and energy to control the mind, vital and physical and to change them or to bring down the higher consciousness or for any other yogic or high purpose.

thinking mind — that part of the mind proper which is concerned with ideas and knowledge in their own right; its function is to observe, inquire, understand and judge.

Totapuri — the Naga sannyasi who initiated Sri Ramakrishna into sannyasa.

transformation — not just a change of consciousness, but the bringing down of the higher, divine consciousness and nature into the lower nature of mind, life and body, and the replacement of the lower by the higher.

trāṭaka — concentration of the vision on a single point or object, preferably a luminous object.

Truth-Consciousness — the Supermind; the consciousness of essential truth of being (*satyam*), of ordered truth of active being (*ṛtam*) and the vast self-awareness *(bṛhat)* in which alone this consciousness is possible.

turīya — the fourth plane of our consciousness; the superconscient; the Absolute.

udāsīna — seated above and indifferent.

Uma — name of the consort of Shiva.

Upanishad — one of a class of Hindu sacred writings, regarded as the source of the Vedanta philosophy.

upari budhna eṣām — their foundation is above.

vairāgya — distaste, disgust for the world and life; a strong dissatisfaction and reaction.

Vaishnava — relating or belonging to Vishnu.

Vaishnavism — Vaishnava religion.

vāsudevaḥ sarvam — Vasudeva (the Divine Being) is all.

Veda — a generic name for the most ancient Indian sacred literature; the term "Veda" is sometimes reserved for the mantras or metrical hymns of the Rig-veda.

Vedanta — a system of philosophy and spiritual discipline based on the Upanishads and teaching the culminating knowledge of the Absolute.

Vedanta Adwaita — Monistic Vedanta; the doctrine of One-Existence or Monism as propounded in the Upanishads.

Vedic — relating to the Vedas.

veil, the — the veil of Ignorance.

Vibhuti — Divine power; a power of God in man; an embodied World-Force or human leader.

vicāra — intellectual reflection; thought in the mind.

vijñāna — the higher knowledge; the power above the ordinary logical reason which gives the direct knowledge; the perception of Truth.

vijñānamaya puruṣa — being of knowledge.

Vishnu — the member of the Hindu Trinity expressive of the

conservative process in the cosmos; the Preserver, Vishnu is the Eternal's Personality of Consciousness.

viśuddha — the throat centre of consciousness, governing the externalising mind.

vital, the — the life-nature made up of desires, sensations, feelings, passions, energies of action, will of desire, reactions of the desire-soul of man and of all that play of possessive and other related instincts, anger, greed, lust, etc., that belong to this field of nature. The vital part of man is a true instrument only when its feelings and tendencies have been purified by the psychic touch and governed by the spiritual light and power. The vital has three main parts:

higher vital — the mental vital and emotional vital taken together. The mental vital gives a mental expression by thought, speech or otherwise to the emotions, desires, passions, sensations or other movements of the vital being; the emotional vital is the seat of various feelings, such as love, joy, sorrow, hatred and the rest.

central vital or **vital proper** — dynamic, sensational and passionate, it is the seat of the stronger vital longings and reactions, such as ambition, pride, fear, love of fame, attractions and repulsions, desires and passion of various kinds and the field of many vital energies.

lower vital — made up of the smaller movements of human life-desire and life-reactions, it is occupied with small desires and feelings, such as food desire, sexual desire, small likings, dislikings, vanity, quarrels, love of praise, anger at blame, little wishes of all kinds, etc. The material vital is that part of the lower vital turned entirely upon physical things, full of desires and greeds and seekings for pleasure on the physical plane.

vital mind — *see* **mind**

vital physical — the nervous part of the being, the life-force closely enmeshed in the reactions, desires, needs, sensations of the body.

vital plane — the plane connected with the life-world or desire-world, a plane in which life and desire find their untrammelled play and their easy self-expression and from there throw their influences and formations on our outer life.

Vivekananda, Swami — monastic name of Narendranath Dutta

(1863-1902), the most famous disciple of Sri Ramakrishna and one of the great spiritual teachers of modern India.

wideness — the expansion of consciousness that comes when one exceeds or begins to exceed the individual consciousness and spread out toward the universal; it is felt as a great substantial vastness giving the sense of oneness free and infinite.

will — a force put upon a thing to be changed.

Will, Divine — something that has descended here into an evolutionary world of Ignorance, standing at the back of things, pressing on the Darkness with its Light, leading things presently towards the best possible in the conditions of a world of Ignorance and leading it eventually towards a descent of a greater power of the Divine, which will not be an omnipotence held back and conditioned by the law of the world as it is, but in full action and therefore bringing the reign of light, peace, harmony, joy, love, beauty and Ananda.

Witness, the — the witness Purusha, a consciousness or Purusha calm and detached from the outer actions of Nature.

Yajna — sacrifice.

Yajnavalkya — a famous Rishi who figures prominently in the Brihadaranyaka Upanishad.

yama-niyama — the first two limbs of Patanjali's system of yoga, aimed at purifying the character and mind. The *yama*s (restraints) are rules of moral self-control, the *niyama*s (observances) are regulating moral habits.

Yoga — joining, union; union with the Divine and the conscious seeking for this union. Yoga is in essence the union of the soul with the immortal being and consciousness and bliss of the Divine, effected through the human nature with a result of development into the divine nature of being. Yoga is a generic name for any discipline by which one attempts to pass out of the limits of his ordinary mental consciousness into a greater spiritual consciousness. *See also* **Integral Yoga**

Yoga-force (Yogic Force) — a higher consciousness using its power, a spiritual and supraphysical force acting on the physical world directly.

yoga-siddhi — the perfection that comes by the practice of Yoga.

Yogi (Yogin) — one who practises yoga; but especially one who has attained the goal of yoga and is already established in spiritual realisation.

yuktāhārī yuktanidraḥ — one who eats and sleeps suitably; one who is in union with the Divine in food and sleeping.

Zoroaster — the Persian prophet (628-551 BC) who founded the Zoroastrian religion.

OTHER TITLES BY SRI AUROBINDO

Bases of Yoga (New U.S. edition)	p	6.95
Bhagavad Gita and Its Message	p	15.95
Dictionary of Sri Aurobindo's Yoga (compiled)	p	11.95
Essays on the Gita (new US edition)	p	19.95
Gems from Sri Aurobindo, 1st Series (compiled)	p	8.95
Gems from Sri Aurobindo, 2nd Series (compiled)	p	12.95
Gems from Sri Aurobindo, 3rd Series (compiled)	p	10.95
Gems from Sri Aurobindo, 4th Series (compiled)	p	8.95
Growing Within	p	9.95
Human Cycle: Psychology of Social Development (new US edition)	p	14.95
Hymns to the Mystic Fire (new US edition)	p	17.95
Ideal of Human Unity (new US edition)	p	17.95
Integral Yoga: Sri Aurobindo's Teaching and Method of Practice (compiled)	p	14.95
The Life Divine (new US edition)	p	29.95
	hb	39.95
Lights on Yoga	p	2.95
Living Within (compiled)	p	8.95
Looking from Within (compiled)	p	6.95
The Mother (new US edition)	p	2.95
A Practical Guide to Integral Yoga (compiled)	p	7.95
The Psychic Being: Soul in Evolution (compiled)	p	8.95
Rebirth and Karma (new US edition)	p	9.95
Savitri: A Legend and a Symbol (new US edition)	p	24.95
The Secret of the Veda (new US edition)	p	19.95
The Synthesis of Yoga (new US edition)	p	29.95
	hb	34.95
The Upanishads (new US edition)	p	17.95
Vedic Symbolism (compiled)	p	6.95
Wisdom of the Gita, 2nd Series (compiled)	p	10.95
Wisdom of the Upanishads (compiled)	p	7.95

available from your local bookseller or
LOTUS PRESS, Box 325, Twin Lakes, WI 53181 USA
262/889-8561 • www . lotuspress.com
email: lotuspress@lotuspress.com

Sri Aurobindo:
Secret of the Veda

SECRET OF THE VEDA by Sri Aurobindo

In this ground-breaking book, Sri Aurobindo has revealed the secret of the Veda and illustrated his method with numerous translations of the ancient hymns. *Secret of the Veda* has been acclaimed by scholars and yogins as the ultimate key to revealing the hidden sense and secret inner meanings of the original spiritual revelation of the Veda. The Rig Veda provides an inner spiritual and psychological practice to achieve realization. It is the foundation upon which the Upanishads were later developed.

Now in it first US edition.

LOTUS PRESS   ISBN 0-914955-19-5 581p pb $19.95

ESSAYS ON THE GITA by Sri Aurobindo

Sri Aurobindo:
Essays on the Gita

The Bhagavad Gita stands alone in the spiritual tradition of humanity by being at the same time a Scripture, a teaching , a poetic utterance and a practical guidebook to the problems of life in the world. For this reason, the Gita is a powerful aid to anyone who wants to integrate the life of the Spirit with the issues of life in the world. It does not "cut the knot" but systematically works to untie it. In so doing, it helps us clarify the issues alive within ourselves. Sri Aurobindo understood these issues and in his famous *Essays on the Gita* he was able to reveal many subtle and hidden aspects of the teaching of the Gita. He entered into the spirit of the original and created a commentary that has stood the test of time in its lucidity and value for anyone wishing to truly understand the Bhagavad Gita. *Essays on the Gita* has been widely acclaimed for opening up the deeper sense of the Bhagavad Gita.

Now in its first US edition

LOTUS PRESS   ISBN 0-914955-18-7 588p pb $19.95

THE MOTHER by Sri Aurobindo

Sri Aurobindo
The Mother

Sri Aurobindo has created, in this small book, a powerful guide to the practice of spirituality in life. To discover this gem is to gain a constant companion whose guidance remains forever meaningful. Its power of expression and meaning are so concentrated and far reaching that many have called it "Matri Upanishad", the Upanishad of the Mother. Sri Aurobindo's Matri Upanishad is the text which reveals this power and energy of creation in its universal and personal sense, providing both truth of philosophy and truth of yogic experience at one and the same time.

Now in its first US edition

LOTUS PRESS   ISBN 0-941524-79-5 62p pb $2.95

SAVITRI: A LEGEND AND A SYMBOL by Sri Aurobindo

Sri Aurobindo
Savitri
A Legend and a Symbol

Savitri is an inner guidebook for the soul. These mantric verses imbue even the body with potent spiritual resonance. In this epic spiritual poem, Sri Aurobindo reveals his vision of mankind's destiny within the universal evolution. He sets forth the optimistic view that life on earth has a purpose, and he places our travail within the context of this purpose: to participate in the evolution of consciousness that represents the secret thread behind life on earth. Sri Aurobindo's verses describe the origin of the universe, the appearance of sentient beings and the stages of evolution, as well as speak to many of mankind's unanswered questions concerning pain and death.

Now in its first US edition

LOTUS PRESS   ISBN 0-941524-80-9 816p pb $24.95

available from your local bookseller or
Lotus Press, PO Box 325, Twin Lakes, WI 53181 • 262-889-8561
www.lotuspress.com
email: lotuspress@lotuspress.com

REBIRTH AND KARMA by Sri Aurobindo
In depth study of the concepts of rebirth, karma and the higher lines of karma.
One of the best introductions to this area we've ever found.

LOTUS PRESS ISBN 0-941524-63-9 190p pb $9.95

Sri Aurobindo
Rebirth and Karma

THE LIFE DIVINE by Sri Aurobindo
The Life Divine is Sri Aurobindo's major philosophical exposition, spanning more than a thousand pages and integrating the major spiritual directions of mankind into a coherent picture of the growth of the spiritual essence of man through diverse methods, philosophies and spiritual practices.

LOTUS PRESS ISBN 0-941524-61-2 1113p pb $29.95

Sri Aurobindo
The Life Divine

THE INTEGRAL YOGA
Sri Aurobindo's Teaching and Method of Practice
by Sri Aurobindo (compilation)
"These carefully selected excerpts from the writings of Sri Aurobindo provide a wonderfully accessible entre into the writings of one of the great masters of spiritual synthesis."
Ram Dass

LOTUS PRESS ISBN 0-941524-76-0 416p pb $14.95

Sri Aurobindo
The Integral Yoga
Sri Aurobindo's Teaching and method of Practice

SYNTHESIS OF YOGA, US EDITION by Sri Aurobindo
In The Synthesis of Yoga Sri Aurobindo unfolds his vision of an integral yoga embracing all the powers and activities of man. First, he reviews the three great yogic paths of Knowledge, Works and Love, along with Hatha Yoga, Raja Yoga and Tantra, and then integrates them all into a great symphony. "Truth of philosophy is of a merely theoretical value unless it can be lived, and we have therefore tried in the The Synthesis of Yoga to arrive at a synthetical view of the principles and methods of the various lines of spiritual self-discipline and the way in which they can lead to an integral divine life in the human existence".

LOTUS PRESS ISBN 0-941524-66-3 899p hb $34.95
LOTUS PRESS ISBN 0-941524-65-5 899p pb $29.95

Sri Aurobindo
The Synthesis of Yoga

available from your local bookseller or
Lotus Press, PO Box 325, Twin Lakes, WI 53181 • 262-889-8561
www.lotuspress.com
email: lotuspress@lotuspress.com